12 ⁵⁰

Nicholas M. Albertson
March 23, 1946

CORNELL UNIVERSITY:
FOUNDERS AND THE FOUNDING

LONDON: HUMPHREY MILFORD
OXFORD UNIVERSITY PRESS

CORNELL UNIVERSITY:
FOUNDERS AND THE FOUNDING

SIX LECTURES
DELIVERED AT CORNELL UNIVERSITY
ON THE MESSENGER FOUNDATION IN THE YEAR 1943
IN RECOGNITION OF THE 75TH ANNIVERSARY
OF THE OPENING OF THAT INSTITUTION
IN THE YEAR 1868: TOGETHER WITH
FIFTEEN INTERESTING BUT HITHERTO UNPUBLISHED
DOCUMENTS RELATING THERETO

THE WHOLE further adduced in explanatory and commentative
NOTES and supported by exact REFERENCES TO THE ORIGINAL
SOURCES according to the practice of the most eminent historians;
WITH ALL OF WHICH is included an address entitled 'THE CORNELL
TRADITION,' delivered on April 27, 1940, in recognition of the 75th
anniversary of the SIGNING OF THE CHARTER

BY

CARL L. BECKER

PROFESSOR EMERITUS OF HISTORY AND UNIVERSITY HISTORIAN
IN CORNELL UNIVERSITY

INTER FOLIA
FRUCTUS

Ithaca, New York
CORNELL UNIVERSITY PRESS
1944

First Printing, November 1943
Second Printing, April 1944

PRINTED IN THE UNITED STATES OF AMERICA
BY THE VAIL-BALLOU PRESS, INC., BINGHAMTON, N. Y.

By doubting we are led to questioning, and by questioning we arrive at truth.

ABELARD

PREFACE

THE MESSENGER FOUNDATION was established to provide each year for a series of twelve lectures, or two series of six lectures each, on some aspect of the history of civilization. Since 1943 is the seventy-fifth anniversary of the opening of Cornell University it was thought appropriate that one of the series of lectures for that year should be devoted to the founding of the institution, not only because the subject would have a special interest for all Cornellians, but because the founding of Cornell University had a notable influence on the history of higher education, that is to say on the history of civilization, in the United States.

The task (not that "task" is the right word) of preparing these lectures has been facilitated by the assistance of many people— Miss Mary Hull, who placed at my disposal the notes and papers relating to Ezra Cornell collected by her brother, Charles H. Hull; Mrs. A. W. Smith and Mrs. Franklin C. Cornell, who gave me information about the nature and disposal of certain papers left by Mr. Cornell and placed at my disposal certain books and documents; Miss Harriett Naylor of the City Historian's Office in Rochester, who examined for me the Rochester *Democrat* and *Union and Advertiser* in connection with the Cornell University bill of 1865; Miss Dorothy C. Barck, who gave me information about the O'Reilly papers in the New York Historical Society Library; Mrs. Nellie B. Smelzer, who greatly facilitated my examination of the Cornell Papers in the De Witt Historical Society Library; Mr. E. R. B. Willis of the Cornell University Library, whose familiarity with the contents of "the vault" and the manuscript collections in the library is indispensable to any one who has to use them; Professor Paul Gates, whose wide and exact

Preface

knowledge of the subject has saved me much time and research; and Mr. Woodford Patterson, who prepared the manuscript for the printer, and whose extensive and exact knowledge of Cornell University and its early history has saved me from a number of errors.

The explanatory notes for Lectures III, V, and VI are unusually full, either because the information is not to be found elsewhere in print, or because the conclusions presented in the lecture are not those that have been commonly accepted.

C. B.

Ithaca, New York
July 1943

CONTENTS

ILLUSTRATIONS

CORNELL UNIVERSITY:
FOUNDERS AND THE FOUNDING

I

Life and Learning in the United States

It shall be the duty of the General Assembly, as soon as circumstances will permit, to provide by law for a general system of education, ascending in a regular gradation from township schools to state university, wherein tuition shall be gratis, and equally open to all.
INDIANA STATE CONSTITUTION, 1816

I HAVE often wondered what the United States would be like if it had been first settled at another time and by other people—if it had been settled, say, in the thirteenth century, the eastern seaboard by the Norman French, the western by the Chinese, with the two frontiers subsequently meeting on a line running roughly from New Orleans to Minneapolis through Kansas City and Omaha. It's an intriguing thought. Unfortunately, we must be resigned to the prosaic fact that the settlements of greatest importance for the future history of the United States were made chiefly by Englishmen, and in the seventeenth century.

Whether the institutions of the United States were inherited from Europe or newly devised to meet the novel conditions of the American wilderness is much disputed. I cannot decide that dispute; but certainly the first settlers had acquired in England certain ideas about politics, morality, and religion that must have had a decisive influence in determining the original form of the institutions they established in Virginia and New England and elsewhere. Among the ideas thus brought to America were the ideas then prevailing in England about schools and universities. In this respect the seventeenth century might be thought a bad time for the United States to begin its institutional career. At

3

almost no other time, certainly not in the thirteenth century, could the first settlers have brought to these shores a set of ideas more restricted or less promising for the promotion of learning in the new world.

In seventeenth-century England, as in Europe generally, the prevailing idea was that schools and universities should teach nothing that would discredit the established religion or the authority of kings and magistrates. There were, it is true, some voices raised in protest. Francis Bacon protested, and with good effect, against an arid scholasticism and a slavish worship of ancient writers. Milton complained that professors "take from young men the use of reason by charms compounded of metaphysics, miracles and absurd scriptures"; the result of which was that at Cambridge he had misspent his own youth trying to digest "an asinine feast of sow-thistles and brambles." John Hall, himself a teacher at Cambridge, maintained that the advancement of learning was thwarted by incompetent teachers teaching outmoded subjects. But such voices were for the most part unheeded, and what they said was scarcely understood. Even Leibnitz opposed academic freedom, and Hobbes thought the chief use of universities was to teach subjects their duty to the king. So much was this the prevailing idea that even Hartlib, friend of Milton and Comenius, and himself a reformer, held it without being aware that he did so. "The readiest way," he said, "to reform church and commonwealth is to reform the schools therein." [1]* No doubt; but he differed from Hobbes only in his conclusion. The premise of both was the same; namely, that teaching and learning, so far from being free, should be subordinated to political ends.

This totalitarian conception of schools and universities was brought to the new world by the first settlers. The unexamined assumption that made it acceptable to them was that learning is

---

* The author's notes, numbered consecutively throughout each of the six Lectures, are all assembled at the end of the book (References and Notes, p. 219).

essentially dangerous; and they were aware that, so far as schools and universities were concerned, the danger could be met in one of two ways, either by not having any schools or by preventing them from teaching any but familiar and accepted ideas. William Berkeley, Governor of Virginia, preferred the first way. "Thank God there are no free schools nor printing, and I hope we shall not have these hundred years; for learning has brought disobedience and heresy . . . into the world, and printing has divulged them. . . . God keep us from both." [2] But generally speaking, in Virginia as well as in the other colonies, the first settlers, being either less pessimistic or more courageous than Governor Berkeley, preferred the second way. They believed that the danger inherent in learning could best be met by schools teaching, under proper control, the right things—the mechanic arts, the learned tongues, and Christian philosophy.

Schools in this sense were perhaps more necessary in New England than elsewhere, because there the first settlers came with the deliberate intention of establishing, as Winthrop said, "a due form of government both civil and ecclesiastical." What this due form of government was, the leaders knew with great certainty, and they took care accordingly that their followers should be like-minded men—the "sifted wheat" for the new planting. Yet in spite of every precaution unlike-minded men were found among them. "Many untoward servants," says William Bradford, "were brought over"; parents in England were glad to be rid of children that "would necessarily follow their dissolute courses"; ship masters, making a business of transporting settlers, "to advance their profit, cared not who the persons were, so they had money to pay them"; and so, the kindly governor ends on a plaintive note, "the country became pestered with many unworthy persons, who, being come over, crept into one place or other." [3] Besides, even like-minded men were apt to turn perverse. There was Roger Williams, who believed in soul-liberty, and even went so far as to say that the land belonged to the Indians. There was that "anciently religious woman," Deborah

5

Moodie, who cavilled at infant baptism; and Mistress Anne Hutchinson, who, "speaking from the mere motion of the spirit," criticised the ministers for preaching a covenant of works. Obviously, having no schools or printing would not meet the danger inherent in learning, since the Devil was always around to mislead the people anyway.

Of this profound truth the founders of Massachusetts Bay were well aware. Accordingly, the General Court enacted a law to the effect that, "it being one of the chief projects of that old deluder Satan to keep men from a knowledge of the Scriptures, as in former times by keeping them in an unknown tongue, so in these later times by persuading from the use of tongues," there should be established a free school in each town in the province.[4] This was in 1642. In the same year Harvard College held its first Commencement, graduating nine men. If we may go by the printed rules of the College, these nine men had been instructed, intermittently and superficially, in Logic, Mathematics, Physics, Politics, Rhetoric, Moral Philosophy, Divinity, History, and the nature of plants; and, more constantly and thoroughly, in those tongues (Greek and Latin) in which the old deluder Satan wished to keep the Scriptures hidden. But the chief aim, apart from which all this learning was a vain thing, was that every student should be "plainly instructed and earnestly pressed to consider well the main end of his life and studies, . . . to know God and Jesus Christ, which is eternal life." To this end every student was required to "exercise himself in reading the Scriptures twice daily"; and "if in anything they doubt, they shall enquire as of their fellows, so (in case of nonsatisfaction) modestly of their Tutors."[5] What the tutors should do if in anything they doubted, the rules do not say; but it is recorded that in 1654 President Dunster, having doubted the doctrine of infant baptism, was admonished on Lecture Day, and forced to resign his office.

Harvard College was founded to promote learning, but not quite in the sense understood by Abelard, one of the founders of the University of Paris in the twelfth century. "By doubting," said Abelard, "we are led to questioning, and by questioning we arrive at truth." At Harvard College, in the seventeenth century, doubt was evidently regarded as the chief obstacle to learning. There the rule was: by doubting we run into error, we arrive at truth by enquiring, modestly, of the tutors.

Until the eighteenth century Harvard College was rather a promise than a performance. For lack of funds there were few tutors for the fifteen or twenty students to enquire modestly of; and there was no professor at all until 1721. At that time two other colleges were in existence—William and Mary, founded in 1693, and the Collegiate College, a kind of wandering academy that finally, in 1716, consented to settle down at New Haven, and that was incorporated, in 1745, as Yale College. During the next twenty-five years six other colleges were founded—Princeton, the University of Pennsylvania, King's (Columbia) College, Brown, Rutgers, and Dartmouth. In the eighteenth century the due form of government had become rather more civil than ecclesiastical, and the colleges had in some measure responded to this change. But in the eighteenth no less than in the seventeenth century, the colleges were supported by the ruling classes (a flexible, mixed aristocracy, composed of the educated and wealthy families who thought of themselves as "the better sort") in order to provide the leaders of the community with a liberal education; and it was taken for granted that a liberal education would safeguard them against subversive political ideas, and fortify their faith, if not in the tenets of any particular sect, at least in what the Prospectus of King's College called "the Great Principles of Christianity and Morality in which all true Christians in each of the denominations are generally agreed." [6] Certainly nothing was further from the intention of the founders of these institutions than that their most distinguished alumni should become the leaders of a revolution dedicated to the principle that all men are endowed by their Creator with an inalienable right to abolish any form of government, civil or ecclesi-

7

astical, which did not in their opinion derive its authority from the consent of the governed. Yet this is what came to pass; and if we ask where Jefferson, the brace of Adamses, and their confreres got these subversive ideas, the answer is that they got them in part in college, by reading works in those tongues in which, according to the founders of Massachusetts Bay, the old deluder Satan had hidden the Scriptures.

To establish centers of learning on the assumption that, properly supervised, no subversive ideas will be generated in them is to take a great risk. The founders of the first American colleges took that risk. They were intelligent and courageous men, but in subtilty and resourcefulness they were no match for the old deluder whom they were out to circumvent. Their fatal error, I suspect, was to suppose that the old deluder wished to keep men from a knowledge of the Scriptures, either by hiding them in an unknown tongue or by persuading from the use of tongues. Certainly he must have known that to read the Scriptures is to become acquainted with various and sundry ideas, forms of government, idolatries, moralities, and with every species of pessimism and the most devastating doubt. If he did indeed have anything to do with recording the Scriptures in an unknown tongue, it must have been for another purpose than to keep them hidden. His purpose must have been (this is only my private opinion) to have the boys of Harvard, Yale, and Princeton exposed to Tully, and such-like classical authors, so that they might become infected with the most ingenious ideas and plausible sophistries ever invented to bedevil the minds of men and beguile them into disobedience and heresy.

That the old deluder had really anything to do with all this I do not affirm as a fact: I only refer you, as a good historian should, to the authentic official documents. But it is a fact that Jefferson, the brace of Adamses, and many other leaders of the American Revolution attended one or other of the colleges and there learned to read and prize the classical authors. They read the Scriptures too, no doubt, but they seem to have liked the pagan better than the Christian writers—preferring Demosthenes to Deuteronomy; Cicero to Solomon and St. Augustine; Plutarch and Livy to Eusebius or Orosius. Reading the pagan authors, they found the content more interesting than the grammar, no doubt because the content confirmed them in the notion, already current in the eighteenth century, that history and politics were both more interesting and more relevant than theology. The experience of young John Adams was more or less typical. While studying in Harvard College he failed to find in the Scriptures any precept "requiring . . . creeds, confessions, oaths, subscriptions, and whole cart-loads of trumpery that we find religion encumbered with these days." Concluding, therefore, that "the design of Christianity was not to make . . . good mystery-mongers, but good men, good magistrates, and good subjects," he was drawn to "that science by which mankind have raised themselves from the . . . state in which nature leaves them, to the full enjoyment of the social union." [7]

In classical literature Adams and his fellows found an engaging if not entirely true account of what the social union was in ancient Greece and Rome, and took it as in some sense a model of what the social union should be in modern times. Reading the classical authors they learned to admire the fortitude and civic virtues of the republican heroes of that time—the Spartans who died with Leonidas at Thermopylae, the Athenians who stood at Marathon, Brutus who drove out the Tarquins, Regulus who returned to Carthage, and that other Brutus, noblest Roman of them all, who from pure love of freedom struck Caesar down in the Senate house. Admiring the ancient republican heroes, it seemed to them that the golden age of freedom and enlightenment had ended when Caesar crossed the Rubicon, to be followed by a thousand years of despotism and superstition. But from this long Dark Age the world was in their own time emerging, the eternal struggle against tyranny was again the central issue, and in resisting the unwarranted measures of the British government were they not themselves standing at Armageddon? What better then could honest men do than to cultivate the civic virtues of the ancient republican heroes, each in his own way becoming a latter-day Valerius or Poplicola? John Adams, elected a delegate to the First Continental Congress, had his eye on Demosthenes. "When Demosthenes (God forgive me for recollecting his example) went ambassador from Athens to the other states of Greece, to excite a confederacy against Phillip, he did not go to propose a Non-Importation or Non-Consumption agreement!!!" [8] Doubting whether even non-intercourse measures, then regarded as radical, were radical enough for a true patriot, John Adams did not enquire modestly of the tutors. He enquired, none too modestly, of Demosthenes.

So long as Adams and his compatriots were concerned only to defend, against British legislation, the rights of British subjects, it was enough to rest their case on precedent, and to fortify their courage by recalling the virtues of the ancient republican heroes. But resistance to British measures presently involved them in war with the mother country, and war imposed upon them the hard necessity of declaring that the colonies "are and of right ought to be free and independent states." But by what right? The rights of British subjects were not sufficient to justify rebellion. To justify rebellion it was necessary to invoke a more inclusive principle than the rights of British subjects; and this more inclusive principle was found, not in precedent, nor yet in the traditional Christian philosophy of man's origin and destiny, but in the revolutionary doctrine of the natural and imprescriptible rights of man.

The American republic was thus founded on a revolutionary political philosophy—a fact of profound significance for the history of life and learning in the United States. Since the sixteenth century the advancement of learning in Europe had been a difficult business. It was carried on for the most part by scholars who were often excluded from the colleges and universities, and often proscribed by governments, because the doctrine of natural law and right reason which they accepted as the first premise in the search for truth was ostensibly at war with the Christian story of man's origin

10

and destiny which the community accepted as the necessary foundation of morality and public authority. But in the eighteenth century, for the first time since the Middle Ages, the principles officially affirmed as the foundation of civil government were coming to be identified, and in the American and French Revolutions were identified, with the premises accepted by scholars as essential to the advancement of knowledge.

In the eighteenth century, therefore, as one may say, established political philosophy and current science made a marriage of convenience. Both accepted the doctrine of natural law as God's revelation to men; both were committed to the theory that the nature of man and the institutions best suited to his happiness and welfare, so far from being divinely revealed in sacred scripture, and to be authoritatively interpreted and enforced by church and state, could only be progressively discovered by man himself through the free application of reason to experience and available knowledge. In so far as political philosophy was translated into practice, the constituted authorities were, therefore, obligated to guarantee freedom of opinion, and to regard colleges and universities as centers for the increase of knowledge rather than merely for the preservation and transmission of familiar and accepted ideas. In such institutions the rule would then presumably be that if pupils or professors in anything doubted they would consult, modestly or not (that was their affair), not the tutors, not the clergy or the magistrates, or even the "Great Principles of Christianity and Morality in which all true Christians are generally agreed," but the best right reason available to intelligent men.

Marriages of convenience, as is well known, are rarely entirely happy. The doctrine of natural law and right reason, however useful for effecting a separation from Great Britain, did little to dislodge from the minds of average men faith in the traditional Christian story of man's origin and destiny. For this reason the liberal ideas of the Enlightenment were less generally accepted, and their implications for education less well understood, among the mass of the people than among the political leaders, among the administrators than among the distinguished alumni of the colleges; and I need scarcely say that ingrained habits and settled ideas of professors were not all at once transformed by the doctrines enshrined in the Declaration of Independence. Nevertheless, before and during the American Revolution we can note the beginnings of such a transformation—the beginnings of those social and intellectual influences that were, during the course of another century, to bring about a liberal and democratic transformation of higher education in the United States.

Long before the middle of the eighteenth century Professor Samuel Johnson found in the Yale College Library copies of Newton's *Principia* and Bacon's *Advancement of Learning;* and from these and other works of similar import he discovered that mathematics and physics were instruments of vast importance for interpreting the ways of God to man: reading Bacon's *Advancement of Learning,* he said, was an experience like that "of a person suddenly emerging from a glimmer of twilight into the full sunshine of day." [9] In subsequent years Samuel Johnson became so well known for his interest in the natural sciences that he was called to be the first President of King's College in New York. According to the Prospectus of 1754, which he himself drafted, the college would provide instruction, not only in mathematics and the classical languages, but also in the arts of "surveying and navigation, of geography and history, of husbandry, commerce, and government, and in the knowledge of all nature in the heavens above us, and in the air, water, and earth around us . . . and of everything useful for the comfort, the convenience and elegance of life, in the chief manufactures relating to any of these things"—all to the end of leading students "from the study of nature to the knowledge of themselves, and of the God of nature, and their duty to Him, themselves, and one another." [10] This ambitious project, expressing so well the sentiments of an eighteenth-century *philosophe,* was apparently not very cordially received by the faculty, and was at all events aban-

doned altogether when President Johnson retired in 1762; but in
1785 the curriculum of the college (Columbia as it was then called)
was again revised to include the natural sciences, navigation, the rise
and progress of language, "history and chronology as low as the
fall of the Roman Empire," and the origin, extent, power, commerce, religion and customs of the principal kingdoms of the
world.[11]

The founding of the University of Pennsylvania may be regarded
(for our purpose, although not perhaps for the purpose of a loyal
alumnus of that institution) as the result of a movement started by
the publication, in 1749, of Benjamin Franklin's pamphlet on the
education of youth in Pennsylvania. Franklin maintained that the
time spent on the study of Greek and Latin might be better spent
on the study of more practical subjects, since for the majority of
young men, "in such a country as ours," a practical education would
be more useful.[12] Money was raised, within a few years an academy
was founded, and in 1756 the first Provost of this institution, later
known as the University of Pennsylvania, was appointed. The man
selected was the Rev. William Smith, one of several citizens of New
York who had been much interested in the founding of King's
College two years before, and had approved of the liberal ideas of
its first president.[13] Under the direction of William Smith the University of Pennsylvania offered a course of study that conformed in
many respects to the ideas of Samuel Johnson and Benjamin Franklin; and for many years that university was the most advanced of
American colleges in the emphasis it placed on the natural sciences,
politics and history, and the modern languages.[14]

No one in the eighteenth century advocated more novel measures for reforming higher education than Thomas Jefferson, and in
1779 his prestige in Virginia was sufficient to effect a complete re-
organization of William and Mary College. Knowledge of the classical languages was no longer required for entrance. Students were
free to elect any courses in any order, and to come up for their degrees when they thought themselves sufficiently prepared to pass

the examinations. New professorships were established in law and politics, in anatomy and medicine, in natural philosophy and the modern languages; and the chair of divinity was abolished because, as James Madison informed President Stiles of Yale, "an establishment in favor of any particular sect was thought to be incompatible with the freedom of a republic." [15]

Other colleges were less influenced by the liberal ideas of the time. If in some of them more attention was given to history and the natural sciences, it was less because of changes in the curriculum than because some or other professor happened to be interested in these subjects. Under President Leverett, according to Professor S. E. Morison, the liberal tradition was established at Harvard, which means that Harvard was "kept a house of learning under the spirit of religion, not, as the Mathers and their kind would have had it, the divinity school of a particular sect." The liberal tradition at least permitted the first Hollis Professor, Isaac Greenwood, to promote interest in the natural sciences, very much as Samuel Johnson did at Yale, by "giving lectures with demonstrations 'of the discoveries of the incomparable Sir Isaac Newton.'" [16] After 1735 French was intermittently taught at Harvard, but as late as 1814 George Ticknor could only with difficulty find a German dictionary or grammar in the Boston book shops or the college library.[17]

These were tentative beginnings in the liberal spirit of the Enlightenment; but the liberal movement, even in the colleges of William and Mary, Columbia, and the University of Pennsylvania, had largely spent its force before the end of the century. This was partly because the revolutionary war had weakened and impoverished the colleges as well as the country; but chiefly because the revolutionary upheaval, especially in France, had discredited the liberal philosophy of the pre-revolutionary period. At the opening of the nineteenth century the educated and governing classes, both in Europe and America, were in a mood to regard the word "revolution" as synonymous with the word "Jacobinism," and "Jacobinism" was for them much the same thing as political and moral anarchy. Mr. Thomas Paine, once highly respected as the author of *Common Sense* and *The Crisis,* was suddenly transformed, by the publication of *The Age of Reason,* into "old Tom Paine the free thinker." Even the author of the Declaration of Independence was fallen from his former high estate. In the North he was vilified as little better than an agent of international Jacobinism; while in the South his religious ideas were deplored, and explained on the convenient hypothesis that in his youth, most unfortunately, he had been led astray by the atheistical French writers.

This reversion to timidity in the community was equally pronounced in the colleges—perhaps even more pronounced in the colleges, since they were the guardians of youth. The fact may be symbolized by the contrast, in temper and outlook, between two presidents of Yale College: Ezra Stiles (1777–1795) and his successor Timothy Dwight (1795–1817). The genial curiosity and catholic sympathies of Ezra Stiles, always disposing him to try anything once, enabled him to smuggle into fixed classical courses much enlightening discussion of history, law and politics; and into a course on ecclesiastical history at least one lecture on ventriloquism.[18] Timothy Dwight, a man of vast learning, incredible energy, and skill as a teacher and administrator, is one of the heroic figures in the history of Yale College. That he did much for Yale College may be readily admitted. He obtained money for the college, enriched its library, enforced discipline, converted the students, made them study and like it, and even appointed Benjamin Silliman as Professor of Chemistry—something that we can hardly suppose he would have done could he have foreseen that the study of natural science would undermine religion as he understood it.[19] He did much to toughen the body of Yale College, but singularly little to enrich its spirit; for when all is said it must be said that he devoted his great learning and dynamic energy to the Canute-like enterprise of commanding the swelling tide of liberal thought to recede. As president and teacher his principal concern seems to have been to keep the students undefiled by the dangerous political ideas of

Thomas Jefferson, and the still more dangerous intellectual and religious ideas of the most distinguished writers of the eighteenth century. One of his notable efforts was the Baccalaureate address to the class of 1797: not one but two long sermons on *The Danger of Infidel Philosophy*. The infidels refuted were, among others, Shaftesbury, Hobbes, Bolingbroke, Hume, Voltaire, and Diderot. The argument refuting them was elaborate, uninspired, and notable for the careless distribution of undistributed middles throughout. The two sermons were sufficiently approved at the time to be printed and widely read but in retrospect one can only regard them as a pathetic, if valiant effort to make Yale College one of the homes of lost causes.

Not that Yale was any more the home of a lost cause than other colleges. In 1820 the curriculum of Columbia was no more liberal than it had been in 1786, while that of the University of Pennsylvania was less liberal than the one devised by its first Provost in 1756. By 1820, or thereabouts, and for half a century thereafter, all of the leading colleges, with the exception of the University of Virginia in so far as it conformed to Jefferson's plan, were so much alike, so standardized and set in respect to personnel, methods of instruction, and course of study, that no one but a loyal alumnus could easily distinguish one from another.

The course of study consisted of a thorough four-years' drill in the classical languages, supplemented by a little superficial instruction in natural science, history and politics, and modern literature. A few professors (such as Ticknor at Harvard, Silliman at Yale, and Lieber at South Carolina) gave stimulating lectures in the class room; but to hear a lecture by a distinguished scholar or man of letters the students had for the most part to go outside the college to the town Lyceum. Inside the college they prepared and recited the daily lesson. They were rarely invited to examine the content of any classical author, much less any, such as Plato or Lucretius, whose ideas might have led them in something to doubt by arousing them to unaccustomed thought. They received a good mark each day if they had learned the vocabulary and mastered the grammar of the assigned passage, or could turn into respectable Latin some respectable passage of English prose. They learned history and modern literature by memorizing each day, more or less verbatim, four or five pages of the prescribed textbook. In mental and moral philosophy the chief thing was to master the fine distinction between the ordinary, the primary, the predominant, and the primary-predominant choices of the will—choices which, if right, made the man right, here and hereafter. "Mr. Blank," said Professor Parks to a supposedly obtuse Dartmouth student, "if Peter had died when he was cursing and swearing, where would he have gone?" "Gone to Heaven, sir." "Doubtless, but how would he have gotten there?" "Got there on his primary-predominant." The student was not so obtuse after all, since his answer, being the right one, satisfied the professor.[20]

College faculties were composed, with some notable exceptions, of men who were entirely competent to teach by this method, since they had suffered an extremely competent training in it. Some of them were learned men, attending diligently to *hoti's* business; some, learned or not, were best known for personal eccentricity; and virtually all were cultivated and well informed men of unquestioned integrity and genuine devotion to their profession. If there were not among them as many uneducated specialists as may be found on faculties today, neither were there as many really original minds. Rarely troubled by doubt, and always disposed to rely on the recognized authorities, their chief distinction was to know and to enforce all of the right answers rather than to know or to ask any of the right questions. "I would rather have ten settled opinions, and nine of them wrong," Professor Taylor of Yale was accustomed to say, "than to be like my brother Gibbs with none of the ten settled." The attitude was typical at a time when, according to the younger Timothy Dwight, "the idea was so widespread and all-controlling that the teacher's work was . . . to bring Cicero into adjustment with Andrews and Stoddard's grammar, that no one, however free and gifted, could make it his great effort to put Andrews and Stoddard in accord with Cicero." [21] Boldness was not indeed the primary-predominant choice of professors in those days. But, lacking originality, they could be dogmatic; and there was no great danger of their being admonished on Lecture Day, since, for them, all of the really vital questions had been settled, and for every emergency (in the class room, in the market place or the political forum, in polite conversation or serious discourse) their minds were furnished with an ample supply of Latin tags to see them triumphantly through to the prejudged conclusion.

Anchored in the classics and stayed by authority, college faculties were for the most part impervious to the rising demand for more thorough study of natural science, history, and modern literature. Brander Matthews said that as late as his time in Columbia but one term was given to English literature, and that he was not introduced to any English author or told to read any. Henry Cabot Lodge said that at Harvard he "never had his mind roused to . . . anything resembling active thought"—except, he added, in Henry Adams's course in Mediaeval history. For fifteen years Benjamin Silliman, the most distinguished and best loved member of the Yale faculty, worked in a damp, ill-lighted underground laboratory, which he could enter only by backing down a ladder through a trap door; and he used to say that when he went to Philadelphia to lecture he carried all of Yale's geological specimens with him in a candle box. At Princeton instruction in natural science was more perfunctory and less competent than it had been in the eighteenth century under President Witherspoon. The scientific specimens were too bulky to be taken to Philadelphia (supposing that any one at Princeton had wanted to go to Philadelphia) in a candle box; but James McCosh, when inaugurated as president in 1868, pronounced them all fit only to be burnt.[22] Natural science made its way in the medical schools, through the Smithsonian Institution, and in special schools such as the Rensselaer Institute and the Lawrence and Sheffield schools at Harvard and Yale. But such schools were regarded by the college proper as not quite out of the top drawer. In the eighteen-fifties Andrew D. White spent three years at Yale without being more than vaguely aware that "Sheff" was a part of it; and one day, watching through the dusty window of an unfamiliar building some fellow manipulating a test tube, he wondered how any one could interest himself in such matters.

The lost cause, so explicitly defined and ably defended by the famous and influential Yale Report of 1828, was not the small college, still less the study of the classical languages and literature. The cause that was lost was the traditional conception, deriving with slight modification from the seventeenth century, of the purpose of learning and the function of colleges in the community. According to that conception, the function of such institutions was to preserve and transmit rather than to increase knowledge; and more especially to prepare a select group of young men, taken for the most part from the educated and governing classes, for the learned professions by giving them a limited command of the classical tongues, and transmitting to them the factual knowledge and ideas about man and the world in which he lived that would lend support to the political institutions, the moral habits, and the religious convictions acceptable to the best progressive-conservative thought of the time. The end desired, as the Yale Report said, was the disciplined and informed mind; but a mind disciplined to conformity and informed with nothing that a patriotic, Christian, and clubable gentleman had better not know.[23]

For half a century opposition to this conception of higher education became more widespread and insistent. The opposition was inspired by different motives, supported by different classes of people, and directed to different ends. An increasing number of scholars (foreign born and trained, or Americans returning from study abroad) were primarily interested in expanding the American college into centers of research and publication on the model of the best German and French universities. Others were primarily interested in liberalizing the course of study in the college itself, by giving more time and attention, as the Amherst Report of 1827 suggested, to "the modern languages, history, civil and constitutional law," and those physical sciences that "have a practical application to the useful arts and trades." [24]

But far more important than these limited demands for reform was the growing conviction, among the people throughout the country, that the older colleges were "undemocratic," and in any case unsuited to the needs of an industrial and agricultural community. As early as 1830 the workers of Philadelphia declared "that there can be no freedom without a wide diffusion of intelligence; that the members of a Republic should all be instructed alike in the nature of their rights and duties as human beings, and as citizens; . . . that until means of equal instruction shall be equally secured to all, liberty is an unmeaning word, and equality an empty shadow." [25] The idea is more explicitly expressed in the constitutions of many of the newer states, and nowhere better than in the constitution of Indiana, adopted in 1816: "It shall be the duty of the General Assembly, as soon as circumstances will permit, to provide by law for a general system of education, ascending in a regular gradation from township schools to state university, wherein tuition shall be gratis, and equally open to all." These are but two examples, out of innumerable ones that might be given, of the widespread conviction that in a country, as Franklin said, "such as ours" (a great, sprawling, sparsely settled country, whose people were committed to the principle of equality and largely engaged in agricultural and industrial pursuits), what was needed was a system of education that would enable the ordinary citizen, at slight cost or at public expense, to prepare himself for the practical occupations and to assume the political obligations of free men in a democratic society.

The concrete result of this widespread dissatisfaction with the older colleges was the multiplication of colleges and the establishment of state universities, especially in the newly settled and more remote sections of the country. But for many years most of these institutions were poorly endowed and incompetently staffed; and if it were necessary to fix a date when the general demand for educational reform began to win notable victories all along the line, the year 1865, when Governor Fenton signed the charter for Cornell University, would serve as well as any other. During the last quarter of the century, at all events, there occurred a striking expansion and transformation of the colleges and universities throughout the country. The most obvious change was quantitative—more students and professors, more and larger buildings, more and more varied equipment, more books in libraries, and endowments rising to heights never before dreamed of. Equally obvious was the rapid liberalization of the curriculum, and the adoption of the elective system in place of the fixed, required course of study. Less obvious, but more significant, was the expansion of a few state universities and some of the old colleges into universities properly so called— institutions that included—besides the college of liberal arts—professional schools, and graduate schools for the promotion of scientific research and publication in all branches of knowledge. Most significant of all was the fact that the best colleges and universities, accepting frankly the principle of freedom of learning and teaching, were able to find a place for those exceptional individuals whose function it is to advance the frontiers of knowledge, and thus to become, what the best European universities already were, centers for the promotion as well as for the preservation and transmission of human learning.

In this educational renaissance Cornell University played its part, and that not an insignificant one. Better than any other institution it may be said to have represented, in its organization and in its aims, all of the dominant trends of the time. Located neither in the old East nor in the newer West, it was shaped by the interests and currents of opinion that prevailed in both regions. It was not altogether a state university, like those of Michigan and Illinois, or altogether a privately endowed university, like Harvard and Yale, but a curious combination of both. It managed, with great ingenuity, to obtain munificent gifts from private individuals while holding lands granted by the federal government for a rise in price, and then to induce the state legislature to make additional and substantial appropriations for its support. It was founded by a shrewd, hard-headed farmer and business man with a practical outlook and a Quaker conscience, and organized by a Michigan professor of history who had graduated from Yale and was familiar at first hand with European universities; and as a result of their united efforts it was deliberately designed to meet the three cardinal demands of the time—the demand for a liberalization of the college of arts, for the promotion of scientific research, and for advanced professional training in agriculture and the mechanic arts.

The event that led directly to the establishment of this representative institution is connected with the demand for schools of agriculture and the mechanic arts. In a country so predominantly agricultural, and possessing immense stretches of free land, it was inevitable that the people should request the federal government to set aside a part of the public domain for the endowment of agricultural education. The most important response to this demand was the Morrill Land Grant College Act of 1862; and so far as New York State is concerned Cornell University was the direct result of the Morrill Act. In the next lecture I shall deal with the origin and nature of the Morrill Act.

II

The Morrill Land Grant College Act

The one class have schools, seminaries, colleges, universities, apparatus, professors . . . for educating them . . . for the peculiar profession which is the business of their life; and they have already created, each class for its own use, a vast and voluminous literature, that would well nigh sink a whole navy of ships. But where are the universities, the apparatus, the professors and the literature, specifically adapted to any one of the industrial classes? Echo answers, where?

JONATHAN B. TURNER

FEW things give historians more deep satisfaction, spiced as it is with a trace of malice, than to dig up evidence to prove that this or that celebrated document, until then supposed by every one to have been the work of some well known and honorable man, was really the work of some other fellow whom no one ever heard of before. It is because of this that I have to ask the question: Who was the originator of the so-called Morrill land grant college plan (until the point is determined it will be well to call it the so-called Morrill plan), and who was the author of the bill by which it was enacted into law? Not that it really matters very much, of course. But all the same, the question has been much and ardently debated; and since the honor of sovereign states is involved, and the right to wear laurels is at stake, I think we have a right to know what has been going on behind the scenes.

As every one knows (this is the lecturer's friendly way of calling the attention of his listeners to something he supposes they don't know)—as every one knows, the so-called Morrill Act provided for a federal grant of public land to each of the states as an endowment for education in agriculture and the mechanic arts. And as every one knows, the act became a law on July 2, 1862. But perhaps every one does not know that some years later, when it became a distinct merit to have had something to do with the famous act, Senator Morrill (as he then was) said that the phraseology of the act was wholly his own; and he intimated that the plan itself was wholly his own too. "I do not remember," he said in 1894, "of any assistance in framing the bill prior to its introduction." And again: "Where I obtained the first hint of such a measure, I am wholly unable to say." [1] But he as good as said that the measure was essentially the result of his own personal experience (that of a poor boy, the son of a village blacksmith), and of pure excogitation on his part. Thus Senator Morrill, after a lapse of years, gave the world to understand that he was the sole originator and author of the so-called Morrill Land Grant College Act. What more then do we want?

Well, in due course there were bound to be inquisitive historians who wanted a good deal more. They wanted to know whether, after a lapse of years, Senator Morrill hadn't forgotten some things. Had he not perhaps forgotten that in 1848, as a trustee of Norwich College, he was associated with its founder, Alden Partridge, and must have learned from him that many men throughout the country were discussing the need of agricultural colleges and the possibility of endowing them by grants of land from the public domain? More particularly, had he not forgotten that in 1856, the year before the so-called Morrill Act was first introduced in Congress, he was himself a delegate to the meeting of the United States Agricultural Society, and must at that time have heard the delegates discuss at length a specific plan for establishing an agricultural university in each state in the union, and for endowing each university with a federal land grant of a value not less than five hundred thousand dollars? This plan certainly did not originate with Mr. Morrill. It was drafted and promoted by Jonathan B. Turner, a professor in Illinois College; and those who are concerned for the honor of

Illinois say that this plan was the original form of the so-called Morrill Act. They say that the bill was not introduced by an Illinois congressman because Professor Turner and his friends thought it would have a better chance if introduced and sponsored by the representatives of some eastern state. They even say that Professor Turner and his friends requested Mr. Morrill to introduce the measure, turned over to him all of their documents relating to it, and, generally speaking, employed him as front man and mouth-piece for getting their plan enacted into law. And then, they say, the mere introducer of the bill got all the credit, whereas the laurels, such as they are, should rightfully be worn by Jonathan B. Turner of Illinois.[2]

So they say. And there is a good deal in what they say, but not, after all, as much as they would like us to think. I can well believe that Senator Morrill was unable, not only after a lapse of years but at any time, to say where he got the first hint for his bill. I doubt whether Professor Turner would have been any better able to say where he got the first hint for his plan. It was not a question of any-thing so illusive as hints. When the so-called Morrill Act was first introduced in Congress in 1857 the idea and the practice of endow-ing schools by federal land grants was a commonplace. It had by then become the settled policy of the federal government to set aside, in each state as it was admitted to the union, a part of the public domain for the support of education in that state. More than sixty million acres had already been set aside for the support of common schools; and four million acres had already been granted to fifteen states for the endowment of state universities. If any one needed a "first hint" for a plan essentially similar to the so-called Morrill Act, here were hints in God's plenty. Strictly speaking, no one originated the so-called Morrill Act. It was an obvious adapta-tion of ideas widely current and of practices long established. And for this reason, and because it is customary to attach to a law the name of the man who introduced it in Congress, we shall do no great violence to historic truth if we now revert to the established practice, and henceforth call the so-called Morrill Act the Morrill Act.

Let us not fail, however, to give all due credit to Jonathan B. Turner and Illinois. For some fifteen years prior to the introduction of the Morrill Act there had been a more or less active movement for the establishment of agricultural colleges. The movement was not started, nor much supported, by the farmers themselves. "The great and insuperable trouble," said James B. Angell, writing as late as 1869, "is to inspire farmers with the belief that science has anything to offer them." [3] But there were prominent men in most states (more especially in New York and Massachusetts, in Michigan and Illinois) who realized that science had much to offer the farmers. They were acquainted with recent advances made, chiefly in Europe, in the chemical and biological sciences; they knew that in the older communities the farms were being exhausted, and in the newer communities wastefully cultivated; and they believed that science could do much to improve the quality of the farms and advance the profits of the farmers, if only the farmers themselves could be sufficiently educated to understand their own business. They were convinced, therefore, that an agricultural college in each state would serve a double purpose: it would be a center for advancing the science of agriculture, and for teaching the farmers how to make a practical application of that science.

By no one was this program urged with more persistence, or with more picturesque volubility, than by Professor Jonathan B. Turner of Illinois College. Some of the leaders of the movement believed that the need could be adequately met by establishing courses in agriculture and the mechanic arts in the older colleges; and certain colleges had done something in that way. But Professor Turner soon became convinced that all such efforts would fail. The old colleges, he said, "have hauled a canoe alongside their huge professional steamships and invited the farmers and mechanics to jump on board and sail with them; but the difficulty is, they will not embark." His own ideas were first clearly formulated in an address delivered before a convention of farmers at Granville, Illinois, on November 18, 1851; and this address, afterwards published and widely circulated, contained most of the suggestions in what came to be known as the "Turner Plan." [4]

Professor Turner began his address by pointing out that the professional classes already had "colleges, universities, apparatus, professors . . . for educating them . . . for the peculiar profession which is the business of their life; and they have already created, each class for its own use, a vast and voluminous literature, that would well nigh sink a whole navy of ships. But where are the universities, the apparatus, the professors and the literature, specifically adapted to any one of the industrial classes? Echo answers, where?" To fill this empty, rhetorical "where," Professor Turner presented his plan—a plan that was perhaps a bit visionary, but not lacking in vision and imagination for all that. There should be, he thought, and potentially there already was in the Smithsonian Institution, a central directing organization at Washington. What was lacking was a national hook-up of this central organization with a network of institutions throughout the country—that is to say, "a university for the industrial classes in each of the states, with their consequent subordinate institutions, lyceums, and high schools in each of the counties and towns."

Professor Turner then went on to describe in much detail the kind of university he had in mind—an industrial university with its specially trained professors, its specialized library, its laboratories for conducting experiments in all the relevant scientific fields, and of course its model farm to demonstrate the advantages, to farmers and to the community as a whole, of husbandry conducted in a scientific manner. The central purpose of his entire plan was to make the university an integral part of the life of the community, a fact which might well be played up a good deal at Commencement time. Commencement exercises should be, Professor Turner thought, in the nature of an annual fair, lasting several days, during which agricultural products from all parts of the state would be exhibited, and prizes awarded for the best specimens of every sort. And maybe (Professor Turner does not say, but I would not put it past him) horse races, and contests with horseshoes to see who could throw the most ringers. In short, a glorified state fair conducted by the university on a scientific basis, and with an Arcadian simplicity and expansiveness—the spirit of ancient Olympian games reborn in the Illinois cornfields!

But the endowment for these universities—what of that? In his Granville address Professor Turner said that, so far as Illinois was concerned, the lands already granted to the state, if not diverted to other purposes, were "amply sufficient." Very shortly, however, he and his friends were urging something more than that; and on February 8, 1853, the Illinois legislature adopted a resolution that may have been drafted by Professor Turner and his friends, and at any rate expressed their ideas on the subject. The resolution directed the Illinois representatives in Congress to work, in cooperation with representatives of other states, for "a law of Congress donating to each state in the Union an amount of land, not less in value than $500,000, for the liberal endowment of a system of industrial universities, one in each state in the Union, to cooperate with the Smithsonian Institution in Washington, for the more liberal and practical education of the industrial classes and their teachers; a liberal and varied education adapted to the needs of a practical and enterprising people." [5] This resolution may be taken to be the Turner Plan in its final and essential form; and in the same year Professor Turner and his friends organized "the Industrial League" to obtain support for it in Congress and throughout the country.

The first step, obviously, was to prepare a bill for congressional action. In 1854, at the request of Representative Yates of Illinois, Professor Turner himself drafted such a bill and sent it on; but for various reasons it was not thought advisable to introduce it at that time. In 1857 the circumstances seemed more favorable, and in October of that year Professor Turner wrote to Senator Trumbull suggesting that the bill be introduced by the Illinois representatives at the coming session. In reply, Senator Trumbull said that he would gladly support such a bill—so much land at the disposal of Congress was, he thought, a perennial source of patronage and corruption, and the sooner the federal government got rid of the land the better; but, he said, Congress was just then reluctant to make any new grants of land, and particularly so if the request for them came from the western states, since so much of the public domain had already been turned over to those states. For this reason, Senator Trumbull thought, it would be advisable to have the bill introduced and sponsored by the representatives of one of the eastern states.[6] This was in October, 1857; and two months later Mr. Morrill of Vermont introduced the Morrill bill.

That Mr. Morrill was at that time familiar with the Turner Plan can hardly be doubted. We know that he was a delegate to the meeting of the United States Agricultural Society in 1856, where the Turner Plan was discussed at length. We know that as late as 1856 he was still advocating the establishment of national agricultural colleges on the model of the West Point military academy —something quite different from the colleges contemplated in the Morrill bill. It is reasonable, therefore, to suppose that in framing the Morrill bill he took over the essential feature of the Turner Plan —that is, the proposal to endow an agricultural college in each state by a federal land grant. But there is no good reason to suppose that Professor Turner asked Mr. Morrill to introduce the Turner bill, or that he turned over to him all of his papers relating to it. This is a claim that was made much later. At this later time there is reference to a "voluminous correspondence" between Professor Turner and Mr. Morrill, the only evidence that such a body of letters ever existed being the assertion that it must have been lost. About all that is extant, at all events, is a brief, formal note from Mr. Morrill, dated December 30, 1861, acknowledging the receipt of a letter from Professor Turner—such a note as a public man of many acquaintances usually writes in reply to a letter from some one whose name, he vaguely feels, ought to mean something to him but in fact doesn't.[7]

So far as the crucial years 1857–1859 are concerned there is no contemporary evidence that Professor Turner himself ever claimed, or that any one ever claimed for him, any credit for framing the Morrill bill, or for getting it introduced in Congress. On the other hand, there is a letter from Professor Turner to Senator Trumbull, dated January 4, 1858, which clearly indicates that he had nothing directly to do with the Morrill bill, and was not in any case very well satisfied with it. "I thank you much," he writes, "for copy of the industrial university appropriation bill. I like its main features, but hope it may have *some* amendment. I send by this mail another copy of our reports, thinking you may not have one at hand and may desire to refer to the action of our state." [8] This, to say the least of it, does not sound like the letter of a man who had asked Mr. Morrill to introduce his bill for him, had turned over all of his papers relating to it, and generally speaking was, with his Illinois friends, standing by watching and directing the whole performance. It is the letter of a man who, two weeks after the Morrill bill was introduced, learns for the first time what the provisions of the bill are, and wonders what, if anything, can be done at that late date to make it conform more closely to his own plan.

However that may be, one thing is certain: the bill actually introduced by Mr. Morrill differed from the Turner Plan in one very important respect, and the difference was highly prejudicial to Illinois. According to the Turner Plan each state was to receive an amount of land equal in value to $500,000; according to the Morrill bill each state was to receive 20,000 acres (in the final act increased to 30,000) for each senator and representative in Congress to which it was entitled by the preceding census. No wonder Professor Turner hoped the bill "would have *some* amendment," since the difference was by no means a negligible one. It meant, for example, that New York would receive more than twice as much land as Illinois, and approximately one tenth of the entire grant.

This method of allocating the lands was adopted to win the support of the eastern states. "Many easterners," says Professor Paul Gates, "were now ready to support free homesteads and liberal land grants to railroads in exchange for [western] support for high tariffs, favorable immigration laws, a national banking system, and ship subsidies." [9] But they felt that the western states had been granted more than their fair share of the public domain. The provision of the Morrill bill for allocating the lands was thus just an ordinary political bargain—give us a share-plus in the public lands, and we will give you your agricultural colleges.

The people of the West wanted agricultural colleges, but as it turned out were extremely reluctant to pay the price demanded in the Morrill bill. The bill, introduced December 14, 1857, was passed by a bare majority (25–22 in the Senate; 105–100 in the House), and the adverse vote came largely from the South and the West. Vetoed by President Buchanan, February 24, 1859, the bill was reintroduced, with slight modifications, three years later, passed by a larger majority (32–7 in the Senate; 91–25 in the House), and signed by President Lincoln July 2, 1862. As before, the favorable vote came chiefly from the eastern states, the adverse vote chiefly from the western states; and if the adverse vote was greatly reduced, that was because many of the southern states were not then represented in Congress.[10] It seems odd, certainly, that there should have been so much opposition to the Land Grant College Act by the very states that most approved of those provisions that make it seem to us admirable, and that alone have made it famous. The reasons for this opposition need to be understood in order to appreciate certain circumstances connected with the foundation of Cornell University; but in order to understand them we must first have a somewhat detailed knowledge of the act itself.

The Morrill Act has the following title: "An act donating public lands to the several States and Territories which may provide colleges for the benefit of agriculture and the mechanic arts." [11] The act is comparatively short, and if I wanted to be accurate at all costs

I could very well quote the chief passages verbatim. But since I want to make the act intelligible, I will venture, even at the risk of some slight error, to summarize its chief provisions in language that the non-legal mind can understand. To safeguard myself still further, I ought to say that in the course of drafting and passing the bill the framers appear to have suffered a slight attack of amnesia: the title of the act expresses the intention of donating lands to the several territories, but the act itself fails to donate them any.

The Morrill Act provided, first of all, that each state should receive 30,000 acres of public land for each Senator and Representative in Congress to which it was entitled by the apportionment of 1860. For this purpose public land was defined as "land subject to sale and private entry at one dollar and twenty-five cents per acre"; and if land acquired by any state had, at the time of entry, doubled in value as "a consequence of railroad grants," the number of acres donated to that state should be proportionately reduced. But how were the lands to be transferred to the states? Here a distinction had to be made. Within the limits of some eight western states there was still a sufficient amount of public land to cover the donation to those states. In all such cases, therefore, the land donated to each state was to be selected from the public land within the limits of that state, and the state itself could acquire title to the land and either sell it at once or hold it for a better price.

But in many states (New York for example) there were no public lands at all; in others (Illinois for example) there were still some public lands, but not enough to cover the total donation. For donating lands to these states another method had, therefore, to be adopted. Carefully concealing this important distinction as long as possible, the act ever so casually slips it to the reader in the third clause of a long-winded sentence defining the method of donation: "and the Secretary of the Interior is hereby instructed to issue to each of the states in which there is not the quantity of public lands . . . to which it is entitled . . . land scrip to the amount in acres for the deficiency of its distributive share." Just so. This means, to take a concrete example, that New York State, instead of being given title to its share of public lands (989,920 acres), would be given 6,187 pieces of federal government land scrip (each piece good for 160 acres) which could be used by private persons to acquire title to that number of acres of public land in any of the states and territories where there was any.

But why not permit the state itself to use its scrip to acquire title in its own name? Well, it would never do of course to allow one sovereign state to walk in majesty and peace into the domain of another sovereign state and take possession of public lands therein. It could in effect get possession, that was the intention of the act; but it could do it only by indirection. The act therefore further provided: "said scrip to be sold by said States and the proceeds . . . applied to the uses . . . prescribed in this act." To make what was perfectly clear a little clearer the act went on to say: "Provided, that in no case shall any State to which land scrip may thus be issued be allowed to locate the same within the limits of any other State, or Territory." But then, thinking perhaps that a little obscurity would after all be good for the lay mind, the act added: "but their assignees may thus locate said scrip upon any of the unappropriated lands of the United States . . . but not to exceed one million acres in any one State." What is obscure is the meaning of "assignees." If a state sold the scrip to a private person the purchaser would be its assignee; but if, wishing to endow a particular college, it gave its scrip to that college, as Rhode Island gave its scrip to Brown University, would that college be its assignee within the meaning of the act? The act does not say, but the legal mind says not; it says that the clause "said scrip to be sold by said States" is mandatory, so that in giving its scrip to Brown University Rhode Island violated the act. I hope this is clear, or as clear as may be, since it was by the authority of this provision (a somewhat more ingenious and complicated manipulation of the provision than a strict interpretation of the act would seem to warrant) that Cornell University obtained by far the larger part of its endowment.

We now come to the central and controlling provision of the Morrill Act—the provision defining the purposes for which the lands and scrip were donated to the several states. The act states that all proceeds from the sale of lands or scrip "shall be invested in . . . safe stocks, yielding not less than five percentum upon the par value of said stocks; and moneys so invested shall constitute a perpetual fund . . . the interest of which shall be inviolably appropriated . . . to the endowment, support, and maintenance of at least one college where the leading object shall be, without excluding other scientific and classical studies, and including military tactics, to teach such branches of learning as are related to agriculture and the mechanic arts, in such manner as the legislatures of the States may respectively prescribe, in order to promote the liberal and practical education of the industrial classes in the several pursuits and professions of life." And that this purpose might be faithfully fulfilled, certain subsidiary provisions were included. These were: (1) that each state should formally accept the act as a condition of benefiting by it; (2) that if the invested funds were lost or diminished the state concerned should replace the amount; (3) that if any state failed, within five years, to provide "at least not less than one college [admirable phrase!], as described in . . . this act," it should pay back to the United States all proceeds received from the sale of lands or scrip; and (4) that not more than ten per cent of the proceeds of the sale of lands or scrip should be used to purchase land for experimental farms or sites for college buildings, and that no part of the proceeds or interest should be used for the purchase, erection, or maintenance of any buildings.

Such was the Morrill Land Grant College Act. Land Grant College Act is a proper name for it, since it was, obviously, two distinct measures joined together—a measure for granting public lands, and a measure for endowing colleges. What especially strikes one, in following the debates in Congress, is the singular indifference of the representatives to those educational provisions that have made the act famous. Representative Morrill, it is true, defended the first bill on the ground that it was a great educational charter—a measure that would "enable the farmer to raise two blades of grass instead of one" (not a difficult thing to do one would suppose), that would do something for "cheap education," that would do something for all men "who love intelligence and not ignorance." Whether he was voicing his own deep conviction, or merely defending his bill at its least vulnerable point, is none too clear. But what is clear is that the Morrill bill, both in its earlier and in its later form, won support or incurred opposition chiefly because of its advantages or disadvantages as a measure for distributing public lands. The eastern states gave the bill very nearly a unanimous support, and their reasons for supporting it were well expressed in a resolution of the New York legislature, in 1858, instructing its representatives not to vote "for any further appropriations of public lands to the newer states until just provisions be made by which the original states shall receive their equitable proportion of said lands." [12] The Morrill bill gave them what they regarded as their equitable proportion, and they therefore voted for it, less because it gave them colleges than because it gave them lands.

The representatives from the western states were not in a position to vote with much enthusiasm either for or against the act, since they regarded the method of granting the lands as a bad means of obtaining a good end, which was the endowment of agricultural colleges. Those who voted for the measure did so in spite of the bad means; those who voted against it did so in spite of the good ends. The means were bad, they all thought, partly because the eastern states were given more than their proper share of the endowment, but chiefly because the method of granting the lands would open a free field for unscrupulous land speculators, of whose activities they had seen more than enough. The evil was already notorious, especially in Illinois and Iowa, where enormous tracts of land were held by absentee owners for a rise in prices. The Homestead Act was the result of a long effort to end this evil by reserving public lands in small farms for actual settlers, and the western states supported it for that reason. How then could they support the Morrill Act, which was so obviously calculated, in effect if not in intention, to defeat the purposes of the Homestead Act? Senator Lane declared that the Morrill Act was "in contradiction to the Homestead proposition," and that it "contained the ruin of the state" of Kansas which he represented. Senator Wilkinson of Minnesota voiced the general opinion in those states that still had vast tracts of unappropriated public lands within their borders. "The scrip," he said, "will pass into the hands of speculators, a remorseless class of vampires, who care little for the general prosperity, and still less for the cause of education." [13]

It is scarcely an exaggeration to say that in 1862 the Morrill Act was less well known as a land grant college act than as a land grant grab act. And not without reason, as it turned out. For our purpose the point is important, since it helps to understand certain circumstances connected with the founding of Cornell University. It was this attitude towards the Morrill Act that gave credit and currency to the charges against Ezra Cornell. He was charged with being an ordinary land speculator. He was charged with conspiracy to rob the state. He was charged with being primarily interested in grabbing land for the enrichment of the Cornell family rather than for the endowment of Cornell University. As it happens the charges were false, because Ezra Cornell happened to be an honest man; but that was something which, in that golden age of free economic enterprise, no one but a Diogenes would have thought it worth while to light a lantern to look for among the buoyant, pushing crowd of western land buccaneers.

We need not be surprised, therefore, to find that an act so impregnated with the odor of the political trader and the land speculator was not hailed throughout the country as a great educational charter. It is true that in 1862, when the country was engaged in a desperate civil war, there was less interest in education than there had been in 1858. But even the avowed friends of agricultural education found singularly little to say in commendation of the Morrill Act. It was in no sense played up in the newspapers, or even much commented upon in the agricultural journals. The *New England Farmer* ignored it altogether. The *American Agriculturalist* gave it a twelve-line summary, and promised to comment later, but did not, for some reason, find time to do so for more than a year. As late as 1891 the founders of Poole's *Index to Periodical Literature* could find no more than six articles on the subject that were worth listing. Indifference to the act is reflected in the general belief that not many states would think the value of the grant worth the obligations they would assume in accepting it. Even Horace Greeley, who defended the act with more spirit than most, seems to have shared this belief: he could only say that the act would have been worth while if even five states took advantage of its provisions.[14]

As it turned out, most of the states then in the union did accept the act, but not with much eagerness, or any conviction that they were embracing a splendid opportunity to promote the cause of agricultural education. And after all there was no good reason for any such conviction. The grants were in fact less munificent than we (here at Cornell at any rate) are apt to think. To say that ten million acres of public land was made available for agricultural education sounds very impressive; but when the acres are translated into dollars the result is much less impressive. So much land suddenly dumped on the market inevitably depressed the price, so that quotations fell as low as forty-three cents an acre. Indiana, a fairly typical case, sold its 390,000 scrip acres for an average price of fifty-three cents per acre, netting $206,700; a sum which, invested even at seven per cent (a possibility at that time) would provide an annual income of $14,469.[15] Fourteen thousand dollars is fourteen thousand dollars, no doubt; and no college at

37

that time would think it a bagatelle—a little loose change which might be slipped to the Superintendent of Grounds for beautifying the campus. But even so, fourteen thousand dollars was only about one fifth of the income of the University of Michigan in 1867, or of the Massachusetts Institute of Technology in 1871 [16]— that is to say, quite inadequate, even at that time, for maintaining a first-class college. In accepting the grant, therefore, any state was confronted with the not too agreeable fact that the obligations involved, if adequately met, might very well cost it more than the value of the land received.

Generally speaking, the states did no more than was necessary to meet the obligation. Unwilling or unable to make the appropriations necessary for founding a new college, they commonly followed the line of least effort by selling the land or scrip for what it would bring, and turning over the proceeds, such as they were, to whatever existing college was prepared, or could at least make a formal show of being prepared, to give instruction in agriculture and the mechanic arts. In many cases the proceeds were less than they might have been. Some states managed the business badly, others were swindled by speculators, or by government officials in cahoots with speculators. "The story of the disposal of the agricultural scrip by the states," according to Professor Gates, "is one of neglect, carelessness, and something closely akin to corruption." So closely akin as makes no matter, one is apt to think in view of the specific examples given by Professor Gates in support of his statement. His conclusion, at all events, is that "the meager returns received from the land and scrip were [so] discouraging" that "the early history of many of the agricultural colleges is marked with promising beginnings, followed by quick retrenchments." [17] The carelessness and neglect, the "something closely akin to corruption," might have been avoided, no doubt. But that would not, after all, have added a great deal to the sums actually obtained. The truth is that, apart from some extraordinary good luck or the exercise of a questionable ingenuity, it was not

38

possible, under the existing conditions, for any state to derive a very large endowment from its share of the Morrill land grant, or to make an effective use of its share without substantial appropriations on its own account.

Of all the states, New York was the most favored by the Morrill Act. Its share of the gift was approximately one tenth—to be exact, 989,920 scrip acres. On March 4, 1863, the New York legislature passed an act "declaring the acceptance . . . of the provisions" of the Morrill Act, and then on May 5 of the same year it passed an act authorizing the Comptroller to receive the scrip and to sell it under certain conditions.[18] There was at that time no reason to suppose that New York would manage its scrip better than other states did, or get more for it per acre. The general expectation, inside and outside of the legislature, was that the scrip would soon be sold, and that it would bring in at most a sum of $600,000, so that there would be available annually a sum of from thirty-five to forty thousand dollars to be turned over to one or more of the existing colleges.

There were plenty of colleges. According to the Regents' Report for the academic year 1863–1864, there were, subject to the visitation of the Regents, 236 academies in the state. Of these, some twenty odd were classed by the Regents as colleges, with a total registration of 1,527 students. To any one of these colleges, with the possible exception of Columbia, an addition of $35,000 to its annual income had all the appearance of inexhaustible manna from Heaven, and most of them, having no expectation whatever of obtaining the entire grant, were in favor of having it divided among them all.[19] But there were two colleges that could make a plausible claim for the entire grant, since each one was founded to give instruction in those subjects (agriculture and the mechanic arts) specifically mentioned in the Morrill Act. These were the Agricultural College at Ovid, and the People's College at Havana (now Montour Falls). It is true that in 1863 neither college had any students, nor was either college in a position to meet the conditions imposed by the Morrill Act; but any friend of either college could point to its charter and say that its intentions were of the best, since they conformed so exactly to the purposes for which the grant was made.

Such was the situation and such were the expectations in New York in regard to the Morrill land grant in 1863. No man in his right mind supposed that the scrip could be made to yield any such fantastic sum as five million dollars. There were indeed only two ways in which any state could realize from its scrip any such sum as that. One way was to violate the law, as Illinois apparently did, by locating its scrip in another state on its own account, holding it for fifteen or twenty years for a rise in price, and gamble on getting away with it. The other way was to sell its scrip to some individual sufficiently public spirited to locate the land and hold it for a similar period, and then turn the proceeds over to the college selected by the state as the beneficiary of the act. No state could count on there being, at the right time, just that sort of altruist with sufficient ability and capital to carry the business through. New York could not, and did not, count on it either. Yet that is precisely what happened. At precisely the right time, in 1864 and 1865, Ezra Cornell, a member of the Senate much interested in agricultural education, was wondering what he could best do for the public good with some four or five hundred thousand dollars more than he thought his family would need.

The presence of Ezra Cornell, with the settled conviction that he ought to spend his extra cash for the public good, was certainly a most fortunate circumstance for New York, and for higher education in the United States, since it was one of a series of related events which led to the founding of Cornell University. In itself, however, it would not have been sufficient to achieve that result. In 1863, when the Morrill Act was accepted by New York, Ezra Cornell had no intention of founding a new university. He was then working to obtain the proceeds of the land scrip for the State Agricultural College at Ovid; and in 1864, when it seemed impossible to obtain all of it, he introduced a bill in the legislature to divide the proceeds between the Agricultural College and the People's College. It had not yet seriously occurred to him that anything more than six hundred thousand dollars could be realized from the scrip, and he seems to have thought that by adding his extra cash to that sum, or to half of it, for the rehabilitation of the Agricultural College, he would be doing all that he could for the promotion of agricultural education in the state of New York.

The presence of Ezra Cornell was perhaps the most important, but after all only one of many odd chances, designs of fate, or interventions of Providence (call it what you like) that seemed, during the crucial years from 1863 to 1865, to be always conspiring to prevent the state of New York from making any but the best use of its gift from the federal government. That fate, or Providence, or the laws of probability should have thus exhibited, at many crucial moments, such unaccustomed interest in the public good is an arresting thought—something that obviously needs to be carefully looked into. But an inquiry into the mysterious behavior of the higher powers is always, or should be, a delicate matter. There are those, of course, who think otherwise—those who regard such an inquiry as in the nature of a bold frontal assault, with vast and heavily armored generalizations, in the hope of reducing the behavior of the higher powers to some simple, invariable law, such as the conflict of economic classes for material gain, or the foreordained, perennial conflict between the clearly discernible forces of light and of darkness. The advantage of proceeding in this way is that, by reducing the individual man to a mere chance deposit on the surface of the world, and the odd chance and recalcitrant event to a negligible exception to the rule, the historian is relieved of the hard task of thinking on his own account—has no longer to make terms with the fact that human life is always exceedingly complex and often inexplicable, or take into account those curious conjunctions of fortuitous circumstances and exceptional individuals which, to the unsophisticated, so frequently seem to be the trivial causes of great events.

The founding of Cornell University seems to fall into this category. In relating the story of its founding I shall, therefore, at the risk of being classed with the unsophisticated, ignore the invariable laws of history, and proceed to inquire into the interesting and apparently fortuitous conjunction of circumstances without which it seems extremely unlikely that Cornell University would ever have existed. And this inquiry into the mysterious behavior of the higher powers may well begin, I think, by exploring the minor mystery of Ezra Cornell, a rich but honest man who could make a case of conscience out of the prosaic fact that he had five hundred thousand dollars more than he thought his family would ever need.

III

Circumstances and the Man: Ezra Cornell

My greatest care now is how to spend this large income to do the greatest good to those who are properly dependent on me, to the poor and to posterity. EZRA CORNELL

I DO not know why it should be so often thought necessary to slander poor people by saying of one's hero that "he was born of poor but honest parents." For once let us take the honesty for granted. Both of Ezra Cornell's parents were poor, and both were of New England stock. Perhaps it should be added that both were Quakers: that admirable fellowship whose members have fared well in the world by adhering to three fundamental articles of faith—the inner light, the brotherhood of man, and, in the City of Brotherly Love at least, as I have been told, five per cent ground rent. Elijah, the father of Ezra, conformed well enough, I dare say, to the first two articles, but he had little occasion to practice the third. Born in Swansea, Bristol County, Massachusetts, he became a journeyman potter and sometime school teacher. From Swansea he moved to Westchester Landing on the Bronx River, and there, on July 4, 1805, he married Eunice Barnard, whose father belonged to the adventurous company of New England sea captains sailing out of New Bedford for the Grand Banks. It was here, at Westchester Landing, to these good people of New England ancestry and Quaker convictions, that Ezra Cornell was born on January 11, 1807.

During the boy's early years the family moved about a good deal, seeking better fortunes in various nearby towns; but finally in 1819 they moved out west to De Ruyter, New York. Ezra was

43

then twelve years old, the eldest of six children, the youngest an infant in arms. The long journey was made by the family of eight in a covered wagon, drawn by two horses, and loaded with household goods and potter's implements. Whenever possible they stopped for the night at a farmhouse; more often they had to make do with cooking their meals over a fire by the roadside and sleeping, huddled together, in the wagon. For three weeks, in the chill days and nights of November–December, they thus lived and travelled, moving on to the frontier, land of opportunity.

At De Ruyter Elijah turned to farming, and during the winter months taught the district school, with Ezra one of his pupils. Ezra tells us that "reading, spelling, arithmetic, geography, and grammar were the only branches taught, and it generally required the first month of every winter to regain the knowledge lost during the summer vacation." We may guess that Ezra was the brightest and most diligent pupil. Then or later, certainly, he learned all of these branches of knowledge well enough. But he seems to have taken a special interest in arithmetic. At the age of sixteen, at all events, he got himself a "Cyphering Book" in which he did sums —"I have just got 503 sums to this date," so the record runs in 1824. This was his last year of schooling, and to pay for it he and his brother cleared four acres of forest, cutting the timber for lumber and firewood, pulling the stumps and burning the brush.[1]

With his formal education finished at the age of seventeen, Ezra turned to carpentry, which he picked up with such facility that during the next year he designed and built, with a good deal of neighborly applause, a very sound frame house on his father's farm. The same year or the next he set out, with nine dollars in his pocket, to make his fortune, working for some three years at carpentry and other trades at Syracuse and Homer; and then, one day in April, 1828, with a little spare cash in his pocket and a box of carpenter's tools over his shoulder, he walked from De Ruyter to McLean, and the next day went on to Ithaca, catching his first sight of the town, as like as not, as he came up the rise from Free

Hollow (Forest Home) round Beebe Lake. The first thing he did, according to his brother-in-law, Otis E. Wood, was to enter a hotel and indulge in "one of his Quaker capers. He said to the landlord: 'If a decent young man were to come along and say that he had had no breakfast and had no money to pay for one, what would you do?' 'I would tell him to come in and have something to eat.' 'Well,' said Ezra, 'here's your chance.' When he came out after he had had his breakfast, he put down twenty-five cents. 'I thought you didn't have any money,' says the landlord. 'No, I didn't say so. I just wanted to know what you would do if I didn't have any.' " [2]

When Ezra Cornell came to Ithaca, at the age of twenty-one, he was a tall, angular, physically powerful man. A picture taken at the time discloses a large head, with deeply lobed, protruding ears and high cheek bones. The dark hair, carefully brushed down for the occasion, surmounts and partly conceals a high, well shaped fore-head. Beneath prominent but unaggressive brows, wide-set eyes look out with attention, appraisingly, yet with a certain detach-ment, as if they were reserving judgment: an impression confirmed by the strong nose and chin, and a mouth that is wide, firmly set, and a bit grim at the corners without being either tight or bitter. Altogether a face that reveals character—the self-reliance of a man who has learned to take it, who proposes to meet without fear or elation a world that he knows to be exacting and unromantic, and to make the most of whatever it may have to offer to one upon whom Fortune has conferred no extraneous favors, no favors at all except good health, tempered courage, and sound common sense. [3]

Such qualities, however, being the essential ones, served the young man well enough. On July 16, 1828, he began to work in Mr. Eddy's cotton mill, located on the site of the present Cas-cadilla Hall. [4] The next year he obtained what proved to be a permanent job in Jeremiah Beebe's plaster and flour mill near the Fall Creek bridge over the present lower lake road. Two years later, on March 19, 1831, he married Mary Ann Wood, whom he had met at her home in Dryden before coming to Ithaca. To be near the mill, he built a house called "The Nook" about two hundred yards north of Fall Creek, and there his nine children were born. Since Mary Ann was not a Quaker, Ezra was expelled from the fellowship for marrying out of meeting; and it is said that a good Quaker, in the way of duty, walked the forty miles from De Ruyter to inform brother Ezra that he had committed a grave fault, but that he might be reinstated if he would say he was sorry. Ezra replied, with some firmness, that he would never be sorry for the best act of his life. The reply was characteristic. As a young man, and throughout his life, Ezra Cornell formed opinions and reached decisions with a most serene indifference to what others might think or do, and once having formed his opinion or reached his decision he was not disposed to think any better of it because others approved, or any less well because others opposed it. This trait Andrew D. White once described by saying that, in respect to a certain matter, "Mr. Cornell was what he calls 'firm,' but what we rather called 'obstinate.' " [5]

One essential quality of Ezra Cornell's intelligence was a Yankee flair for manipulating material things and mastering practical affairs—a talent that soon won for him the confidence of his employer and his fellow townsmen. "I commenced working for Mr. Beebe," he says, "in 1829 at repairing his plaster mill at Fall Creek. After the mill was repaired . . . I took a contract of him to grind and measure out to customers 600 tons of plaster for fifty cents per ton. . . . The next first of May, I commenced working for him by the year, taking charge of all his business at Fall Creek at a salary of $350 per annum. . . . The summer of 1830 I . . . blasted the tunnel through the rock to take water from the dam above the falls for the mill. . . . In 1831 we lowered the tunnel four feet, and built a new dam across the creek." Under Ezra's management the business seems to have prospered greatly, so that in 1838–39 he

46

designed and supervised the construction of a larger factory, "the most complete of any in the state at that time." [6]

Meantime, the rising young business man took an active part in the affairs of the community. He subscribed for ten shares in the Tompkins County Bank. He joined the Whig party, and was often to be seen on the counter of John J. Speed's store of an evening, as Theodore Cuyler remembered him, "a shrewd, managing chap—unfolding schemes for carrying the township for the Whig ticket." He was sufficiently esteemed to be elected, in 1837, a delegate to the county convention, and to be asked, in the same year, to address an audience of business men on the subject, highly important at the moment, of bank failures.[7] At the age of thirty Ezra Cornell was obviously on the way to become a leading citizen of the community; and on his record one might have expected him to be, at the age of forty-five, the rich man of the town, owner of the principal mills, trustee of the bank, local political tycoon, and no doubt the envied owner of a mansion, on Buffalo Street perhaps, more mistakenly Gothic and pretentious than any that now survive to render that noble thoroughfare gloomy and forbidding.

But this is all pure fancy. At the age of forty-seven Ezra Cornell was, as he tells us in his Cyphering Book, sunk under a mountainous debt of fifty thousand dollars.

Now this, surely, is an odd thing to have happened to a shrewd, hard-headed, prudent young business man; and we naturally ask what could have brought about such an astounding defeat of the practical intelligence and its grasp of affairs. Both circumstances and the man contributed to the defeat, but the man more than the circumstances. The initial circumstance was the panic of 1837,[8] as a consequence of which in 1841 Ezra Cornell, at the age of thirty-four, lost his job. A reverse certainly, but surely not, at the age of thirty-four, a disaster. An ordinary shrewd, prudent young business man would have begun again, got another job in the community, saved his money, and then gone on in the conventional way to become a solid citizen. But Ezra Cornell was not an ordinary business man, and he did not act quite as an ordinary business man would have done.

Ezra Cornell might be described succinctly as a tough-minded idealist. There are a couple of revealing letters written by him at the age of forty or thereabouts to his son Alonzo, then a lad of about fifteen. He advises the boy, as fathers are apt to do with unnecessary repetition, to study hard; but he recommends to him two rules which he thinks especially useful for the guidance of one's life. The first is the Golden Rule: "As ye would that others should do unto you, do ye also unto them." The second he thinks almost equally important: Keep a daily expense account book, do not spend a cent without "putting it down . . . with the name of the article." [9] A modern version of "trust God and keep your powder dry"! The first rule Ezra observed as well as most men, rather better, in fact; but I suspect that the second was so strongly recommended to the son because it was a counsel of perfection which the father himself could not follow. The daily expense account book is for the near in spirit, who live in hourly fear that on some unguarded occasion a nickel may slip unobserved through their fingers. Ezra Cornell was not at all that kind of man. He was too large-handed to be always pinching the pennies; his own daily expense account books—the few that have been preserved [10]—are rather sad affairs; and even in his major undertakings he was often astonishingly casual in attending to financial details.

The point is that Ezra Cornell cared singularly little either for business or money-making. He had indeed the Yankee flair for gadgets, a hard practical intelligence, a dry salty humorous appreciation of the foibles of men, and a certain talent (not nearly as good as he often thought) for beating them (or, as he said, for "tiring them out") at their own game. In all this he was as native to these states as Ben Franklin or the Man Who Corrupted Hadleyburg. But with all his grasp of the practical there was in him a marked strain of Quaker mysticism, a fine Quaker feeling that

48

success in life is not to be attained by prudential insurance against material mischances. His brother-in-law called him a "visionary"; [11] and so, if his grand enterprises had failed, as they came very near doing, he would have been regarded. Above all he was not a prudent man intent upon a small security; or a vain man living in the opinion of others and vulnerable to ridicule; or a self-regarding man reluctant to expose himself by going out on a limb. Not the least dominant of his characteristics, perhaps inherited from his seafaring ancestor, was the impulse to chance it, the dour determination to accomplish at all hazards something out of the ordinary, something that would do him credit and the world no disadvantage. Both his failures and his successes were the result of his serene self-confidence, his willingness to back his own judgment and, throwing prudence to the winds, to gamble, win or lose all, for high stakes.

Let us now return to the activities of the young business man who has lost his job, in order to understand how these various qualities contrived to make him at the age of forty-seven a bankrupt, at the age of fifty-seven a millionaire, and from that moment until the end of his life an open-handed philanthropist.

Having lost one safe job the young man did not scurry around to find another, because a safe job was never what he had most in mind for himself. As early as 1833 he wrote to his father requesting a loan of $800 "to doo business with." He refers to "my tavern house," which he insured for $750, and "my barn" adjoining it, which he insured for $100. What after all was a safe job to a man of property with a tavern house and a barn? To a man who was at the same time running Mr. Beebe's farm, buying fine stock for the farm, and hiring Henry Brooks to work for him for $19 a month, and "keep himself"—yes, and "keep my brother Benjamin" to boot! Besides, he had other interests. In 1841 he visited eastern cities, as an authorized agent, to "dispose of water privileges for manufacturing and other purposes." He himself built a pottery factory, subscribed for shares in a new company to establish a woolen mill at Fall Creek, and bought for $160 the patent rights, for Maine and Georgia, of Barnaby and Mooers' recently invented "double mole-board side hill and level land plow." Let the safe job go! All else failing, he would seek his fortune in Maine and Georgia with the double mole-board plow.[12]

And so, late in 1841 Ezra went to Maine, and in 1843 to Georgia, walking most of the way—a means of travel he preferred to any other. And why not? A strong man, maintaining a good clip, could easily cover forty miles in thirteen hours, thus leaving, out of the twenty-four, two for meals, seven for sleep, and two with nothing whatever to do. An exhilarating and a leisurely life, really, besides enabling one to see the country to best advantage. In this leisurely and care-free way Ezra arrived, in 1843, in Georgia, but only to find, unfortunately, that the only plow needed in that great agricultural state was a hoe in the hand of a slave.[13]

All this time Mary Ann and the children remained at The Nook, doing the best they could with the garden, and the income from the tavern house and the farm and miscellaneous rentals collected, or not as the case might be, from persons living in "the sellar room" and such odd places. Judging from the letters of E. L. Stuvins, to whom Ezra intrusted the management of his properties during his absence, they were not doing any too well; so that Father Wood had to "come with his lumber wagon loaded with things to carry the family along." So at least we are told by Ezra's brother-in-law, Otis E. Wood. And we are also told that when Ezra returned from Georgia, "instead of bringing at least a sack of flour or something practical, he brought a trunk full of gilt-edged books." [14]

Leaving the books to the family and the family to Father Wood and Mr. Stuvins, Ezra then went a second (or it may have been a third) time to Maine, hoping to sell his plow there. In Portland he looked up his friend F. O. J. Smith, whom he found on the floor of his office trying, with a piece of chalk, to explain to another man the kind of machine he wanted devised and constructed. "Cornell," said Smith, "you are the very man I wanted to see." It seemed

EZRA CORNELL

Photograph by Kurtz, New York, made about 1870 to assist Francis
Bicknell Carpenter in painting a portrait which Cornell University acquired.
Copied here from a print kindly loaned by John L. Senior, to whom the print
was given in 1910 by Miss Mary Cornell and Mrs. Charles H. Blair, daughters
of Ezra Cornell.

that Smith had obtained the contract for laying an underground cable of wires between Baltimore and Washington to test S. F. B. Morse's electric telegraph invention; and for that he thought he needed two machines, one to dig the trench and lay the cable, the other to cover the cable after it was laid. Could Cornell help him? Cornell could. "A little reflection," says Mr. Cornell, "convinced me that he did not want two machines. . . . I, therefore, with my pencil sketched a rough diagram of a machine. . . . The pipe, with the wires inclosed, . . . was to be coiled around a drum or reel, from whence it was to pass down a hollow standard . . . directly in the rear of the coulter or cutter, which was so arranged as to cut a furrow two and a half feet deep and one and one fourth inch wide. Arranged something like a plow, it was to be drawn by a powerful team, and deposit the pipe in the bottom of the furrow as it moved along. The furrow being so narrow would soon close itself." [15] It was as simple as that, and, let us note, as simple as that to describe.

The outcome of this chance meeting was that Smith authorized Ezra to design and construct the plow, and then offered him the job of laying the pipe. Convinced that the telegraph was to be a "grand enterprise," and that it would, if he became identified with it, lead him "on the road to fortune," Ezra accepted the offer, and early in October, 1843, left Portland for Baltimore.

The plow worked admirably, but with some ten miles of the pipe laid it was found that, on account of defective insulation, all the work so far done was wasted effort. To let this be known would prejudice the entire undertaking, and make it difficult to obtain additional appropriations from Congress; and one day Professor Morse, in great distress, called Ezra from his plow to ask him if he could suggest any way of suspending operations without giving the true reason. Ezra's ingenuity made little of so slight a difficulty. Stepping back to the plow, he directed the teamsters to start up the mules; and, watching for an opportunity, with simulated clumsiness canted the point of the plow into a ledge of rock and broke it to pieces. The next day it was reported in the newspapers that on account of this "unfortunate accident" the work would have to be suspended for a few weeks. The weeks dragged on while Professor Morse and Alfred Vail and F. O. J. Smith experimented with other methods of insulating the wires in the pipe. Meantime, Ezra spent his spare time boning up on electricity, and came to the conclusion that the simplest and cheapest way would be to abandon the underground system altogether and string the wires separately on poles, insulating them at the cross bars by wrapping them around glass knobs, such as might be found on bureau drawers. After still further delay, and consultation with Professor Henry at Princeton, this method, used to this day, was finally adopted; and Ezra was employed as Professor Morse's assistant at $1,000 a year to build the line, which he did with such dispatch and economy that the work was completed in May, 1844, without any need of an additional appropriation from Congress.[16]

Thus at the age of thirty-seven Ezra Cornell became identified with the "grand enterprise." He was then, I will not say in towering high spirits, but as nearly so as it was in the nature of Ezra Cornell ever to be. To Mr. Beebe he wrote saying that he would soon be a wealthy man, and to Mary Ann saying that "Old Dame Fortune was bestirring herself to make amends."[17] His optimism was misplaced. The story of his venture on the road to fortune during the next twelve years is not one of success attained by the orderly and progressive mastery of difficulties encountered. On the contrary, it is the story of repeated and magnificent failures. The story cannot be told in detail here; but the high lights need to be presented in order to understand how Ezra Cornell acquired a fortune, as one may say, by misadventure, by violating all the rules of prudence and common sense and adhering, with stubborn tenacity, contrary to experience and all sound advice, to a settled conviction. The settled conviction was that the telegraph business was bound to be a phenomenal success; and the key to the story is that the telegraph business turned out to be something very near a complete failure while Ezra Cornell was actively engaged in promoting it, and became a phenomenal success only after he had retired from active connection with the enterprise.

In 1844 Ezra Cornell evidently thought that his services in building the Washington-Baltimore line would make him useful if not indispensable to the men who, as owners of the Morse patent, were in a position to control the telegraph business. These men were Morse and Alfred Vail, who together owned three fourths of the patent right, and F. O. J. Smith, who owned the remaining one fourth. After the federal government had declined an offer of all rights for $100,000, Morse and Vail intrusted the management of their interests to Amos Kendall, but F. O. J. Smith preferred to manage his own. In May, 1845, Smith and Kendall organized the Magnetic Telegraph Company to complete the line from Baltimore to New York. In the years following other companies were organized by them for connecting the principal eastern cities—notably the New York, Albany and Buffalo Company. But F. O. J. Smith, who quarrelled with every one, proved to be a thorn in the side of Morse and Kendall; so that in 1847 it was agreed between them that thereafter Kendall should have the right of disposing of the patent rights for lines built in the East and South, while Smith should have a similar right for lines built in the northern states west of Buffalo. Under this agreement the patent right was variously leased, under contracts so loosely worded as to be the occasion of endless litigation, and lines were rapidly and flimsily built throughout the country.[18]

Ezra Cornell's part in these early enterprises was less than he had hoped. He managed to scrape together $500 for twenty shares of stock in the Magnetic Company. In 1845 he supervised the construction of seventy miles of the line from New York to Philadelphia, making little or nothing from it. But in 1846 he built under contract the line from New York to Albany, which netted him the substantial profit of $6,000. This, together with some two thousand dollars in the bank, made him a capitalist, capable of venturing as a promoter on his own. He could now afford an insurance premium of $34.40. He could even afford a "dress coat"— purely as an investment, no doubt, useful for making friends and influencing people with money to invest in the telegraph business. To advance his interest he formed a business partnership with his old friend and prominent Ithaca merchant, John J. Speed, Jr., who thus became one of the men with whom he was most closely associated in all of his major enterprises.[19] Another of these associates, unfortunately, was F. O. J. Smith.

Unfortunately, because F. O. J. Smith turned out to be a man of such devious ways that he was commonly known in the trade as "Fog" Smith, and the term "fogsmithery" became current as a synonym for any kind of crookedness in the telegraph business. Cornell and Speed would have done better to have allied themselves with Morse and Kendall, even if Kendall was a bit condescending and Morse more than a bit vain and irritable. But Mr. Cornell had then a double grievance against Morse. He felt that his services in building the first line, and—as he always maintained—in improving the Morse sending instrument, had not been adequately recognized. Besides, a sending instrument which he had himself invented and patented in 1845 and urged Morse to use, was rejected by Morse on the ground that it was no more than a "clumsification" of his own.[20] For these or whatever reasons Cornell and Speed became involved with "Fog" Smith in their two major telegraph enterprises.

The first of these was the Erie and Michigan Telegraph Company, organized to build and operate a line from Buffalo through Cleveland and Detroit to Chicago and Milwaukee. The contract, originally let by Fog Smith to Livingston and Wells, was soon taken over by Cornell and Speed,[21] who completed the line early in 1848, and thereafter obtained a controlling interest in the Erie and Michigan and many other western lines built as feeders to it. The other enterprise was the New York and Erie, running (roughly along the route of the Erie Railroad) from New York through Middletown, Binghamton, Ithaca, and Fredonia to Dunkirk on Lake

Erie. The disposal of the Morse patent rights in this region properly belonged to Amos Kendall; but Cornell had no wish to do business with Morse and Kendall, and Fog Smith made nothing of leasing the patent in his own or another's territory, especially if that other was Kendall. Accordingly, on February 28, 1848, Fog Smith signed with Cornell and Speed the contract for building and operating the New York and Erie line.

Why Cornell and Speed should wish to build the New York and Erie line is obvious: linked up with their western lines it would give them a through trunk line from Cleveland and Chicago to New York. But, one naturally asks (and Amos Kendall asked it with great indignation), why should Fog Smith wish to build a line that would compete directly with the New York, Albany and Buffalo line in which he, to say nothing of his partners Morse and Kendall, had a major interest? The answer is that the New York and Erie, so far as Fog Smith was concerned in it, was a case of "fogsmithery" at its most foggiest. Evidence of this is to be found, with some difficulty it is true, in the terms of the New York and Erie contract in which Fog Smith appears as both vendor and vendee—a contract admirably designed, in short, to enable Smith to risk nothing and lose nothing himself, to do his partners Morse and Kendall out of their fair share of the patent rights, to put all the risk and labor on his partners Cornell and Speed, to take half the profits of their enterprise if it succeeded, and to leave them holding the sack if it failed.[22]

Ezra Cornell's animus against Morse appears to have blinded him to the essential dishonesty of Fog Smith; but he was too astute a man to be deceived by the flagrant "fogsmithery" of the New York and Erie contract. What deceived him was his own optimism —his settled conviction that any risk in the telegraph business was bound to be a safe bet. In 1848, with the Erie and Michigan in operation and the New York and Erie in process of construction, he was therefore in a mood to see himself as the dominant figure in the grand enterprise. The tone of his letters to Alonzo, who was then running the Cleveland office, is assured and at times magisterial. "I have now," he writes in December, "such advantages in the telegraph business that I shall be able to make an ample fortune for myself and each of my children." At that time the Erie and Michigan was just beginning to pay expenses, the New York and Erie still lacked two thirds of the money required for construction, both companies were bound to Fog Smith by contracts that no prudent man would ever have signed—and yet Ezra Cornell could count six ample fortunes as good as made.[23]

No forecast of the immediate future could have been more completely mistaken. Within less than three years Ezra Cornell was reduced to the humiliation of soliciting financial aid from his rival, Amos Kendall. Writing in September, 1851, he told Kendall that all of the real estate he possessed was mortgaged, and that he was in debt "some $15,000 besides." For two years past, he confessed, "I have not received the first dollar for my services, and have not been able to contribute the first cent towards the support of my family. They are wholly dependent on the charity of friends, and every line of telegraph that I have any interest in . . . are [is] running in debt for expence of working, and I can see no prospect for any favorable change. Under such circumstances what is to be done? For my part I cannot answer the question. My wife . . . feels that I have followed the telegraph quite long enough, and that it would be to our interest to abandon it, and direct my energies to some more productive channels." But to abandon the telegraph business was, for Ezra Cornell at least, even more difficult than to go on with it: first, because the lines would not pay his debts even if they could be sold; second, because they could not be sold anyway on account of the "unsettled state of the patent question." [24] He therefore stuck it out, only to see his indebtedness mount until, in 1854, it had reached the appalling sum of fifty thousand dollars.

The principal cause of this crisis in the affairs of Ezra Cornell was the failure of the New York and Erie. From the first everything went wrong with that most cherished of all Cornell enterprises. Instead of $50,000 needed for construction, less than $20,000 was forthcoming. But by borrowing from his friends, pinching his family, personally supervising the construction of the line, working day and night, going sometimes a week at a time without taking off his clothes, he managed somehow to get the line up. To the operators along the line he was a familiar bedraggled figure, known as "Old Bones," not infrequently to be seen rummaging in the petty cash (the only cash there was for the most part) for two bits to buy his dinner. He even managed to pay Fog Smith $4,000 on the patent-right account, which Fog Smith conveniently forgot, so that Morse brought suit against Smith for his share of the patent money, and then Smith brought suit against Cornell for the whole of it. Curiously enough, even Ezra's flair for gadgets failed him for once. Having himself devised the simplest and best method of insulation by means of glass knobs, he now invented and used a contraption known as the "Brimstone Hat," which was not only expensive but, in damp weather, rather worse than no insulation at all. For these and other reasons the New York and Erie was a complete failure. Sold at sheriff's auction in 1852, it was bid in by Mr. Cornell for $7,000, and leased for two years to his rival, the New York, Albany and Buffalo Company. In 1855 it ceased to be operated, and the wires were sold to the Erie Railroad.[25]

Unfortunately for Mr. Cornell, the failure of the New York and Erie came at a time when all of his other lines were ceasing to pay expenses. For this he was himself in part responsible. His optimism had led him to build or acquire control of more lines than he could well manage. In any case, as a manager of complicated enterprises, Ezra Cornell had certain limitations. Generally respected by his associates and subordinates, he was not very well liked by them. He was too austere, too little disposed to take advice, a little too certain that others rather than himself were at fault, to win the warm friendship or command the loyal devotion of those with whom he worked. According to J. H. Wade, he lacked the talent for delegating authority, and as a consequence wasted his time on a multitude of trivial details. "Your God," said Wade, in a long, frank, and sarcastic letter in 1853, "is *economy,* but you make a slight mistake and worship *parsimony* (at a sacrifice to yourself and everything you are able to influence). . . . I have known you to economize by leaving your official chair [as President of the New York and Erie] without even a substitute, for two months at a time, and travel on foot and knee deep in mud, from New York to Dunkirk, and carry on your shoulders a 24 foot ladder, when some *foolish, extravagant* president would have paid an Irishman $12 a month for doing the same thing, while he was staying in his office and attending to his business." [26]

But whatever the limitations of Mr. Cornell as an administrator may have been, it must be said that his lines were not the only ones that were failing. In 1854 even the most able and prudent owners and managers of telegraph lines were facing disaster. The principal reason for this situation was the rapid duplication of competing lines throughout the country—lines using the Morse patent, and lines using the recently patented "printing" instruments of Alexander Bain and Royal E. House. The larger cities were commonly served by three, or even four, rival telegraph offices. But rarely was any of them open after nine o'clock in the evening, and at any time of day the chances were good that one would find on the door of any office the familiar notice: "Closed temporarily, gone to fix the line." In 1854 there was scarcely a business man of credit left who still had any faith in the telegraph business. Nevertheless, Ezra Cornell's faith remained unimpaired: with existing lines failing to pay expenses, he built or acquired control of more lines; with stocks a drug on the market, he bought more stocks. And so it happened that the six ample fortunes which, in 1848, he thought as good as made, had dwindled away to a fifty-thousand-dollar debt incurred by the failure of the New York and Erie, and extensive holdings in the Erie and Michigan and other western lines that could not be sold in the open market at any price. It was indeed true, as he said himself, that if the game had ended then he would have been "swept from the board."

From this precarious situation Ezra Cornell was rescued, one might say in spite of himself, by the formation of the Western Union Telegraph Company. Consolidation of competing lines was the obvious solution, and Mr. Cornell had himself, as early as 1851, suggested it casually in conversation with W. H. Ellsworth.[27] But the men chiefly responsible for the formation of the Western Union were Hiram Sibley and Samuel L. Selden. In 1851, having acquired the House patent rights and $90,000 raised by Sibley from his Rochester friends, they organized the New York and Mississippi Valley Printing Telegraph Company. Sibley had the very sound idea that in any region one line, if solidly constructed and competently managed, would soon force the existing lines into bankruptcy or consolidation. By 1854 his policy had sufficiently proved its worth to make the New York and Mississippi Valley Company (or "the House Lines," as they were called) the most dangerous competitor of all other companies. In letter after letter Mr. Cornell's operators informed him that the House lines were gradually taking what little business remained. "The House folks," wrote W. P. Pew from the Pittsburg office, "like the fiends out of hell," are "bent on your destruction." To avoid destruction on the one hand, and consolidation with the House lines on the other, Mr. Cornell fought, as Otis E. Wood said, "with all his might": came to terms with his old rival, the New York, Albany and Buffalo Company; with its aid acquired control of the Michigan Southern; and even attempted to form his own "grand combination" of all Morse lines against "the common enemy." [28]

But all without avail. The battle was virtually lost in 1854 when, either without Mr. Cornell's knowledge or against his protest, four of his principal associates (Speed, Wade, Haviland, and Cobb) deserted him by selling their Erie and Michigan stock to the House companies and associating themselves with the Sibley crowd. Early in 1855 the Sibley people offered the Erie and Michigan definite terms of union, and assured Mr. Cornell that if he refused consolidation on fair terms they would run him out of business. The terms offered were, according to Mr. Cornell, all to the advantage of the House companies; but, with some modifications that made them less objectionable to him, they were formally accepted by the board of directors in August, 1855. The contract provided for the organization of a new company with a capital stock issue of 500,000 shares, of which the Sibley interests were to receive 350,000 and the Cornell interests 150,000. The new company was incorporated in March and April, 1856, and at Mr. Cornell's request was given the name of the Western Union Telegraph Company. The merger included all of the Cornell lines except the Michigan Southern; but scarcely more than a year later, July 17, 1857, Mr. Cornell abandoned the game altogether by selling the Michigan Southern for shares in the Western Union.[29]

When the merger was thus completed in 1857, the value of the Western Union stock credited to Ezra Cornell was estimated at $50,000. Thirteen years of incessant and heartbreaking effort to acquire a fortune in the telegraph business had brought him a property which, if it could then have been turned into cash, would barely have paid his debts. He had, at all events, the advantage, whatever that might prove to be, of being the largest stockholder in the new company, and for some years he served on its board of directors; but responsibility for the management and phenomenal success of the Western Union Telegraph Company fell mainly to other men.

In this way, not quite as he had intended, Ezra Cornell retired from the "grand enterprise"—returned home, as one may say from the wars, if with something less than a complete victory, at least with honor and peace in his time. Some years before, in the midst of the wars, he had advised Alonzo that in choosing a profession a person should consider how far its permanency "would depend on his own will and how far on the will of others." [30] Certainly Ezra had himself found that the telegraph business depended altogether too much on the will of others; and once rid of it he was well content to turn to other and more congenial interests—to farming and breeding fine stock, to promoting the interests of Ithaca and serving his community in the state legislature, to the affairs of the state Agricultural Society, and especially to the movement for founding a state agricultural college.

Meantime he could begin to pay his debts. One day in October, 1860, he turned up his old Cyphering Book. The last entry in it, made at the age of seventeen, was a bold heading: "Loss and Gain." Under this heading he now, after thirty-five years, thought fit to make an entry: noting that all his life had been a desperate struggle to see which, loss or gain, would win; that in 1854, sunk under a mountainous debt of fifty thousand dollars, the issue seemed a "doubtful one"; but that at the present moment, February 1, 1860, that debt "has mostly been paid . . . with 7 percent interest added, and a yearly income of $15,000 seems to be a reliable guaranty that the credit side has now the victory." Never before had Ezra Cornell been out of debt with an income of fifteen thousand dollars. Yet this was only the first slight trickle of the golden stream that was to come pouring in from the Western Union Telegraph Company. In 1862, with its capital stock raised within three years from 385,700 to 2,994,800 shares, the company paid a valid stock dividend of thirty-six per cent. In 1864, Ezra therefore thought fit to make another entry in the Cyphering Book: "My last quarterly dividend on stock in the Western Union was $35,000, July 20, 1864. The dividend for October quarter will be as large."

Thus within four years Ezra Cornell's income, without effort on his part, had jumped from fifteen thousand to one hundred and forty thousand dollars. But what would Ezra Cornell do with all this money? Live in the gilded luxury to which he was not accustomed? No. For Ezra Cornell, with his dour, hard-bitten New England conscience, with his fine Quaker feeling for justice and humanity, there was just the one obvious thing to do with his superfluous wealth. And so he sets it down, with great simplicity, in the Cyphering Book: "My greatest care now is how to spend this large income to do the greatest good to those who are properly dependent on me, to the poor and to posterity." [31]

Like many other men of that time Ezra Cornell believed profoundly in a better time coming for the poor and for posterity. Some twenty years earlier he had told Alonzo that it was clear to all reflecting minds that a great revolution was about to begin—"a revolution by which the down trodden millions will be elevated to their equal and just rights, and each led to procure and enjoy that degree of happiness that all men and women are entitled to as the fruit of their labor." [32] Among the downtrodden millions were the farmers and the industrial workers; and what better could be done to elevate them to their equal and just rights than to provide them with the means of obtaining an education suited to their needs? Having acquired an education the hard way himself, Ezra Cornell all his life believed (mistakenly, no doubt) that if books and schools were freely available to the people, any poor boy could make as good use of them as he would have done if they had been available to him. To make these advantages, which he had lacked, available to others—this, clearly, would be to use his large income to do the greatest good to the poor and to posterity.

His first notable contribution to this end was the founding of the Cornell Library (a free public library for the citizens of Tompkins County), which he built and endowed at an ultimate cost of something more than one hundred thousand dollars. As for schools, his lifelong interest in farming led him to read and reflect much on the education of farmers; and after his retirement from the telegraph business he took an active part in founding the State Agricultural College at Ovid, and was the most influential member of its board of trustees. The college first opened its doors to students in December, 1860; but eleven months later it was forced to close them because the president, Brigadier General M. R. Patrick, had been called to the army and many of the students had enlisted. In 1863, when the Morrill Act was accepted by the state, the college was still closed. At that time it consisted of a charter, an empty building capable of housing one hundred and fifty students, and a farm of four hundred and fifty acres in good condition. The trustees estimated that the farm and building had a current value of $101,780; but against this had to be set a mortgage debt of $70,000.[33] With this much to show, the trustees applied to the legislature for the Morrill land grant, and the prime mover in the business was Ezra Cornell. At that time it had not occurred to him that the Morrill land grant could be made to yield more than thirty-five or forty thousand dollars a year; but he thought that if in addition to this the legislature would pay the debt and provide adequate buildings and equipment, the purposes of the Morrill Act would be realized to the best advantage. In that case he did not know of anything better to do with his large income than to add what he could (perhaps two hundred thousand dollars) to the college endowment.

As it turned out, fortunately we must suppose, the legislature was not sufficiently interested in agricultural education to make any appropriation for it; and there were plenty of colleges in the state more than willing to accept the Morrill land grant without any additional appropriations from the legislature.[34] One of these was the People's College, designed by its founders to give instruction in "those branches of science immediately and vitally essential to agriculture and the mechanic arts." The college had been chartered in 1853, but for lack of funds nothing further had been done until 1858, when Charles Cook, a wealthy resident of Havana (now Montour Falls) promised substantial financial aid if the college should be located in his home town. This offer was accepted, the Rev. Amos Brown was elected president, and on September 2, 1858, the corner stone of the main building was laid with appropriate ceremonies. The aid promised by Mr. Cook turned out to be so much less than munificent that in 1863, although the main building had been erected, no student had as yet darkened its door,

63

and supposing one should do so there were no adequate facilities, in fact virtually no facilities at all, for teaching him agriculture and the mechanic arts. Nevertheless, on May 14, 1863, the legislature appropriated the entire Morrill land grant to the People's College.[35]

What in this instance determined the legislative mind (a difficult thing to fathom at best) is not clear. Senator Cook (as he then was) undoubtedly used all of his considerable influence (he was known as "the leader of the third house"), and it is said here and there that he even resorted to "political trickery." That may well be, no doubt; but in any event he was unable, fortunately, to obtain the grant for the People's College except on certain conditions. The conditions were that the college should have, within three years, at least ten competent professors, buildings adequate to house two hundred and fifty students, a farm of two hundred acres free of encumbrance, shops suitable for teaching the mechanic arts, a library, scientific apparatus, and "cabinets of natural history." [36]

The People's College evidently lacked a good deal—according to the Regents' Report two years later, what it lacked would require $242,000 to remedy; [37] but it was generally expected that Senator Cook would donate the necessary sum, for why should he have resorted to political trickery, or whatever it was, to obtain the grant if he did not intend to put the college in a position to accept it? Senator Cook may have intended, at the time, to do just that. But then one of those fortunate odd chances again intervened to change the course of events. At exactly the most appropriate moment Senator Cook suffered a stroke of paralysis, and thereafter refused categorically and repeatedly to give any further financial assistance to the college.[38] So long as Senator Cook remained in this unamiable frame of mind there was slight chance that the People's College would get the grant after all. It seemed certain, therefore, that the legislature, at the next session, would have to burden its mind once more with the difficult problem; and Ezra Cornell had decided that it would be worth while to introduce a bill for dividing the grant, leaving the People's College in possession of one half of it, and giving the other half to the State Agricultural College at Ovid.

This was the situation when, on the first of January, 1864, a newly elected senator from Syracuse entered the chamber for the first time and took his seat. He was a young man—thirty-one years old; slight in stature, alert in bearing; with fine, wavy brown hair parted nearly in the middle, worn rather long, and running to sideburns; in appearance and demeanor a man suggesting, in some undefinable way, the intellectual and the aristocrat. To the seasoned senators he must have seemed somewhat fragile and a bit dandified; and I should think the more cultured among them may have wondered whether it might not be that Mr. Matthew Arnold, mistaking the time and place, had dropped in to deliver a lecture on sweetness and light. It was not so. The young senator was Andrew Dickson White.

Taking account of his colleagues, Mr. White noticed, sitting not far away, "a man of about sixty years of age, tall, spare, and austere, with a kindly eye, saying little, and that little dryly. He did not appear unamiable, but there was about him a sort of aloofness: this was Ezra Cornell." [39] Of all the odd chances or designs of fate that seemed in those years to be always conspiring for the public good, this conjunction of men and circumstances was the most fruitful; for the result of it was that Ezra Cornell and Andrew Dickson White became fast friends, exchanged their ideas, joined their forces, and thereby became the effective creators of Cornell University.

IV

Circumstances and the Man:
Andrew Dickson White

*From my first years in college it has been the steady aim of my life to
aid in founding and building a worthy American university.*

ANDREW D. WHITE

"SAYING little, and that little dryly"—so Andrew D. White noted
one of the salient characteristics of Ezra Cornell. That an intelligent man should say little must always have seemed strange to
Andrew D. White: he was himself, on every occasion, so well prepared and eager to say a great deal.

One day in the fall of 1917 George Lincoln Burr took me to see
Mr. White at his house on the campus. He was then eighty-five
years old. We found him in his library, sitting before the fireplace,
surrounded by his beloved books. Three walls were lined with
books from floor to ceiling, and a large table was piled two or three
high with the newest books, one of which Mr. White had been
reading. He received us with unstudied courtesy and an air of
pleased anticipation, as if we were both old and valued friends, the
two men in the world whom he most wanted just then to see. He
began talking before we were fairly in the room, and kept on talking for an hour and a half, not so much to us or with us as for us
and for himself, and for the pure joy of practicing the art, as if cultivated conversation were God's best gift to men. He spoke of the
good fortune of Cornell in inducing me to join its faculty, and of
my good fortune in being associated with his friend George Burr
whose learning and wisdom he had himself found of unfailing

ANDREW DICKSON WHITE

Photograph made in 1878. In dress and otherwise this is, nevertheless, very much the way Mr. White looked at the opening of the university in 1868.

assistance; spoke of the new book he was then reading, and of other new books he had recently read by authors unknown to him, and asked us what we thought of them, and then, before we could start anything, told us what *he* thought of them; spoke of the war and the Fourteen Points and of Bismarck whom he had known and liked, but now thought in some sense responsible, with his blood and iron, for the war; spoke of early Cornell days and difficulties, and of Ezra Cornell, a remarkable and lovable man, and of the realization of his early dreams for the university, and of its future prospects, which would always be good so long as the most eminent scholars could be got to come to it; spoke of many other things besides—a copious flow of narrative and commentary, of incidents and anecdotes and judgments light and serious, moving on, without haste, without rest, like a prairie river in spring, gently irresistible, swelling up and around and over all obstacles, all conversational reticences and awkwardnesses, filling all silences, carrying us and himself serenely along on the broad surface of his knowledge and experiences recalled.

We said, and needed to say, and had a chance to say, very little.

The voice was warm and persuasive, infinitely persuasive, so that one wanted nothing better than just to listen and take it in. The voice was also a little husky, as if it may have been going on in just this happy way, except for the minimum of unavoidable cessations, for eighty-three years, ever since the first full-blown sentence was uttered at the age, maybe, of two. It has occurred to me that Ezra Cornell, after having become closely associated with Andrew D. White, may have found it even less necessary than before, and on occasions perhaps even less possible, to say very much, however dryly.

There they were then, meeting in the Senate in 1864 for the first time—the two men, superficially so different: Ezra Cornell, the large, slow-moving, self-contained man, a bit dour and austere in appearance, as well weathered as a hickory knot by fifty-seven years of harsh experience in the world of men and affairs, knowing much, saying little; and Andrew D. White, the slight, nervously active, buoyant and vital man, a young intellectual Lochinvar out of the academic world, fully equipped and armored with ideas newly polished and pointed by the battle of the books, eager champion of good causes, expatiating and expounding at length with friendly confidence and persuasive facility. I like to think of them in those first days walking down the Capitol steps, or sitting in the plushy room of the Delevan House: Ezra saying little, content to listen, benevolently wondering what the talkative youngster may be good for, wondering whether, under all this bookish lore and spate of words, the fastidious professor may possibly have after all some saving grace of guts and common sense.

It turned out that the professor had plenty of both; and in spite of superficial differences, perhaps because of them, the two men were soon drawn together in close friendship. There was every reason why they should have been, for in all essentials they had much in common. They were both honest men, ambitious to use their wealth to do some striking good in the world; and they were both profoundly convinced that nothing better could be done in the world than to make freely available to the people in it the means of acquiring an education. But apart from all this, there were in January, 1864, particular circumstances that would have thrown them together whether they liked it or not. Ezra Cornell was made chairman of the committee on Agriculture; Andrew D. White was made chairman of the committee on Literature (that is to say, education); and both committees were bound to be concerned in the immediate question of how the Morrill Act could best be used in case, as seemed likely, the People's College failed to meet the conditions imposed by the act of May 14, 1863. We know that Ezra Cornell had formed, as a result of his experience in life and affairs, certain fairly definite ideas about education. It was a happy circumstance that Andrew D. White, having had a quite different experience, had formed quite different, although not necessarily

68

conflicting ideas about it. What then was this experience, and what were these ideas?

Andrew Dickson White was born November 7, 1832, in Homer, New York.[1] His ancestors, on both sides, came to that region in the late eighteenth century from Massachusetts, the Whites from Munson, the Dicksons from Middletown. Great-grandfather Dickson was a member of the Great and General Court of Massachusetts Bay; Grandfather—"Squire"—Dickson was a prosperous business man and a member of the New York legislature. There was a tradition, which Andrew had not the time or the interest ever to verify, that the Whites were descended from the Peregrine White who came over on the Mayflower. Grandfather White was at all events once counted the richest man in Homer Township; and although a fire destroyed his mills and his fortune, his son Horace sufficiently retrieved the disaster to become the leading business man of the county. Andrew had not the advantage, therefore, of belonging to the great American aristocracy of poor boys who make good. "My first recollections," he says, "are of a big, comfortable house of brick, in what is now called 'colonial style,' with a 'stoop,' long and broad, on its southern side, which in summer was shaded with honeysuckles. . . . Spreading southward from this was a spacious garden filled with old fashioned flowers, and in this I learned to walk." Here, in this comfortable house and garden, he must also have learned to talk, and I like to think that his first intelligible word was "book."

Since the Whites were given to reading there were books enough in the house, and for the young Andrew the "Rollo Books," *Sandford and Merton,* and *The Children's Magazine* were thought the right sort of thing. In later life Mr. White could not remember a time when he could not read; but he could remember being frequently, at the age of three, in school, not as a pupil, but in charge of a colored servant who used to slip into the school in order to learn to read, and took the boy along, not knowing what else to do with him. He remembered also attending the public exercises of the Cortland Academy, and being impressed to the point of awe when he saw "Principal Woolworth, with the best students around him on the green, making astronomical observations through a telescope." When Andrew was seven the Whites moved to Syracuse; and there he was sent first to the public school, and then, at the age of twelve, to the preparatory department of the Syracuse Academy, where he had the good luck to be taught by "the best teacher of English branches" he was ever to know, Joseph A. Allen, who introduced him to proper selections from Shakespeare and Milton, and to Gray's *Elegy*, Goldsmith's *Deserted Village*, and other classics much favored at the time.

That Andrew should go to college was no doubt preordained from the time of his birth; and as a preparation he was of course drilled in Andrews and Stoddard, and learned to translate Caesar and Virgil correctly—well enough at least to recognize that a fellow pupil was off the rails when he turned *Arma virumque cano* into "Arms and a man and a dog." Besides preparing his Latin and mathematics in school, he appears to have read at this time a great variety of books, among others the Waverley Novels, *Robinson Crusoe, The Pilgrim's Progress,* Rollin's *Ancient History,* and Lander's *Travels in Africa.* Then, at the age of seventeen, came the first real frustration of Andrew's life.

He had set his heart on going to one of the famous eastern colleges; but his father, guided by the rector of St. Paul's Church, sent him to Geneva (Hobart) College, an Episcopal institution that claimed to be able, on account of the limited number of students, to "exercise a direct Christian influence upon every young man committed to its care." To this college, therefore, Andrew reluctantly went. There he found some excellent teachers, and a library of four thousand volumes, the largest collection of books he had ever seen. But he found also that the "Christian influence" was insufficient to prevent the boys from raising perpetual pandemonium —carried to the point, on one occasion, of burying a professor under a "heap of carpets, mattresses . . . and blankets," and, on another, of valiantly keeping the president himself "at bay with a shower of beer bottles."

At the close of the year, deciding that he had had enough of this sort of Christian influence, Andrew urged his father to send him elsewhere. Unfortunately, he had done very well in his studies, so that his father insisted on his returning to Geneva. It was at this point that Andrew showed what he was good for in a way that would have brought to the eye of Ezra Cornell, could he have known of it, the famous "twinkle." The incident is worth relating because it illustrates so well those qualities which, often exhibited in later life, were largely responsible for Andrew D. White's achievements. The qualities in question were precise knowledge of the end to be attained, inflexible determination to attain it, and rare diplomatic skill in dealing with those who might assist or oppose him.

On this occasion his purpose was to go to Yale College. He could not go without his father's consent. A frontal attack on his father having failed, he was therefore obliged, as he says, "to make a *coup d'état*." What he did was not a *coup d'état,* but rather in the nature of an elaborate and well-conceived flank movement. Shortly after arriving at Geneva in the fall of 1850, he quietly left the place and took refuge with a former tutor, then the principal of Moravia Academy, and there waited for the enemy to move. The enemy moved quickly, wrote at once to say that he was inexpressibly shocked, regarded Andrew's career as a thing wrecked, and refused to take any further interest in a son guilty of such flagrant disobedience. Andrew atoned for his disobedience by studying "more earnestly than ever before," but still waited, knowing all the time that there was, within the enemy country, a competent and reliable fifth-columnist. The fifth-columnist, needless to say, was Andrew's "dear mother," who wrote to him affectionately, and bided her time for three months until one day when Mr. White, who was passionately fond of music, expressed his intention of

71

going to New York to hear the famous "Swedish Nightingale," Jenny Lind. Then Andrew's dear mother, with that feminine guile with which there is no contending, suddenly exclaimed, as if it had just that moment occurred to her, "What a pity that the boy cannot hear this; how he would enjoy it." Poor Mr. White was no match for two such masters of finesse. "Tell him to come home and see us," was his eminently male way of giving in.

So Andrew came home, and it was understood that after Christmas his father would take him to Yale College. The battle seemed won, but was not quite; for on the train to New Haven Mr. White got into conversation with a student returning to Trinity College at Hartford—a college which, according to the student, was a most wonderful and truly Christian place. Still hoping, Mr. White tried once more. Would it not be well, he suggested to Andrew, to go on to Hartford and take a look at this Christian college before deciding definitely for Yale. Taken off his guard by this base betrayal of the Moravia Pact, Andrew countered by affirming confidently, without knowing anything at all about it, that Yale had "an infinitely finer library than Trinity." Mr. White then played his last card, threw in, as it were, the Old Guard: "My boy," he said, "if you will go to Trinity College I will give you the finest private library in the United States." Said Andrew roundly: "No, I am going to New Haven; I started for New Haven, and I will go there." A boy of eighteen! Mr. White gave it up. In thick, oppressive silence father and son rode on to New Haven.

Andrew remained at Yale College three years, and must, I think, have had a good time there. He was a member of the Psi Upsilon Society, and was variously known to his intimates as "Toots" and "Jock." He won a literary competition with an essay entitled "Greater Distinction in Statesmanship," for which he received a medal, very pleasing to his father, who wrote the boy that he would "rather have it than $1,000 in money." He tried his hand at essays on other subjects, such as modern history and the dilemma of theology. He took part, I have grave reasons for believing, in the

"Burial of Euclid" in November, 1852; and in the Commencement exercises he appeared in the afternoon, the sixteenth on the program, with a dissertation on "Ancient and Modern Oracles." ² There was surely nothing in all this to displease him; and surely he must have had a good time reading voraciously in the library that was "infinitely finer" than the library of Trinity College, in learning how to make friends and influence people, and in discoursing at length in a correct, easy manner on the state of the bright new world. I think he must have had a good time savoring Cicero and Seneca, and even, if the truth were known, in getting the better of Andrews and Stoddard.

So I think it must have been. But fifty years later, in the light of all that had occurred in the meantime, the Yale experience recollected, not altogether in tranquillity, seemed to Mr. White thin and unrewarding. There were, as he recalled, gifted professors—Woolsey and Porter, Silliman and Dana—whose personalities sometimes broke through the system which made "everything of gerund-grinding and nothing of literature." But only sometimes. Even Woolsey taught history by hearing men "recite the words of a text book," and that text book the Rev. John Lord's *Modern History*. During his whole time at Yale there was not a single "lecture on any period, subject, or person in literature, ancient or modern." Even the teaching of Silliman and Dana, masterly as he thought it, was "listlessly heard and grievously neglected" by the students, because the system put a premium on the neglect of all "studies that did not tell upon 'marks' and 'standing.'" One day a Latin tutor said to Andrew: "If you would try you could become a first rate classical scholar." To which Andrew replied: "Mr. B——, I have no desire to become a classical scholar, as scholarship is understood here." Such was Andrew's experience at Yale as he remembered it years later.

The remembrance was no doubt distorted a good deal by what he saw and heard in Europe during the next three years. A short visit to Oxford left its inevitable impression—an impression of

ancient towers and cloistered gardens, of excellent, leisurely din-
ners and cultured, donnish conversation evoking the enigmatic,
provocative spirit of John Ruskin and other famous men. In Paris
he lived with a professor's family where nothing but French was
spoken; and was soon listening at the Sorbonne to lectures on history and literature that confirmed his idea of what a university
should be. In Paris he acquired a lifelong interest in the French
Revolution—visited all the historic spots, practiced his budding
French on veterans of the revolutionary wars hanging about the
tomb of Napoleon, conversed with civilians old enough to remember the thundering Girondin orators of the Convention, and began to collect the library that would some day be at least one of
the finest private libraries in the United States. From Paris he was
fortunate enough to be taken, as an attaché of the American Le-
gation, to reside for six months with Governor Seymour at St.
Petersburg. There he witnessed the coronation of Alexander II,
upon whom was devolved from Heaven all power over his subjects; and there he read Gibbon, made a special study of Guizot's
History of Civilization, and discussed at length with Governor
Seymour the ideas of Jefferson and the significance of American
history.

Leaving the land of the Tsars, with his "democratic creed" much
deepened and strengthened, he went to Germany and matricu-
lated at the University of Berlin. There he learned German well
enough to listen with some profit to professors then eminent—
Lepsius, August Boeckh, Friedrich von Raumer, and Carl Ritter.
There he also listened to the most famous of all historians, Leo-
pold von Ranke, whom he could not follow, however, because the
great man had the unfortunate habit of "becoming so absorbed
in his subject, as to sink down in his chair, hold his finger pointing
toward the ceiling, and then, with his eyes fastened upon the end
of it, to go mumbling on in a kind of rhapsody" which even the
German students, listening "as priests might to a Sibyl on her
tripod," admitted they could not understand. It was an experience

worth while, no doubt—such an experience as, according to William James, Harvard undergraduates enjoyed in listening to Royce, the experience of not at all understanding what was said, but of having a vague and salutary sense that something big was going on. From Germany he went to Italy, in intimate company with two Latin scholars, one of whom, Henry S. Frieze, was later, from his class room at Ann Arbor, to do more than any other man to "make classical scholarship a means of culture throughout our western States." Italy was another world, and there he met James Russell Lowell, who was studying German literature in preparation for a professorship at Harvard. And so, in 1856, with three years of travel and study to his credit, Andrew returned to Yale College to "take the master's degree in course."

With so much knowledge and fruitful experience accumulated at the age of twenty-five, young Mr. White was bound, as any one can see, to become a professor. But where, and what of? Not that there was any difficulty in choosing a subject or in finding a place to teach it. While still at New Haven taking his master's degree in course, his friends Gilman and Porter virtually assured him a position at Yale in the art department to be presently created.[3] But he was less interested in art than in history, and in any case he felt that he would be "fettered" at Yale by the "old fashioned orthodoxy" of the system of instruction. One day, by some odd chance glancing in through the open door of a class room, he heard Francis Wayland, President of Brown University, say to some students: "The best field of work for graduate students is now the West." That decided him. He went home and wrote to sundry friends saying that he was a "candidate for a professorship of history in any western college where there was a chance to get at students." Two offers were shortly forthcoming—one of them from the University of Michigan, which was promptly accepted. Thus it happened that in October, 1857, Andrew D. White went to Ann Arbor determined to "get at students" by teaching them history in unconventional ways.

It was certainly unconventional to prescribe, as text books, such formidable works as Robertson's *Philosophical View of the Middle Ages* and Guizot's *History of Civilization in Europe;* unconventional to require students to read widely in such classics as Gibbon and Hallam, Lingard and von Ranke, Thierry and Macaulay. To master these was the student's task; the highest duty of the professor, needless to say, was "giving lectures"—courses of interpretative lectures on the grand subjects, such as "The Development of Civilization During the Middle Ages," "The French Revolution," and "German History from the Revival of Learning." The young professor ventured boldly to lecture without manuscript, or even notes—a venture that occasioned, on his first entrance to the crowded class room, some inner trepidation and weakness of the knees. But President Tappan, who was present to introduce the new professor, gave him the right clue: "Never stop dead; keep saying something." To keep saying something was never difficult for Mr. White; and was all the easier in this instance since he could always fill in by reading or exhibiting the "original sources" collected in Europe for his private library. With a little practice all went smoothly enough. Both lectures and lecturer were immensely liked by the students: for one reason because the lecturer was so obviously in love with his subject; for another, because the great object and point of the whole business was "to promote the better training in thought regarding our great national problems," such as the evil institution of slavery or the false doctrine of protection. The great object of it all was to present history as philosophy teaching by example the purposes of God in the world. There were, it is true, some "storms"; the doctrine of free trade, for example, being regarded by some Michigan Republicans as no essential part of God's purpose for the United States. But these were mere trifles. The period of six years at Michigan could be later recorded as "one of the most fruitful in useful experience and pregnant thoughts" that Andrew D. White had ever known.

The "pregnant thoughts" maturing in the mind of Andrew D.

White at this time, and indeed throughout his life, came easily to birth. In the intellectual, no less than in the financial sense, Mr. White always lived, as one may say, in easy circumstances. There is no evidence that he ever experienced, even in the mildest form, any intellectual or spiritual crisis, or even that he was ever seriously troubled by doubt or disillusionment. He exercised in the happiest, unconscious way the will to believe. Never given to the critical examination of fundamentals, all of his thinking was in the nature of a facile manipulation of wide knowledge and varied experience in the support of certain general ideas which he, like so many men of his generation, appropriated from the main current of thought, and cherished with the emotional conviction that commonly sustains a religious faith.

These general ideas were what may be called the tenets of the nineteenth-century liberal-democratic creed. Mr. White believed that history is God's revelation to men, and that it can be properly understood only as a progressive, dramatic conflict between good and evil forces. He believed that the good would triumph ultimately, and that it had in his time already won the essential victories: evidence of which was to be found in the unprecedented progress recently made in material prosperity, in the increase and diffusion of knowledge, in the practical application of science to human needs, in the increase of humane sentiment and religious toleration, above all in the rapid spread throughout the world of democratic government in place of monarchical absolutism, of freedom of speech and the press in place of political and ecclesiastical censure of opinion, and of free economic enterprise in place of a regimented economy. The essential meaning of history, the essential test of civilization and the good life, was revealed in this progressive emancipation from age-old tyrannies and superstitions; so that any man might be sure that he was on the side of God and the right, might feel that he was leagued with the force, not ourselves, that makes for righteousness, by working for freedom of opinion in order that the truth might prevail, for freedom of status

77

and occupation in order that careers might be open to talent, and for freedom of government in order that no man might be compelled against his will.

The doctrine of Karl Marx, that the emergence of democratic government and the freedoms it sanctioned was no more than a conditioned reflex induced by the economic factors of production —such a philosophy of history Mr. White repudiated as a blasphemy against God's beneficence and the nobility of human nature. Nothing would convince him that men did not make their own history, or that they could not by deliberate purpose make it fair or foul, or that the course of events had not in epochal moments been shaped, for good or ill, by the responsible action of great heroes or great villains. He believed that eternal vigilance is the price of freedom, and that accordingly the essential condition for preserving the freedom of a republic was a sturdy and literate people, and leaders whose education enabled them to appropriate for themselves, and whose patriotism commanded them to place at the disposal of the community, the best that has been thought and said and done in the world. For a republic, therefore, the indispensable foundation was education—common schools for the people, colleges and universities for the leaders.

By this straight intellectual route Andrew D. White arrived, while teaching in the University of Michigan, at the most fruitful of his "pregnant thoughts"—the settled conviction that he could do nothing better with his talents and his fortune than to "aid in founding and building a worthy American university" for the increase and diffusion of learning and the intellectual and moral training of young men for leadership in the United States.

The beginning of this conviction Mr. White himself traced back to the day when, as a freshman in Hobart College, he came across Huber and Newman's illustrated book on the English universities. Poring over the "engraved views of quadrangles, libraries, halls, chapels—of all the dignified belongings of a great seat of learning," the limitations, both intellectual and aesthetic, of the drab little American college became so obvious and so disheartening that he began at once to build "air castles," to dream of a great American university "worthy of the state and the nation." In this impalpable structural enterprise he continued for many years, until it became an "obsession"; and his subsequent experience, at Yale and Oxford, in Paris and Berlin, served only to make the airy structure at once more vivid and more clearly defined. On the "queenly site above New York's fairest lake" it stood, this imagined university—with its distinguished professors in every field, its "library as rich as the Bodleian," its "towers as dignified as those of Magdalen and Merton," its "quadrangles as beautiful as those of Jesus and St. John." Yes, and also, "as a leading feature, a gate tower . . . adorned with statues in niches and on corbels," and a "lofty campanile . . . a clock-tower looking proudly down the slope, over the traffic of the town, and bearing a deep-toned peal of bells."

Not that the great American university, although in outward semblance resembling Oxford and Cambridge, would in essentials be a mere imitation of them. In essentials the great American university would necessarily be adapted to American conditions and American needs of the present and immediate future time. Ample provision would, therefore, have to be made for other studies besides mathematics and the classical languages—provision for the "great modern literatures," for modern history, and for architecture; and also (as Mr. White's experience at the University of Michigan had convinced him) for natural science, the mechanic arts, and agriculture. These were for the time advanced, but not revolutionary ideas; but in two respects Mr. White would boldly commit the great American university to more radical policies. The great American university would be rigidly non-sectarian, and it would be hospitably co-educational.

One evening, it may have been in the year 1858, sitting before the fire in his Ann Arbor home, Mr. White related his dream to a distinguished visitor from the East—George William Curtis. In his address at the opening of Cornell University, Mr. Curtis recalled this midnight conversation. On that evening, he said, the young Michigan scholar, "in the warmth and confidence of his friendship, unfolded to me his idea of the great work that should be done. . . . Surely, he said, in the greatest state there should be the greatest of universities; in central New York there should arise a university, which, by the amplitude of its endowment and . . . by the character of its studies in the whole scope of its curriculum, should satisfy the wants of the hour." Of all this Mr. Curtis expressed his entire approval; and the two men, parting at a late hour, were encouraged to think that, since they lived "in a country open to every generous idea," the young scholar's dream "one day might be realized." [4]

Thus Andrew D. White's dream slipped into the realm of the practical. But in the realm of the practical the first hard fact was the need of money. Fortunately, Mr. White was himself not a poor man. Upon the death of his father in 1862 he inherited about three hundred thousand dollars; and the greater part of this he was willing to devote to the establishment of a university in central New York (preferably, as he then thought, in Syracuse, on the rising ground where Syracuse University now stands) if a wealthy philanthropist could be found to bear the main burden. Hearing from Samuel Joseph May that Gerrit Smith "had thought of endowing a university," Mr. White sat down on August 12, 1862, and drafted a long letter to him. In this letter, carefully revised and sent off on September 1, Mr. White set forth at length the need of a "worthy American university," solicited Mr. Smith's aid in founding it, and pledged himself to "throw in the bulk" of his own inheritance, which would be sufficient to found an adequate library, or "equip the finest observatory and laboratory in the world," and further promised that to Mr. Smith, if he would join in this noble enterprise, should go "all the glory." [5] Unfortunately, Mr. Smith "gave reasons why he could not join in the plan"; and with this rebuff

Mr. White's cherished scheme for the moment faded away, as he says, "like the baseless fabric of a vision." This was very much his state of mind when, in January, 1864, he took his seat in the Senate chamber at Albany. And there, as if by the Providence of God, was Ezra Cornell.

Mr. White had never before seen Ezra Cornell, but he had heard of him, and favorably, as a man who by his own efforts had acquired a fortune, and then instead of living at his ease was willing to serve the state in the legislature by promoting measures for the public good, and instead of hoarding his wealth for his family was prepared to spend it lavishly for the benefit of his fellow men.[6] Such would describe, to Mr. White's way of thinking, the ideal citizen of a republic. For Ezra Cornell Mr. White had, therefore, the greatest respect and admiration. Nevertheless, the first thing he did in the Senate was to oppose with all his might Mr. Cornell's pet measure.

The measure had to do with the Morrill land grant, which had been given by an act of the previous session to the People's College on certain conditions. Since it seemed unlikely that the college would be able to meet the conditions, Mr. Cornell was still working, with his accustomed tenacity, to obtain at least some part of the grant for the Agricultural College at Ovid. To this end he asked Senator Folger, chairman of the Judiciary Committee, to draft a bill. January 11, 1864, Judge Folger sent the bill, with a covering note: "Inclosed herewith is the bill to amend the People's College law of last session. You will see that it is simply a restriction of that college to one half of the avails of the law. . . . You could have the bill introduced in my behalf [Mr. Folger was to be absent for a week] and get a reference to the Agricultural Committee if may be. . . . I suggest the Agricultural Committee for obvious reasons, *and also* because I am told that the chairman of the Literature Committee [Mr. White] is in favor of having the whole appropriation go to one institution." The next day, January

12, Mr. Cornell "on behalf of Mr. Folger" introduced a bill "to amend Chapter 511 of the laws of 1863" by which the land grant had been given to the People's College.[7]

The chairman of the committee on Literature, Mr. White, at once and vigorously opposed this bill, on the ground that the educational resources of the state were already too much dispersed. There were, he said, "more than twenty colleges in the state, . . . not one of them doing anything which could justly be called university work." What the state needed was a real university. The Morrill land grant, kept intact and given to no matter which college, provided the opportunity for at least the beginning of such a university; to divide the grant would be to fritter it away and thereby defeat its purpose. When Mr. Cornell asked that the bill be referred to the committee on Agriculture, of which he was the chairman, Mr. White again objected, on the ground that the bill, being concerned with education, should properly be referred to his committee, the committee on Literature. There the matter rested until February 17, when there was presented to the Senate a resolution adopted by the State Agricultural Society on February 10, probably at Mr. Cornell's suggestion, protesting on behalf of the agricultural interests of the state against the grant to the People's College, and urging the legislature to rescind or modify its previous action so that the Agricultural College might "receive its full share of the noble grant." The next day, February 18, Mr. Cornell introduced on his own behalf another bill identical, except for a slight verbal change in the title, with the previous one. This bill was referred to a joint committee composed of the committee on Agriculture and the committee on Literature; and on this double-headed committee Mr. White, to use his own expression, "deliberately thwarted Mr. Cornell's purpose throughout the session," and prevented the bill from being reported.[8]

A vain or self-regarding man might well have been irritated by such prompt and vigorous opposition coming from a voluble young professor, bobbing up in the Senate before his newly won seat was fairly warm. But Mr. Cornell appears to have taken it all in good part, with his accustomed serenity. Instead of becoming irritated, he considered how he could meet the objection without letting the Agricultural College down. This he thought might be done by adding to the half of the land grant an equal amount from his own pocket. Saying nothing of his intention, he invited Mr. White to attend the coming meeting of the trustees of the Agricultural College at Rochester in September. The principal business of the meeting was the report of the financial committee, which turned out to be a "melancholy exhibit of the . . . bankruptcy" of the college. After various plans for relief had been discussed, Mr. Cornell read a short statement to the following effect. He had listened, he said, to discussions which have "developed the hopeless situation of the college, and shown so little encouragement of its future prospects, until I have come to the conclusion that the trustees would be justifiable in changing the location of the college if it can be done with the approval of the citizens of Ovid." If then the trustees would locate the college at Ithaca, he would give it a farm of three hundred acres within ten minutes walk of the post office, and donate three hundred thousand dollars, "on condition that the legislature will endow the college with $30,000 per annum from the Congressional Agricultural college fund, and thus place the college upon a firm . . . basis, which shall be a guarantee of its future prosperity . . . and give to the farmers' sons of New York an institution worthy of the Empire State." This noble gift, we are told, "at once relieved the trustees of all embarrassment." [9] It did not, however, satisfy the visitor, Mr. White. "Much to the disgust of the meeting," he says, "I persisted in my refusal to sanction any bill for dividing the fund, . . . but promised that if Mr. Cornell and his friends would ask for the *whole* of the grant—keeping it together, and adding three hundred thousand dollars, as proposed —I would support such a bill with all my might."

An obdurate fellow, this young White—so Mr. Cornell must have thought. And so, indeed, he was. But Ezra Cornell was an obdurate fellow himself, and one sure way to win his respect and liking was to stand up to him, always provided one had anything to stand up to him with. Mr. White had something. His argument against dividing the land grant was, after all, a sound one, and Ezra Cornell could appreciate the fact as well as any one. His conception of a great American university was a sound one too; and during the year 1864 Ezra Cornell must have heard him expounding it many times, and at length. He listened attentively, no doubt, and no doubt he said little. But if Mr. White could say a lot to good purpose, Mr. Cornell could listen and say little to good purpose also. Although slow to change his opinions, Ezra Cornell was a man of intelligence and imagination, quick to grasp the essentials whether of general ideas or grand enterprises; and I think he must have realized, much sooner than he let on, that Mr. White's idea of a university was both more comprehensive and better worth working for than his own relatively limited idea of a college primarily designed to give the sons of farmers instruction in agriculture and the mechanic arts. Not that he would forego his dream of an agricultural college; but I think he learned from Mr. White to see it as part of a larger institution, and all the more effective for being on the same campus with schools of literature, history, and political science. And if it should have a quadrangle of its own, as beautiful as those of Jesus and St. John, so much the better; and if young Mr. White had a fancy for gate towers with statues in niches and on corbels, and a lofty clock-tower looking proudly down the slope and bearing a deep-toned peal of bells—well, that wasn't the main thing, of course, but there could surely be no harm in it.

At all events by January, 1865, Mr. Cornell had come, by whatever route, to Mr. White's way of thinking.[10] His method of announcing the fact was characteristic. "I was one day going down from the State Capitol [this is Mr. White's account of it] when Mr. Cornell joined me. . . . After some little general talk, he quietly said: 'I have about half a million dollars more than my family will need: what is the best thing I can do with it for the State?' " Andrew D. White could answer that one—no man better, since for ten years he had been looking for a chance to tell some rich man what he could best do with his money. "Mr. Cornell," he said, "the two things most worthy of aid in any country are charity and education; but, in our country, the charities appeal to everybody. . . . As to education, the lower grades will always be cared for in the public schools by the State; but the institutions of the highest grade, without which the lower can never be thoroughly good, can be appreciated by only the few. . . . It seems to me, then, that if you have half a million to give, the best thing you can do with it is to establish or strengthen some institution for higher instruction." He then discoursed at some length on the need for "a larger institution for such instruction than the State then had"—emphasizing the fact that "a university worthy of the State would require far more in the way of professors and equipment than most men supposed; that the time had come when scientific and technical education must be provided for in such an institution; and that education in history and literature should be the bloom of the whole growth."

To all this Mr. Cornell, so Mr. White says, "listened attentively, but said little," so that the matter seemed to end there. But not long afterward he came to Mr. White and said: "I agree with you that the land-grant fund ought to be kept together, and that there should be a new institution fitted to the present needs of the State and the country. I am ready to pledge to such an institution a site and five hundred thousand dollars as an addition to the land-grant endowment, instead of three hundred thousand, as I proposed at Rochester." With this announcement Mr. White was, as he says, "overjoyed"; and he immediately set about (no doubt with as much satisfaction as he ever experienced) to "sketch out a bill" for the new institution.

But meantime, as both men realized, it would be well before presenting any bill to the legislature to obtain as much support for it as possible. The Agricultural Society and the trustees of the Agricultural College could be trusted to follow Mr. Cornell's lead in the matter; if the trustees of the People's College, or some of them, could be won over, it would be a great help. To this end the trustees of the two colleges were invited to attend a meeting at Albany on January 12, 1865. So far as is known none of the trustees of the People's College accepted the invitation. One of them, Horace Greeley, had his reasons. "I do not choose to be present at Albany just now," he wrote to Amos Brown, the President of the People's College. "If Senator Cornell and the agriculturists will invite the People's College men to a conference with the single intent to blend the two bequests in one grand institution I will either attend or record my assent. If, on the other hand, he proposes to go his own gait, and thinks himself strong enough to override us, I prefer to wait here." [11] Waiting in New York Mr. Greeley must have been reassured; for the meeting at Albany on January 12, after hearing Mr. Cornell's proposal, adopted a resolution in the very sense of his letter to Amos Brown. "Resolved, that a committee be appointed to correspond with gentlemen concerned in the management of the People's College, and with other persons prominent in the educational interests of the State, and invite them to meet the gentlemen concerned with the management of the State Agricultural College to take into consideration a plan for joint action in regard to the proffer of $500,000 for educational purposes by the Hon. Ezra Cornell." [12]

In accord with this resolution the committee, consisting of Andrew D. White, William Kelly, and B. T. Johnson, at once sent out invitations to the gentlemen concerned to meet in Albany on January 24. True to his promise, Horace Greeley was present at this meeting; but other trustees of the People's College, as Mr. White intimated with a certain amount of irritation, made excuses—"couldn't get there," the "trains wouldn't connect," and so on.[13] It was a disappointment, certainly, since the principal purpose of the meeting was to obtain some sort of official commitment from the People's College in support of the new institution. Nevertheless, the meeting made the best of a bad situation by adopting unanimously the following resolution: "Resolved, that it is the opinion of this meeting that the courses of the Agricultural and People's Colleges, be united in a single institution; that such institution be placed under a single Board of Trustees selected mainly from the Boards of the existing colleges, and that the institution thus formed be located in such place in the central part of this State as shall, at an early date, present the greatest pecuniary inducement. Resolved, that the institution thus formed ought to be the recipient of the endowment from the United States, known as the Agricultural and Mechanical College Fund." [14]

This resolution could not of course be regarded as an official action by the trustees of the People's College, since Horace Greeley was the only one present to vote for it. But Mr. Cornell said that he "consulted the best and most influential" members of the People's College board, and that they "advised the new organization for the new institution"; and late in February Mr. White obtained, by correspondence, similar assurances of approval from four of the People's College trustees—Horace Greeley, Erastus Brooks, D. S. Dickinson, and Edwin B. Morgan. In addition, the Rev. Amos Brown, convinced that Senator Cook would do nothing more for him or for his college, and perhaps with his eye already on the presidency of the new institution, had assured Mr. Cornell of his support.[15]

Meantime, Mr. White had "sketched out a bill" and had had several conferences with Mr. Cornell (at some of which Senator Folger was present as their legal adviser) in order to revise and amplify the sketch in such a way that it would be agreeable to both, and as little offensive as possible to hostile critics. The financial provisions of the bill were determined mainly by Mr. Cornell; the educational provisions mainly by Mr. White. In no essential matter was there any friction or difference of opinion between them. Who first suggested the name "Cornell" for the new university is not certain. In his *Autobiography* Mr. White says that he first suggested the name, and that Mr. Cornell "at first doubted the policy of it; but, on my insisting that it was in accordance with time-honored American custom, as shown by the names of Harvard, Yale, Dartmouth . . . and the like, he yielded." Mr. Cornell's own account, written in 1865, is that after consulting with some of the trustees of the Agricultural and People's Colleges they "tendered the name 'Cornell University.' The name I demurred to, fearing it would be charged that I have an undue ambition in that particular. I was met by assurances that it was eminently proper that the institution should bear my name, and I made no further objection." [16]

One clause in the bill, which was later to provide the basis for the disastrous McGraw-Fiske law suit, Mr. White and Judge Folger were responsible for. "As we were blocking out the bill," Mr. White says in the first draft of his autobiography, "Judge Folger said to me, 'there must be a limit stated as to the amount of property the university can hold. How much will you make it?' My answer was, 'It is understood that the endowment of Harvard is about three million, and that of Columbia about the same. Why not adopt the same figure?' He thought it was very large, and so did I. Neither of us dreamed that the endowment of the university would ever reach any such sum, and both of us feared that its magnitude might alarm the legislature. Still we agreed to try it." [17] The magnitude of three million dollars as an endowment for a university! Fancy that *now*. Yet so the troublesome clause was inserted.

At one of their conferences, or it may have been at some other time, Mr. Cornell "expressed the hope that in the proposed institution every student might find instruction in whatever study interested him. Hence came," says Mr. White, "the legend . . . upon the university seal: 'I would found an institution in which any person can find instruction in any study.'"

Thus the essential features of the bill were agreed upon after many conferences in which Mr. White no doubt said a great deal, and Mr. Cornell no doubt said little, and that little dryly. With that agreeable task completed, it may very well have seemed to Andrew D. White that his long cherished dream of a great American university was about to come true, and to Ezra Cornell that his generous desire to spend his "large income to do the greatest good to . . . the poor and to posterity" was about to be realized. We can then perhaps imaginatively recover, and in some measure share, the profound satisfaction of both men when, on February 7, 1865, Mr. White asked and obtained leave from the Senate to introduce a bill entitled, "An act to establish the Cornell University."

V

The Cornell University: Incorporated, 1865

The leading object of the corporation hereby created shall be to teach such branches of learning as are related to agriculture and the mechanic arts, including military tactics; in order to promote the liberal and practical education of the industrial classes in the several pursuits and professions of life. But such other branches of science and knowledge may be embraced in the plan of instruction and investigation pertaining to the university as the trustees may deem useful and proper. And persons of every religious denomination, or of no religious denomination, shall be equally eligible to all offices and appointments.

CHARTER OF CORNELL UNIVERSITY

FERDINAND BRUNETIÈRE somewhere remarks that official documents, whatever their nature, are not drafted in order that history may be written from them. How profound and disconcerting a truth it is, and how annoying to the historian that those who make history should be so indifferent to the needs of those who have to write it! To this melancholy reflection I am led by the difficulty of finding out exactly what happened to the bill introduced by Mr. White in the Senate on February 7, 1865, for establishing the Cornell University.

The official documents—that is, the Senate and Assembly Journals—say very little about the bill except that it was introduced, debated, amended, voted, and finally, on April 27, signed by Governor Fenton. Of the story behind this bare record—the very human story of interests threatened and passions aroused, of defamatory whisperings bruited about and cloak-room bargains struck and carried out, or not—of all this there is no hint. There is no record even of the formal debates, except Mr. White's speech, which was separately printed. The historian has, therefore, to look elsewhere to learn that the bill encountered strong and concerted opposition from pressure groups with interests to serve and votes to back them up, so that the sponsors of a generous gift for education, in order to get their measure passed in any form, had to pad about behind the scenes stirring up influential individuals to turn on the heat, had to suffer the charge of being "monopolistic" and "swindlers," had on their own account to do a little shopping in political bargains, had even, as a last resort, to scrape up $25,000 in order to dispose of a spot of thinly disguised intercollegiate blackmail. That is not the way laws are supposed to be passed by the representatives of the people in a republic; but that was, in substance, the way the bill for establishing the Cornell University was maneuvered through the legislature of the State of New York.

The story begins with the introduction in the Senate, on February 7, 1865, of Mr. White's bill, the full title of which was: "An act to establish the Cornell University, and to appropriate to it the income of the sale of public lands granted to this State by Congress, on July second, eighteen hundred and sixty-two." [1] The bill was printed, not in the Senate Journal for my convenience, but separately for the use of the Senators, and it is only by the accident that Senators Cornell and White preserved their copies that I am able to say precisely what the original bill contained. [2] The provisions of the bill are set forth in twelve sections, unsystematically arranged; but even a casual reading makes it clear that the purpose of the bill was to do three things: to create a corporation, to endow it with certain property, and to define the purposes for which the endowment should be used.

First, as to the corporation. "Ezra Cornell, William Kelly, Horace Greeley, Josiah B. Williams, William Andrus, John McGraw, George W. Schuyler, Hiram Sibley, J. Meredith Read, John M. Parker, and such other persons as may be associated with them for that purpose, are hereby created a body politic and corporate, to be known as the Cornell University, which university shall be located in the town of Ithaca" (Sec. 1). The management of the corporation was entrusted to a board of trustees, consisting of twenty-five persons. Of these, seven were trustees ex-officio—the Governor and Lieutenant Governor of the state, the Speaker of the house of Assembly, the Secretary of Public Instruction, the President of the State Agricultural Society, the Librarian of the Cornell Library, and the "eldest male lineal descendant of Ezra Cornell." The other eighteen members were to be the ten persons named in section one as incorporators, and eight others to be later "associated with them." And it was further provided that the "said board of trustees shall be so constituted, by election from time to time as the bylaws shall direct, as that at no time shall a majority thereof be of any one religious sect, or of no religious sect" (Sec. 2). Such was the corporation and the governing board of trustees.

Second, as to the endowment. To the corporation there was appropriated "the income . . . which shall be received from the investment of the proceeds of the sale of the lands" granted to the state by the Morrill Act (Sec. 6). But the appropriation was to be made only upon the following conditions: (1) that within six months after the passage of the bill the trustees could prove to the satisfaction of the Comptroller that the corporation possessed a "fund of five hundred thousand dollars at least, given by the honorable Ezra Cornell of Ithaca" (Sec. 6); (2) that the farm and grounds occupied by the corporation in Ithaca should consist of not less than two hundred acres (Sec. 3); and (3) that within two years after the passage of the bill the trustees should have made, "in respect to buildings, fixtures, and arrangements generally," provisions which the Regents of the University of New York would regard as fulfilling the requirements of the Morrill Act (Sec. 7). It was further provided that the corporation should not be permitted to hold "real and personal property" in excess of "three millions of dollars in the aggregate" (Sec. 5); and that the "university grounds, barn, work shops, fixtures, machinery, apparatus, cabinets and library shall not be encumbered, aliened or otherwise disposed of by the said trustees, except on terms such as the legislature of the State . . . shall have approved" (Sec. 8).

Third, as to the purposes for which the endowment could be used by the corporation. The purposes were twice defined. In Section 1: "The object of the corporation hereby created, is the cultivation of the arts and sciences and of literature, and the instruction in agriculture, the mechanic arts and military tactics, and in all knowledge." In Section 4: "The leading object as to the plan of instruction in said corporation shall be to teach such branches of learning as relate to agriculture and the mechanic arts, including military tactics. But such other branches of science and knowledge may be embraced in the plan as the trustees may deem useful and proper." The second definition, couched in the words of the Morrill Act, was no doubt designed to meet any charge that the purposes for which the land grant had been made were not being complied with; the first definition was designed to enable the trustees to interpret those purposes in the most liberal manner possible. The purposes for which the corporation could use its endowment were further defined and limited as follows: (1) "Persons of every or no religious denomination, shall be equally eligible to all offices and appointments" (Sec. 4). (2) "The said university shall . . . be subject to the visitation of the Regents of the University of New York" (Sec. 7). (3) "The corporation . . . shall receive annually one student from each assembly district of this state . . . and shall give them instruction in any, or all the prescribed branches of study . . . free of any tuition fee"; such students to be selected "in consideration of their superior physical and mental ability," to be determined by competitive examination, with preference given, when other qualifications were equal, "to the sons of those who have died in the military or naval service of the United States" (Sec. 9).

Having thus created a corporation, given it an endowment, and defined the purposes for which the endowment could be used, the bill provided that the act of May 14, 1863, by which the land grant had been appropriated to the People's College, "is hereby re-pealed" (Sec. 11).

The introduction of the bill, says Mr. White in his *Autobiography,* "was a signal for war. Nearly all the denominational colleges sent their agents to fight us at Albany; . . . stirred up the secular press . . . in the regions where they were situated, and the religious organs of their respective sects in the great cities." [3] In a confidential letter to Professor E. W. Huffcut, Mr. White was more specific. "Hamilton College was represented . . . by the President who I think was Dr. Fisher, the treasurer, Mr. Williams, and the agent Dr. Goertner. Genesee College was represented . . . by the very powerful body of leading citizens from its neighborhood and by its chief speaker Professor Bennett. . . . Rochester University was perhaps the most vigorous of all in its action on the legislature through the public press. Dr. [President] Anderson became very bitter and Purcell the leading democratic editor kept up a series of most malignant attacks against Mr. Cornell, and all connected with him. . . . As to Hobart and Madison University my impression is that they were represented at some of the meetings before the committee, but their main activity was in the newspapers. The influence of Union against us was felt very strongly at Albany, . . . but Columbia did not, so far as I remember, take any part in the struggle against us." [4]

Mr. White was mistaken about "Purcell the leading democratic editor." Being a good Republican himself, he no doubt took it for granted that opposition to his plans would naturally come from his political rivals. As a matter of fact the leading Democratic paper, the Rochester *Union and Advertiser,* of which William Purcell was the editor, defended the Cornell University bill against the attack made on it by the Rochester *Democrat,* which was the leading Republican paper, and whose editor was Robert Carter. The Rochester *Democrat* posed as the defender of the people against the "moneyed aristocrats"—the moneyed aristocrats being represented, in this session of the legislature, chiefly by the New York

Central Railroad, which was supporting a bill for raising passenger fares, and Ezra Cornell, a rich man whose proposed university was designed to benefit the upper classes rather than the
farmers and mechanics.[5] According to the Ithaca *Journal,* the
Rochester *Democrat* had at this time a special grievance against
Ezra Cornell because, during the preceding summer, it had been
in some way offended by the Western Union Telegraph Company.[6]

It may be that some grievance against the Western Union gave
the Rochester *Democrat* its special zest for vilifying Mr. Cornell.
But the rancor was not confined to the Rochester *Democrat.* In
general the opposition of the small denominational colleges was
characterized by a note of personal animosity that seems excessive,
unless one may attribute it to a deep sense of defeat and frustration. There was, one must admit, good reason for such a feeling
on their part. For three years the small colleges, impoverished as
they were, had been sustained by the lively hope of getting at
least some part of the land grant; and even after the entire grant
had been given to the People's College they felt that all was not
lost, since it seemed unlikely that the People's College would ever
be able to meet the conditions on which the gift had been made.
Then, out of the blue, after all these years of hopeful waiting, the
Cornell-White project was suddenly sprung on them. It must have
been infuriating, and the most infuriating thing about the project
was its inherent merit—the fact that it would be approved by
virtually every one who could take a disinterested view, since it
presented a far better prospect of making a good use of the land
grant than any existing college (unless it might be Columbia, the
one important college that was not offended) could possibly offer. The situation reminds one of those English detective stories in
which many distant, poor relations are waiting hopefully for the
rich lord of the manor to die, when a long-forgotten, scalawag
younger brother suddenly turns up from Australia. Such a situation, as every seasoned reader knows, is always conducive to mur-

95

der, precisely because so long as the legitimate heir lives none of the expectants, not even the favored niece, has a look in.

The favored niece, in this instance, was the People's College. It had, what no other college had, at least a technically valid claim to present. Its friends could say, and did say, that the legislature had already given the land grant to the People's College on condition that it should provide the necessary buildings and equipment within three years; and that to take the grant away now, when some fifteen months of the allotted time remained, would be a flagrant act of "bad faith." [7] To ask for nothing but what the college already had, the nine points of the law, was good political strategy, and none the less so since it was the only thing that could be said for the college anyway.

Taking this technically defensive position, the friends of the People's College enlisted the support of all those who were, for any reason, hostile to the Cornell University bill. The defense was directed from Havana by the Hon. Charles Cook, no longer a senator, half paralyzed and irritable, but still able to command a good deal of political influence at Albany. His faithful lieutenants were Messrs. Hoyt and Webber, representatives in the Senate and Assembly from the Havana district, and Mr. Downs, the brother-in-law of Mr. Cook and the accredited agent of the People's College.[8] The other colleges that were interested came to their support, not that they opposed the People's College less, but that they feared the Cornell University more. Other votes were also to be had—at a price. It happened that the New York Central Railroad was interested in a bill then pending for increasing passenger fares; and, according to Mr. White, the railroad lobby "made an alliance with the friends of People's College which soon became very formidable." [9]

A formidable combination, certainly, but not unbeatable—at least in the Senate. The Cornell University had powerful backing also—Messrs. Cornell and White, a strong team, Mr. Kelly of the Agricultural Society, in a position to speak for the agricultural interests of the state, and many senators who were in a position to regard the bill solely from the point of view of its educational merits.[10] From this novel point of view there was really nothing to be said for the People's College. Nearly two years had passed since the land grant had been appropriated to the institution, and yet, as a report of the Regents to the Senate on February 14 made clear, it had done virtually nothing to provide the necessary buildings and equipment, and had as yet no students at all except a few in the preparatory department. It was generally understood that nothing could be done until Mr. Cook provided the college with an adequate endowment; and as to that Mr. Cook had said that he would, and then had said that he wouldn't, so that no one could know for certain what he would do, but every one was quite sure that he would not do anything like enough.[11] The president of the college, Amos Brown,[12] and four of the trustees, including Horace Greeley, were so sure that he would do nothing at all that they were in favor of, even if not actively engaged in supporting, the Cornell University bill.[13] Mr. White, in a powerful speech before the committee of the whole Senate, on March 10,[14] made the most of this farcical situation by setting forth persuasively the advantages of the Cornell University plan and pointing out with devastating effect the futility of relying upon Mr. Cook or the People's College. Not the least effective of his points was a practical one— the danger of delaying the matter. The Morrill Act had given the state five years to appropriate the grant to an adequately equipped college. "Three years of the five," Mr. White pointed out, "are already gone. If this bill fails now we lose a year more, and then only one is left" to make the necessary provisions, failing which the grant is lost to the state altogether.

There was really no answer to Mr. White's argument. It was not, however, a question of arguments, but of votes. Good political guessers would have said that there were probably not enough votes against the bill to defeat it in the Senate, or enough in favor to carry it in the Assembly. The situation was thus favorable for making a bargain—a bargain in which Mr. Cook and his friends got a little face-saving and time-saving concession in the Senate, and Mr. White and his friends supposed the opposition in the Assembly would be greatly weakened. The bargain took the form of an amendment offered by the friends of Mr. Cook, to the effect that the land grant should be given to the Cornell University only if, within three months of the passage of the act, the People's College should fail to "deposit such a sum of money as, in addition to the amount already expended by them upon or for the purposes of the corporation, shall, in the opinion of the Regents of the University of New York, be sufficient to enable the said trustees fully to comply with the conditions" of the law of May 14, 1863. According to a statement signed by A. D. White, James A. Bell, and A. H. Bailey, the agents of Mr. Cook promised that if this amendment should be adopted "they would withdraw all opposition to the [Cornell] bill in all its stages in the Assembly and elsewhere"; and it was in consequence of this promise that Messrs. White, Bell, and Bailey, "and other senators, voted for the amendment." [15] Accordingly, on March 16 the bill as amended was reported from the Committee of the Whole to the Senate, approved by the Senate, and sent to the Assembly for concurrence.[16]

During these proceedings it was a matter of great regret to Mr. White that the bill had not the active support of Charles J. Folger, chairman of the Judiciary Committee and one of the most influential members of the Senate. Personally Mr. Folger heartily approved of the bill. He had, in fact, helped Mr. White and Mr. Cornell to draft it. He was a close personal friend of both men, and could, like the Walrus and the Carpenter, deeply sympathize. But unfortunately there was, within his district, a small college, and more important still the defunct State Agricultural College at Ovid; so that as a senator Mr. Folger could not officially approve of a bill that took something, however valueless, from his constituents, while giving something likely to be very valuable indeed to the constituents of Senator Cornell. Mr. White recognized that such things are not done, and had resigned himself to his friend's dilemma when there occurred one of those odd chances that Mr. White always regarded as providential—always, that is to say, when they served his purposes. The odd chance was the sudden death of Dr. Sylvester D. Willard, and how Mr. White managed to make a providential use of it is relevant to this story.

For many years Dr. Willard, and before him Dr. Beck, had been deeply interested in the treatment of insane persons in the state, the condition of such persons, huddled together in overcrowded county poorhouses, being generally recognized as nothing less than a scandal. Session after session Dr. Beck—and, after his death, Dr. Willard—had appeared before a committee of the legislature to speak in favor of a bill to create an adequate institution—an institution which Dr. Willard proposed to call "The Beck Asylum for the Chronic Insane." Session after session the bill had failed to pass. And then one day early in April, 1865, Dr. Willard, while making one more passionate plea, suddenly fell dead on the floor of the committee room.[17] The startling event made a profound impression. For some days a certain solemnity pervaded the legislative halls, and the legislators were troubled with an unaccustomed, if perhaps salutary, sense of guilt.

Andrew D. White, shrewd politician that he was, saw at once that a sense of guilt among senators was a force, not themselves, that could be used for righteousness. "I sought out Judge Folger," he says, "and showed him his opportunity to do two great things. I said: 'It rests with you to remedy this cruel evil which has now cost Dr. Willard his life, and at the same time to join us in carrying the Cornell University bill. Let the legislature create a new asylum for the chronic insane of the state. Now is the time of all times. Instead of calling it the Beck Asylum, give it the name of Willard. . . . Place it upon the Agricultural College property on the shore of Seneca Lake in your district. Your constituents are sure to prefer a living State Asylum to a dying Agricultural College, and will support you in both measures.' This suggestion Judge Folger received with favor. The Willard Asylum was created, and he became one of our strongest supporters." Doctrinaires, Mr. White said, "might stigmatize our conduct in this matter as 'log-rolling' . . . even call it a 'bargain.' They may call it what they like." [18]

So they may. I am myself not greatly attached to particular words, but I must confess that if this was not a bargain I don't know what to call it. But bargains are made every day, and no harm in them if both parties are satisfied and no one else injured. In this instance no one was really injured—unless it might be the village of Ovid. At least one hard-grained native of that place was convinced that his home town had decidedly got the short end of the stick. Forty years later, recalling the transaction to Dr. J. Franklin Jameson, he said, with a plaintive bitterness that the passing years had done nothing to assuage, "Why, a university would've been worth three insane asylums!" It is not for me to say that he was wrong. Certainly at that time the inmates of the university were more numerous, the cases milder, and the patients, on the whole, from the president down, rather less in need of constant supervision. Let me then herewith, for Ithaca, apologize to the neighboring village of Ovid, and, for Cornell University, salute the Willard Insane Asylum as a kindred institution, and pass on to the main point. The main point is that the bargain was struck, and thereafter Senator Folger actively and effectively supported the Cornell University bill.

The bill certainly needed all the support it could get. The promise of Mr. Cook's agents "to withdraw all opposition . . . in the Assembly and elsewhere" was not kept; so that there was more, and far more embittered opposition in the Assembly than there had been in the Senate. The tactics adopted by the opposition was to refer the bill to the Committee of Colleges and the Committee of Agriculture, and let it die a peaceful death there unless its friends could muster a two-thirds majority to force the joint committee to report it. Whether this was the best tactics or not is uncertain: it at least gave Mr. Cornell and Mr. White a month to organize their forces and, as Mr. White says, "to enlighten the great body of the senators and assemblymen." To this end Mr. Cornell "invited them by squads, sometimes to his rooms at Congress Hall, sometimes to mine at the Delevan House. There he laid before them his general plan, while I dwelt upon the need for a university in the true sense of the word." The method reminds one of the academic procedure—the large class divided into small discussion groups; and no doubt the professor gave to each group the substance of the speech he had already delivered in the Senate. To enlighten the community at large, this speech had been published in the Albany *Journal* and, through the efforts of Mr. Cornell, widely circulated in pamphlet form. Besides, Mr. Cornell and Mr. White went to New York to solicit editorial support from the newspapers, and obtained from some of them, especially from Manton Marble of the *World,* favorable editorial comment.[19]

Not content with these measures, Mr. Cornell arranged, unwisely as it turned out, for an unofficial debate before the joint committee of Colleges and Agriculture. The meeting, at which many besides the members of the committee were present, was held in the Assembly chamber. For this occasion Mr. Cornell had hired a lawyer to speak for the bill, and Mr. Cook had obtained the services (whether hired or not) of another to speak against it. Unfortunately, the speech of Mr. Cornell's lawyer, according to Mr. White, "was cold, labored, perfunctory, and fell flat. The speech on the other side was much more effective; it was thin and demagogical, but the speaker knew well the best tricks to catch the average man. He indulged in eloquent tirades against the Cornell scheme, as a 'monopoly,' a 'job,' a 'grab,' and . . . denounced Mr. Cornell as 'seeking to erect a monument to himself,' hinted that he was planning to 'rob the State'; and, before he had finished, had pictured Mr. Cornell as a swindler and the rest of us as dupes or knaves."

Through this tirade of abuse Mr. White kept his seat, I can imagine, only with difficulty; but Mr. Cornell took it all in his accustomed manner—calmly, and with a wry humor. Once, when the lawyer's "invective was especially bitter," he turned to Mr. White and said: "I am not sure but that it would be a good thing for me to give the half a million to old Harvard College in Massachusetts, to educate the descendants of the men who hanged my ancestors." [20] Even more characteristic was Mr. Cornell's truly Quaker impulse to clear his own conscience by asking himself what truth, if any, there might be in the charges. The lawyer's claim that he was a wealthy patron of a university designed to serve the rich rather than the poor touched Mr. Cornell deeply—it "led me," he says, "to examine my own position to ascertain if it was obnoxious to the charge of aristocracy." [21] The record of this self-examination is a longish document, in Mr. Cornell's hand, now preserved among his papers in the Cornell University Library. In this document Mr. Cornell sets forth, with simple sincerity, certain facts about himself and his activities: to the following effect—that he was brought up in the Quaker faith, and had departed "from the direct line only by marrying a lady who was not a member of the society, and by falling into the popular form of direct speech"; that he had always been essentially a farmer and a mechanic, and had acquired his wealth by following those pursuits and not by speculating in stocks, not even the stocks of telegraph companies, or by lending money for profit; that his "ruling desire" was to devote the bulk of his property to do the most good to the working classes of his native state; that the Cornell University (so named by no wish of his own) was designed to that end, the evidence of which is to be found in its proposed course of study and in the composition of its board of trustees, which consists of "three mechanics, three farmers, one manufacturer, one merchant, one lawyer, one engineer, and one literary gentleman," besides state officers and persons officially associated with the educational affairs and institutions of the state. From all of which Mr. Cornell concluded that it would be difficult to find a man more closely identified with farmers and mechanics than he had always been, or to found a university more obviously designed to serve their interests, or to "select a board of trustees more likely to foster and protect [their] interests than the one selected." This document was Mr. Cornell's reply to the tirade of Mr. Cook's lawyer, and as such was laid before the joint committee—with what effect, who shall say?

I should guess, however, that it had very little effect—less, certainly, than the tirade of Mr. Cook's lawyer, since the members of the joint committee, adopting the very words of the tirade, posed as "protectors of the State against a monopoly and a swindler," and on that ground were less disposed than ever to report the Cornell bill to the Assembly. For the friends of the Cornell bill, therefore, success or failure depended, not upon securing a majority of the Assembly to vote for the bill, which they could probably do, but upon securing the two-thirds majority required to compel the committee to report it, which there was far less chance of their being able to do. In the end they succeeded in getting the necessary two-thirds majority; not, however, by professing good motives and presenting valid arguments, but by exerting political pressure at two strategic points, and making one substantial and costly political bargain.

The bargain was made with Genesee College, located at Lima about thirty miles south of Rochester. A bill was pending to give the college its "fair share" of the land grant, which its supporters estimated at one hundred thousand acres. In this demand the college was supported not only by the leading citizens of the locality, but by the Methodist Church throughout the state, which favored the grant because Genesee College was a Methodist institution, and in any case was strongly opposed to the Cornell University bill on the ground that, professing to be a non-sectarian institution, it would in effect be hostile to religion. Unless this powerful Genesee-Methodist block of votes could be converted or bought off the chances of getting the Cornell bill out of the committee were none too good. On the other hand, the friends of Genesee College were none too sure of getting any part of the land grant even if the

Cornell bill was defeated. The situation was obviously conducive to bargaining, and a bargain was in fact arranged.

The terms of the bargain are known, but as to which of the two parties proposed it there are two conflicting accounts. One account was given by Angus McDonald, the attorney for Genesee College. Speaking in the Constitutional Convention of 1867–1868, he remembered that when the Genesee College bill for one hundred thousand acres of the land grant was before the Assembly, "Senator White came to us and assured us" that the Senate would on no account divide the land grant, whatever the Assembly might do; "and he suggested whether Genesee College would not be willing to take an endowment for an agricultural chemistry department, and let the [Cornell] bill pass the legislature. . . . He said that Mr. Cornell was willing to endow an agricultural chemistry department with fifteen thousand dollars. After consultation, he said he was . . . willing to say that it should be twenty-five thousand dollars. . . . At the request of friends of Genesee College that was put in the bill as a condition." [22]

A different account was given, at the same time in the Constitutional Convention, by Judge Folger. He remembered that the Cornell bill "went to the Assembly where it met with a very formidable opposition from the agents of a religious body of this state. It became apparent to the friends of Mr. Cornell and the Cornell University . . . that the bill was likely to fail or they be compelled to divide the funds, by reason of the opposition of the friends of Genesee College, while the friends of Genesee College, on their part, did not feel too certain of success. Then a proposition was made outside of the legislature, in the lobby, that if Mr. Cornell would pay twenty-five thousand dollars to the Genesee College, the friends of that institution would withdraw their opposition to the [Cornell] bill and it might go through the Assembly. . . . After consultation was had among the friends of the Cornell University, one of them advised Mr. Cornell that the condition exacted by Genesee College had better be complied with. . . .

But Mr. Cornell (and I approve and applaud him for it) then said that he would do nothing in the dark; that if he was to give this sum for the withdrawal of the opposition it should be made public, and inserted in the bill, so that no man could accuse him of any underhand work. At the request of a particular friend in the Assembly representing his district (Mr. Lord of Tompkins) that condition was, by unanimous consent, inserted in the bill, and in that shape it passed the legislature." [23] This account of the transaction is better supported than the other. It was vouched for at the time by Mr. Alvord; and it is in all essential respects the same as that given by Mr. White in his *Autobiography*.

Such was the bargain with Genesee College. At the time it seems to have been generally understood that the bargain was first proposed by the friends of Genesee College, and that the bargain itself went, as political bargains go, rather beyond the limit. According to the Ithaca *Journal* (not, to be sure, an unprejudiced witness) "one common burst of indignation from the press of all parties was aroused by this outrageous demand. . . . The professorship will be known as the 'Blackmail Professorship,' the 'Captain Kydd Professorship,' the 'professorship of the Christian Foot Pads.' " [24] Whatever the demerits of the bargain, it had at least the merit of being faithfully kept; and it probably did more than anything else to obtain the required votes for the Cornell bill. But two other bargains, or, let us say, political pressure applied discreetly in two instances, had much to do with it also.

One of these instances had to do with the New York Central Railroad bill for an increase in passenger fares. The Rochester *Democrat* charged the Cornell crowd with making a deal with the railroad lobby. The Utica *Herald* denied this, on the ground that "Senator White has spoken and voted against the Railroad bill in all its stages." Mr. White himself had this to say about the matter: "It was I who, when . . . the lobby of the New York Central Railroad opposed us, held up the New York Central bill . . . and persuaded the Senate not to take it up until justice was done us." [25] This cannot mean that Mr. White promised to vote for the New York Central bill, because he in fact voted against it. What I take it to mean is that Mr. White, who was a director on the New York Central Board and well acquainted with the Vanderbilts, let it be known to the proper persons that the railroad bill would be held up in the Senate until after the Assembly ordered the Cornell bill reported out of the joint committee; and some credit is given to this assumption by the interesting fact that just two days after the Assembly ordered the Cornell bill reported out of the committee the railroad bill was passed by the Senate.

The other instance of political pressure exerted to good effect is related by Henry B. Lord, the Assembly representative from Tompkins County. "I was then serving," says Mr. Lord, "on the Committee of Ways and Means. To that committee had been referred a bill providing for the first appropriation for the erection of a new State Capitol. Sufficient opposition to the bill had developed to cause some nervousness on the part of its friends. My associates on the Committee of Ways and Means were all in favor of the bill chartering Cornell University. . . . All proposed to unite with me in notifying certain influential friends of the Capitol Bill that the Committee of Ways and Means could and would hold back the Capitol Bill so long as the Joint Committee held our university bill. Precisely how much influence this notification had, I, of course, cannot say. But I do know that when I moved that the House direct the Joint Committee forthwith to report the bill chartering Cornell University, . . . several friends of the Capitol Bill, among whom the Senator from Albany was conspicuous, were most busily engaged in bringing in their friends to vote for the pending motion." [26]

Mr. Lord's motion instructing the joint committee to report the Cornell bill was offered on April 12. The friends of the bill were well enough assured by then that less than a third of the members would vote against the motion; but they realized that some of those who were committed not to vote against it would prefer to evade all responsibility by not voting at all. When the roll was called such members would no doubt be found conveniently slipping away into the cloak-room. In this strategic position, accordingly, certain friends of the Cornell bill placed themselves and, as Mr. White says, "fairly shamed the waverers back into their places." Thus by virtue of squad lectures and newspaper propaganda, and bargains made, and political pressure applied where it would do the most good, and valiant Horatios guarding the breach in the cloak-room, the Cornell University bill was forced out of the joint committee by a vote of 70 to 22.[27] Among those voting against the motion was the representative from the People's College district, Lorenzo Webber, who had promised Mr. White that all opposition would be withdrawn. But of the twenty-two men who voted against the motion none were from Genesee County, the home of Genesee College, none from Albany where the new State Capitol was to be erected, and only one or two from those regions where the New York Central Railroad may be supposed to have had some influence in persuading representatives that corporate profit is a public benefit.

With this decisive vote recorded, the fight for the Cornell University bill was virtually won. On April 13 the bill was reported from the joint committee to the Assembly, referred to the committee of the whole, and from the committee, with the Genesee College bargain amendment inserted, reported back to the Assembly. The amended bill was approved by a vote of 79 to 25 on April 21, concurred in by the Senate on April 22, and finally signed by Governor Reuben E. Fenton on April 27. On the next day, April 28, the incorporators met for the first time, in the Agricultural rooms at Albany, and did what then could be done—appointed William Kelly chairman and Victor Rice secretary, resolved to accept the "conditions privileges and powers" conferred upon them by the act just passed, directed Ezra Cornell to consult with the Comptroller in respect to the land scrip, and elected seven additional trustees: Andrew D. White, Charles J. Folger, Abram B. Weaver,

George H. Andrews, Edwin D. and Edwin B. Morgan, and Erastus Brooks.[28]

This was all that could be done for the time being. Section thirteen of the act of incorporation declared that "this act shall take effect immediately"; but to the trustees this declaration must have carried something of the flavor of a sour joke, since the act itself made it possible for the People's College to retain the land grant by depositing, within three months, a sum of money which the Regents should declare sufficient for this purpose. In the event that the deposit required should be made, the act for establishing the Cornell University would presumably still be in effect, but to the founders and friends of the institution it would have ceased, to all practical intents and purposes, to have any effect whatever.

Another three months to wait, then, and nothing to be done! The strain, on Mr. White at least, was severe indeed. As often happened when there was something he wanted very much, but could for the time being do nothing about, he became so nervous that he could not sleep. On July 10, when about to leave for Rye Beach for a much needed rest, he somehow became convinced that the Regents had been got at by the People's College men, and were deliberately postponing the business of determining what sum the trustees of the People's College should be required to deposit. On that day he sent off a frantically worded telegram, followed by an equally frantically worded letter, to Mr. Cornell, saying he "greatly feared" that "all was lost," had reason "to believe that influential Regents would be glad to have the whole business fall through," and implored Mr. Cornell to do something about it.[29]

Mr. Cornell, as usual, took it more calmly, hadn't heard anything to be alarmed about, didn't think there was much in it. Mr. Cornell had by now, I think, not only a great respect for Mr. White's intelligence, but a deep affection for the man, and looked upon him very much as if he were a favorite son to be entirely trusted in matters of importance, but apt to go off the handle about trifles, and needing, on such occasions, to be calmed down a bit. From his letters to Mr. White on this occasion and later I get the impression that on such occasions he is saying in effect, if I may transpose his formal phrases into a vulgar key: "Now, now, take it easy, young fellow, take it easy; everything is going to come out all right." More often than not Mr. Cornell was right; and so he was on this occasion. The next day, at Albany, Mr. White had a conversation with the Secretary of the Board of Regents, Mr. S. B. Woolworth, who, as he says, "greatly relieved my mind in regard to the late action of the Regents." [30] This was surely an understatement. Mr. Woolworth must, I should think, have relieved Mr. White's mind altogether, since he must have told him in effect that the Regents, so far from having been got at by the People's College men, had for two months been making a further investigation, and on July 7, three days before Mr. White feared that all was lost, had in fact reached a decision. The decision was that if the trustees of the People's College did not, by July 27, deposit the sum of one hundred and eighty-five thousand dollars, the People's College would automatically lose the land grant.[31]

Mr. White, still suspecting a trick in it, went off to Rye Beach. The days slipped by; July 27, although to Mr. White's impatience it may have seemed a little late, arrived on schedule time, and still no deposit of one hundred and eighty-five thousand dollars, or of any sum at all, had been made by the trustees of the People's College. The land grant would thereupon become the property of the Cornell University as soon as the other conditions imposed on the corporation were complied with. This was promptly enough done. Mr. Cornell transferred to the corporation his bond, secured by Western Union Telegraph stock, for five hundred thousand dollars, and wrote his check for twenty-five thousand dollars in favor of Genesee College. And so in the year 1865, after many disappointments and delays, the Cornell University came into existence.

It existed, but as yet in a somewhat intangible form. It consisted at that time of a charter, a board of trustees, a farm of two hundred acres, and an endowment of approximately one million dollars. But as yet it had neither president nor faculty nor students, nor any buildings, nor a library, nor laboratories, nor equipment of any kind. All of these essential men and things had yet to be assembled, institutionally organized, and informed with a corporate purpose and personality. For the next three years Ezra Cornell and Andrew D. White, with unremitting effort, with unsurpassed zeal and intelligence, and with a resolution that would not be denied, gave themselves to this congenial task—the task of providing the Cornell University incorporated with a habitation and a home.

The Cornell University: Opened, 1868

I hope we have laid the foundation of an institution which shall combine practical with liberal education, which shall fit the youth of our country for the professions, the farms, the mines, the manufactories, for the investigations of science, and for mastering all the practical questions of life with success and honor.　　　　EZRA CORNELL

IN 1865 the Town of Ithaca had a population of something more than seven thousand inhabitants, the Village of Ithaca considerably less than that. Except for some scattered dwellings on South Hill, on upper Seneca and Buffalo Streets, and a small settlement clustered around the mills at the Ithaca Falls, the Village was chiefly confined to the region bounded by the Inlet and by Green, Aurora, and Mill (now Court) Streets. It was served by one railroad, the Ithaca and Owego, and a line of steamboats running on daily schedule between Ithaca and Cayuga Bridge at the northern end of Cayuga Lake. It could boast of various industries—plaster and flour mills, tanneries, a carriage manufactory. It could boast of two newspapers, the *Journal* and the *Democrat;* and of two hotels, of which the Ithaca House was the more ancient and the Clinton House the more splendid, being then regarded by many as one of the finest, both for service and for architecture, in the state. The most conspicuous building in the Village (and by some no doubt regarded as the most beautiful, since there is no accounting for tastes) was the Cornell Library at the corner of Seneca and Tioga Streets. The most distinguished citizen was Ezra Cornell, whose farm, purchased in 1857, and recently donated as the site of the new university, extended eastward from the cemetery between the

Cascadilla and Fall Creek gorges. The old farmhouse, known as Forest Park, and still standing at the Stewart Avenue entrance to the campus, was occupied by Mr. Cornell. Since there were no bridges over either of the gorges, it could be reached only by a road branching off from what is now University Avenue and skirting the north side of the cemetery. This road did not extend beyond the farmhouse; but there was a road running from the farmhouse along what is now Stewart Avenue to what is now University Avenue but was then merely a country highway from Ithaca to Free Hollow (Forest Home), Dryden, Cortland, and Syracuse.[1]

For the inhabitants of Ithaca the fifth of September, 1865, was a day out of the ordinary, a day to take note of and make preparations for, since there were on that day and the following, lodged at Mr. Cornell's home at Forest Park and at the Clinton House and meeting for conference at the Cornell Library, more distinguished strangers than the village had ever before had occasion to welcome. There was His Excellency, Reuben E. Fenton, the Governor of the State, His Honor, Thomas G. Alvord, Lieutenant Governor of the State, the Honorables Andrew D. White and William Kelly, Senators, and Abram B. Weaver, Assemblyman, and Messrs. Erastus Brooks, editor of the New York *Express,* and Edwin B. and Edwin D. Morgan. None of these men had ever been in Ithaca before. Not that the village was, for that time, inaccessible. Mr. Erastus Brooks, for example, could leave New York early in the morning and arrive safely at Ithaca some twelve hours later by either of two recommended routes—either by the Erie Railroad to Owego, changing there to the Ithaca and Owego, and leaving the train at the station at the head of the Inlet; or by taking the New York Central through Albany and Syracuse (where he might have been on the present occasion joined by the Honorable Andrew D. White) to Cayuga Bridge, and thence by steamer to the landing on the Inlet (near the present Johnson boathouse), where he could take a bus, or, for a consideration, a more luxurious vehicle, along

Willow Avenue to the Clinton House.[2] The Village of Ithaca was not inaccessible, but it was after all a small place, and not being on either of the main routes of travel east and west, the Erie and the New York Central, was but little known to the people from other parts of the state, and little visited by them in the way of business or pleasure.[3] The distinguished men who arrived there on the fifth of September, 1865, were not there in the way of pleasure, or in the ordinary way of business either, but in the way of business quite unusual, and regarded by them all as unusually important. They had come to Ithaca to attend the first meeting of the full Board of Trustees of the Cornell University.

The distinguished visitors were well received—a "serenade one evening, followed by a grand reception the next attended by large numbers of the best people." They were of course taken up the hill, and were of course, as they were expected to be, properly impressed by the magnificent view. There was indeed nothing else there to be impressed with, unless it might be Mr. Cornell's prize bulls, contentedly browsing on the hillside, or lumbering heavily down the ravine (where Mr. Cornell's statue now stands) to drink at the spring. What must have impressed them most, I should think, was the absence of all they were required, within two years, to assemble on that rough hillside—adequate buildings and apparatus for teaching agriculture and the mechanic arts, and a competent faculty for teaching them. As yet, not a spade sunk for any foundation —not even the site for any building as yet chosen. With so much to do and so little time to do it in, there was, nevertheless, not much that the trustees could do at this meeting on the fifth of September. Permanent officers were elected—Ezra Cornell, President; Francis M. Finch, Secretary; George W. Schuyler, Treasurer. The necessary committees were appointed—an Executive Committee, a Committee on Buildings, a Finance Committee, and a one-man committee, consisting of Andrew D. White, to draft bylaws. But the chief thing done was the acceptance of Mr. Cornell's proposal to give his bond to the trustees for $500,000, at seven per cent interest, to be secured by Western Union Telegraph stock to the amount of $700,000 par value, and the appointment of a committee to lay this proposal before the Comptroller of the State for his approval.[4]

This was little enough, but more was being accomplished than the formal record indicated. Mr. Cornell had already hit upon a grand idea which, after infinite effort and repeated discouragements, was to provide the university with an endowment far in excess of his original gift of five hundred thousand dollars. As early as March 27, 1865, he had written to Mr. W. A. Woodward: "What I desire . . . is . . . for the Treasurer of the University to take the funds I shall give the institution and buy the scrip of the Comptroller at 50 cents per acre, and enter the lands in the name and for the interest of the university." [5] By holding the lands until they were worth, say, two dollars per acre, the university would have ultimately, in addition to its present annual income of approximately forty thousand dollars, an endowment of about two million dollars. This was Mr. Cornell's grand idea, and he desired Mr. Woodward, as a man with seventeen years of experience in locating and selling western lands, to say whether the idea was a practicable one.

Mr. Woodward replied that the idea was entirely practicable, provided some experienced person—he meant himself—were employed to manage the business. Meantime, Mr. Cornell, finding the trustees not disposed to buy the scrip and locate the lands for the university, had decided to do it himself. On his invitation Mr. Woodward came to Ithaca, late in November, to discuss the matter, and on that occasion, as he remembered some years later, was introduced to some of the trustees—Messrs. Finch, McGraw, Andrus, Williams, and Schuyler—in order to get them interested in the project. But Mr. Woodward found them unwilling even to listen to him. "They were devoting their talk to something else all the time. . . . After . . . about twenty minutes one said: "It's tea time.' Another said: 'I must go, I never keep my wife waiting.' " Mr. Cornell, fortunately, was less interested in his tea than in his

MORRILL HALL IN 1868

View from the present main quadrangle. In the foreground is shown a raw
gully traversed by two rude causeways, the one (*left*) leading to "the shops" and
the other to White Hall, which was then about half built.

grand idea. He gave Mr. Woodward an estimate of his wealth, and asked him whether with that amount he could "carry the matter through." Mr. Woodward assured him that there would not be "any difficulty about that"—always provided, of course, that he would employ Mr. Woodward to manage the business for him.[6]

The upshot of these preliminaries was that Mr. Cornell made an agreement with the Comptroller to buy the scrip and locate and dispose of the lands for the benefit of the university, and for the next six years employed Mr. Woodward as his agent for selecting and entering, with the scrip which Mr. Cornell turned over to him from time to time, valuable pine timber lands in Wisconsin. Mr. Cornell's agreement with the Comptroller was precise and businesslike; his agreement with Mr. Woodward, unfortunately, was not.

Mr. Cornell's arrangement with the Comptroller was made legal by an act of the state legislature, April 10, 1866, which authorized the Comptroller to sell the scrip for not less than thirty cents per acre to the Trustees of Cornell University, or, in case they declined to purchase, to any one who would comply with the condition laid down. Since the trustees declined to purchase, Mr. Cornell signed a contract with the Commissioners of the Land Office, August 4, 1866, which provided: (1) that Mr. Cornell should purchase the unsold scrip (813,920 acres) at thirty cents per acre; (2) that, since thirty cents per acre was one half of the market price of the scrip at that time, Mr. Cornell should, as the lands were sold from time to time, pay into the state treasury an additional thirty cents per acre; (3) that these two sums, totalling sixty cents per acre, should be regarded as the price received by the state for the scrip, and should be kept in a separate fund known as the College Land Scrip Fund, the income of which should be paid to the university and used by it according to the terms of the Morrill Act; (4) that the net profits received by Mr. Cornell from the sale of the lands—that is, the price received minus the sixty cents per acre paid for the scrip, and minus the cost of taxes, management, and the like

—should be paid into the state treasury and kept as a separate fund to be known as the Cornell Endowment Fund, to be used (as the court decided later) for any of the purposes defined in the charter of the university.

By this arrangement the College Land Scrip Fund would be what the state received for the sale of the scrip—$594,000, which was approximately what it had commonly been supposed the state might realize from the scrip. But the Cornell Endowment Fund would be whatever Mr. Cornell could make for the university by locating the land and holding it for a higher price as a private business enterprise. In a letter to the Comptroller, June 9, 1866, Mr. Cornell estimated that this fund would ultimately amount to $1,600,000, which would give the university a total endowment of $2,944,000. The estimate was conservative, being some two million dollars less than the university ultimately realized from the sale of the scrip and the lands alone.[7]

For the present, however, and for some twenty years to come, these advantages existed only on paper, and even on paper they were not regarded as impressive by any one except Mr. Cornell. If Mr. Cornell's estimate of the ultimate value of the lands was too conservative, his estimate of the immediate difficulties of carrying the enterprise was, characteristically, far too optimistic. He was misled in part by Mr. Woodward, who professed a great interest in Mr. Cornell's noble educational plans, but whose real interest was only, with Mr. Cornell's aid, to make a fortune for himself. But he was also misled by an excessive confidence in his own judgment, and by the essential honesty which disposed him to be extremely casual in his business methods. The enterprise in which he employed Mr. Woodward as his agent was a difficult and complicated one, involving the handling, it was estimated, of some two million dollars; and yet we look in vain for a formal contract defining what either principal or agent should render or receive. The two men appear to have drifted into an ill-defined gentleman's agreement, in which there was no intention on either side to deceive, but only every opportunity to do so, nor any wish for mis-understanding, but only the remotest chance that it would not occur. When it did occur it was so complete and baffling that thir-teen hundred and eighty-eight pages of testimony were required to determine whether, and in respect to what matters, there had ever been a meeting of minds between principal and agent. In the end it was decided that that there had been, and that Mr. Cornell owed his agent a good many thousand dollars more than he thought he did.[8]

What Mr. Cornell really owed Mr. Woodward for his services no one will ever know. But the melancholy fact is that with more careful inquiry at the beginning he could have dispensed with the services of Mr. Woodward altogether. The real work of select-ing and locating the lands was done by Mr. Herbert C. Putnam, a clerk in the land office at Chippewa Falls, and after a few years Mr. Cornell learned this fact and thereafter dealt directly with Mr. Putnam. But apart from the money wasted on Mr. Woodward, the necessary expense of carrying the enterprise, even with the most prudent management, was far more than Mr. Cornell had real-ized or could afford; so that in 1867, having purchased and located 511,068 scrip acres, he found it impossible to purchase any more. At that time virtually nothing had been realized by the sale of the lands; and when the university opened in 1868 no one but Mr. Cornell, unless it might be John McGraw and Henry W. Sage, had much interest or any real faith in the grand idea. Cer-tainly President Andrew D. White, a majority of the trustees, and so far as is known all of the faculty would have been glad to sell the lands for whatever they might bring and so get rid of a bad business. Nevertheless Mr. Cornell, encumbered by com-mitments too casually undertaken, but inspired by an indomitable faith in his grand idea, insisted with admirable if sometimes irri-tating stubbornness, and with a good measure of success, on hold-ing the lands for a better price. To Mr. Cornell, therefore, must go the initial credit of providing Cornell University, in spite of the best efforts of its trustees, its president, and its faculty, with an endowment far larger than any one had originally dreamed of.[9]

Since Mr. Cornell and Mr. White had taken the leading part in getting the university incorporated, it was taken for granted by the board of trustees that they should take a leading part in organizing it; and as Mr. Cornell was commonly deferred to in matters of business and finance, Mr. White was commonly deferred to in matters of educational policy. Mr. White was accordingly made chairman of the Committee on Plan of Organization; and on November 21, 1866, he presented to the Board a report of forty-eight pages, which was adopted, and finally put into effect with such slight modifications as may be noted in the first General Announcement issued in 1868.[10]

The report was based on three general ideas: first, that agriculture and the mechanic arts should be regarded as "the peers of any other" subject; second, that the conventional liberal-arts course should be extended to include history, political science, and modern literature; and, third, that students should be given, in respect to choice of studies and in respect to conduct and discipline, a greater degree of freedom than was then customary in most colleges.

In accord with these principles, the subjects of study were organized in two divisions—"The Division of Special Sciences and Arts" and "The Division of Science, Literature and the Arts." The first division comprised nine "departments"—Agriculture; Mechanic Arts; Civil Engineering; Commerce and Trade; Mining; Medicine; Law; Jurisprudence, Political Science, and History; and Education. These departments were, so to speak, in the nature of potential professional schools, designed to fit students for the particular profession indicated, although the department of Jurisprudence was especially recommended for training political leaders in the state and nation, who had hitherto been lacking, the report said, in "the commonest rudiments of knowledge." The second division was intended to replace the traditional college course. Instead of the single required classical course, there were to be three "general" courses, a "science" course, and an "optional" course. The three general courses were variations of the conventional classical course, permitting the substitution of German and French for Greek and Latin, and including a good deal more of history, political science, and modern literature. The science course was designed as preliminary training for those who expected to become proficient in science, engineering, or agriculture. The optional course was a concession to those who were not sure what they wanted, and accordingly permitted them, as one may say, to close their eyes and choose three "subjects of study from all those pursued in the university."

The courses of instruction thus offered called ultimately for forty-six professors—twenty-four in the first division, twenty-two in the second; but for a beginning it was thought that twenty-six would be sufficient. These should naturally be the best obtainable, since the quality of a university depended fundamentally on the quality of its faculty. Unfortunately, the best were not to be had on permanent tenure at any price. "To take Agassiz permanently from Cambridge," the report said, "we must outbid the Emperor of the French, who has recently offered the most tempting prizes in vain." This being the case, Mr. White's happy idea was to secure as permanent, or "resident," professors the most promising young men to be had—at salaries ranging from $1,000 to $2,500— and trust them to achieve distinction; but also to invite men who were already distinguished, such as Agassiz or James Russell Lowell, to give courses of lectures for a term or a year as temporary or "non-resident" professors. This would enable students, faculty, and the citizens of Ithaca to hear many of the most famous scholars in the country, to their own great advantage and to the enhanced prestige of the university. To begin with, the report suggested sixteen resident and ten non-resident professors.

The report discussed at length a great variety of other matters. It touched upon the desirability of providing remunerative manual

labor for students; fixed the student's fees at $25 per year; opposed
the dormitory system; suggested that if the citizens of Ithaca
charged too much for board the university might build a dining
hall and lease it to the students; emphasized the importance of
obtaining, for the faculty, men of "general culture" and good
manners, although a few eccentrics might be tolerated on account
of special distinction in scholarship; declared roundly that "the
university will not tolerate feuds in the faculty"; made much of
establishing close personal and social relations between members
of the faculty and students; and made even more of the library
as an indispensable part of any great university. The report closed
by laying down, as a general test and touchstone of success in all
their efforts, the principle enunciated by Wilhelm von Humboldt
and elaborated by John Stuart Mill: *"The great and leading principle is the absolute and essential importance of human development in its richest diversity."*

Nothing was said in the report about the admission of women.
Both Mr. Cornell and Mr. White approved of it in principle, but
many of the trustees did not, and in any case it was thought to be
out of the question until proper buildings could be provided for
them. For a fleeting moment there seemed to be a bare chance
that this might be done at once. On April 9, 1866, Mr. Henry
Wells wrote to Ezra Cornell asking where he could get a good
quality of brick for a building in which, as he said, "I intend to
educate wives for your boys, allowing they bring good recom-
mendations." Four days later Mr. Cornell replied—very specifically about the brick; but then took the liberty, as an old friend,
to make a suggestion; which was that, since there were already
too many small colleges, it would be better all round if Mr. Wells,
"instead of building one more college at Aurora," should "build
at Ithaca the female department of Cornell University." The hope
that this might come to pass—it must have been pretty thin at
best—was extinguished on May 22, when Mr. Wells gave his
reasons for preferring to build a female seminary at Aurora.[11]

In his report on Plan of Organization Mr. White raised the question of whether the ideal American university needed to have a president, decided, for good or ill, that it did, and recommended that the Board of Trustees should proceed, at an early day, to choose one. But it seems that without Mr. White's knowledge the question had already been decided; for almost immediately after Mr. White's report had been accepted, the board voted unanimously that "the Hon. Andrew D. White of Syracuse" should be the president of the university.

This action, Mr. White says in his *Autobiography,* came to him as a complete surprise. If it seems to us a little incredible that the action should have surprised any one, no doubt the reason is that, looking back on the history of the institution, we find it difficult to suppose that any one else could have been thought of, much less seriously considered, as first president of Cornell University. But in human affairs nothing is predetermined until it has occurred; and in 1866 it was not a foregone conclusion that Mr. White should be chosen. Several other men were in fact thought of in that connection. There is some reason to believe that the Rev. Amos Brown, President of the People's College, thought of himself.[12] Mr. White had various men in mind. He had heard a prominent Massachusetts judge mentioned for the position, and would, he confessed, prefer him "to a clergyman," but thought rather better of Governor Andrews, who had recently declined the presidency of Antioch College. But the man he preferred to all others was Martin Anderson, President of Rochester University, whom he recommended strongly to Mr. Cornell.[13] To all of Mr. White's suggestions in the matter Mr. Cornell listened, but no doubt said little. On one occasion, however, he did go so far as to say that he had a candidate of his own, but preferred not to say who it was until the next meeting of the Board of Trustees; and at the next meeting he presented the name of Andrew D. White in "a very earnest speech."

I think it unlikely, therefore, that Mr. White could have been altogether unprepared for the action of the Board in electing him president of the university. Whether surprised or not, it seems that he nevertheless protested against it, and finally accepted the position, as he says, with "the distinct statement that I should be regarded simply as a *locum tenens* . . . until some man more fit for it could be secured." Reasons for this attitude he had in plenty: he was too young and had not the necessary experience; he was already overburdened with affairs—was at the time a professor in the University of Michigan, State Senator, president of a Syracuse bank and director in two other banks, a director in the New York Central and Lake Shore Railroads and in the Albermarle and Chesapeake Canal, and the executor of two large estates. Besides, so he said, whatever ambitions he had (and in this he was supported by his wife) were "in the direction of accepting a professorship which had been tendered me at Yale." [14]

So he said. And throughout his life he said repeatedly that he was a scholar, and that his greatest desire was to be relieved of business and public affairs, and retire to the peace and seclusion of his study where he could do his proper work. I have no doubt that Mr. White believed, in connection with all this, what he said when he said it. But I am under no such compulsion; and I note that he never declined an offer of any prominent official position, unless it might be a tentative offer—which was in fact not pressed —to be a candidate for Governor of New York, and even this he did not absolutely decline. Mr. White said himself that his chief ambition in life was to aid in founding a great American university; and I cannot think that anything ever pleased him more than to be chosen the first president of Cornell, or ever gave him more satisfaction in later life than to feel that he, no less than Mr. Cornell, or even more than Mr. Cornell, was the effective creator of Cornell University—nothing, that is, unless it might be his appointment as Minister to Germany, where he remained three years hobnobbing with Bismarck and receiving the applause of German universities, in spite of repeated requests from Ithaca that he should by all means return and take up his duties as president, because the university was in a fair way to be ruined by constant and resounding clashes between the rigid conscience of Vice-President Russel and the impervious mind of Henry W. Sage.

Andrew D. White was not, in the modern sense, a scholar, but what used to be called "a gentleman and a scholar"—a very fine gentleman indeed, and in the sense intended a very fine scholar. But scholarship was not his profession. He was essentially a crusader, by profession a promoter of good causes, primarily interested in changing the world rather than in understanding it. If he had been taken at his word, and left severely alone to the peace and seclusion of his study, he would inevitably, in no long time, have been bored by it; the strain occasioned by the silence and lack of bustle would have aggravated his dyspepsia and his sleeplessness, so that he would of necessity have welcomed, for its sedative effect, the first offer to serve on the busy board of no matter what railroad or canal company, or, all else failing, would have found relief in rushing out to organize something—perhaps a society for the promotion of activities and preservation of excitements. Ambitious as he was to aid in founding a great American university, and being neither unintelligent nor shrinkingly modest, I cannot think that he did not know, down in his bones, that he was destined by circumstances and his own interests and abilities to be the first president of Cornell University.

After his election, at all events, we hear nothing more from him about the *locum tenens* business or the Yale professorship, or about anything at all except the pre-eminently important business of organizing the new university, of which no aspect, human or otherwise, was to him indifferent. We find him writing innumerable letters, sending any number of telegrams, and interviewing all sorts of people in the effort to further that business. We find that he has a finger in every pie, and definite and passionate convictions about every matter, whether it be the best type of mind for teaching English literature, or the best type of lens for the great telescope, or the high importance of at once securing the Anthon classical collection, or the proper level for the water tables of the main buildings. We find him suffering from sleeplessness and often on the verge of a complete nervous breakdown—but never more than just on the verge. And so I think we may conclude that he cared for nothing so much as for Cornell University, that he delighted in nothing so much as in being its first president and in working day and night to make it fair and fine. And for my part I also conclude that, for all his frail body and fits of nervous irritability, he must in fact have had a constitution with the flexible toughness of whang leather, besides vitality enough for three ordinary men.

Nothing engaged Mr. White more in these days, or was thought by him to be of so much importance, as the selection of the first faculty. "Better a splendid and complete faculty in a barn," he maintained, "than an insufficient faculty in a palace." [15] Not content with letters of recommendation, he went to New York, New Haven, and Cambridge to consult personally and confidentially with the leading professors about the most promising young men in the various fields of study. While at Cambridge he visited Agassiz at his cottage at Nahant, and had with him long and fruitful conversations "regarding the merits of different candidates." Information obtained in this way, he said, was worth more than "cartloads of credentials"; and to make still more sure he always insisted, if it was at all possible, on having a personal interview with the candidate before making an appointment. [16]

The first promising young men to be nosed out in this fashion —or at least the first to be formally appointed, February 13, 1867 —were Evan W. Evans, in mathematics, and William C. Russel, in modern languages. September 25, of the same year, four additional appointments were made—Burt G. Wilder in natural history; Eli W. Blake in physics; G. C. Caldwell in agricultural chemistry; and James M. Crafts in general chemistry. [17] Young

124

Mr. Wilder, a favorite pupil of Agassiz, apparently took a greater interest in Cornell affairs than the others. In accepting his appointment, he let Mr. White know, in a formal and somewhat elegant English style, that all he had heard of the Cornell University, and of Mr. White himself, "assures me that with the position thus offered is given an opportunity to work in science more than ordinarily advantageous." In November following his appointment he came to Ithaca, was taken by Mr. Cornell for a ride in his dilapidated buggy, and expressed himself delighted with the place and the people, especially with Mr. Cornell, of whom he could not "say enough in admiration." He felt sure, notwithstanding "the smallness of the salary" (which required him to ask for an advance the first year) that a man who could not do good work under such conditions could not do it at all. But one small thing gave him some concern—what type of seats had they planned for the class rooms? He was convinced that "the easier and more comfortable the seats, the closer is the attention and the more rapid the progress of the pupil." He therefore took the liberty of making a rough sketch, in a letter to Mr. White, of the proper type of seat, which had a cushion in the back of it pliable to the natural curve of the spine, and of the improper type of seat, which had only a rigid, unaccommodating bend in it.[18]

From Professor Caldwell, after his appointment, Mr. White obtained information about three other promising young men— Messrs. Miles, Prentiss, and Rothrick. Professor Caldwell thought Mr. Miles the ablest of the three, although he perhaps depended "too much upon a text book"; but he thought Mr. Prentiss a first-class man too, and "more agreeable and elegant than Mr. Rothrick." It seems that Mr. Miles, though tempted, declined an offer, so that the "agreeable and elegant" Prentiss was in fact appointed. From Cambridge Mr. Cornell and Mr. White heard good things of a certain James Oliver, who "for character and purity of life is unsurpassed," and sure to have a great influence on the young, being himself most agreeable and always ready

125

to do good." [19] Young Mr. Oliver was not appointed at this time, but the mistake was remedied later, and for many years James Oliver was the delight of his colleagues, and always ready to do them good, one favorite way being to provide them with the most engaging examples of professorial absent-mindedness ever recorded on any campus. Another unsuccessful candidate, recommended by Moses Coit Tyler, was Hiram Corson, who much desired to come to Cornell because of the prospect that the English language and literature would there "be given the prominence which its transcendent importance demands." [20] Mr. Corson also was appointed later, and also became a center for the collection of myths.

And so with infinite care, but with some mistakes, the first faculty was selected. Yet with every effort to hasten matters it was found that the time allowed for organizing the university was too short, so that it was necessary to get, by legislative act, permission to postpone the opening for one year—to October, 1868.[21] Even so, as late as February 13, 1868, only ten resident professors had been appointed. Meantime Mr. White had been exerting his persuasive charm to induce the settled and the distinguished to accept temporary appointments. At the close of a letter to Mr. Cornell he announces some good news — "P.S. I have secured James Russell Lowell, the foremost literary man in the United States, as one of our non-resident professors." [22] Five other men were likewise beguiled—Louis Agassiz in natural history; Fred Holbrook in agriculture; James Hall in geology; George W. Curtis in recent literature; and Theodore W. Dwight in constitutional law. All six were appointed by the board on February 13, 1868. It was voted by the board that the term of office, unless otherwise determined, should be two years; but Mr. White, allowing always for human frailty even among the distinguished, got a rider inserted to the effect that the agreement might be terminated at any time "for delinquencies." [23]

Mr. White was one of those fortunate if sometimes irritating persons who are predisposed to think that men or things chosen by themselves must be of the best—any doubt on that score being a bar to their going ahead and being right with undiminished confidence. He was therefore well pleased with the men he had chosen for his faculty. He did not, however, go so far as to suppose that these excellent young men, housed in Mr. Cornell's barn, even with the prize bulls removed, would make a "complete university." Additional buildings were necessary; and in the matter of buildings Mr. Cornell was also concerned. Mr. Cornell had been interested in the construction of Cascadilla Place, originally designed as a water cure; and now, as the principal stockholder, he was instrumental in acquiring the gray, massive, prison-like structure as a university dormitory for housing faculty and students. But the main buildings were to be located between the two gorges. As a site for the buildings, Mr. White rather preferred the lower level (no doubt because better adapted for a quadrangle) where the Baker Dormitories now are; but in deference to Mr. Cornell the present site, in spite of its uneven surface and very likely because of the more "magnificent view" afforded, was chosen. For the general plan of the buildings Mr. White was responsible. His idea was a quadrangle, with the main buildings around it, and other buildings to come later located in attractive disarray elsewhere. The architect, Frederick Law Olmsted, who was consulted, protested strongly against this plan, on the ground that it was too conventional and did not sufficiently allow for future expansion.[24] His idea was something less obvious—a plan that would aim at "unity in variety." But Mr. White had too long dreamed of "quadrangles as beautiful as those of Jesus and St. John" to abandon his idea; and so he had his way, and we have the quadrangle—which is well enough. If in the arrangement of the other buildings no great unity is discernible, the buildings themselves at least cannot be said to lack variety.

The plan called for the immediate erection of two buildings on the west side of what would ultimately be the quadrangle—the present Morrill and White (then called the South and North University) Halls, with a more imposing structure between them to be erected later. Mr. Cornell's role was to scrutinize the estimates for construction, which he commonly found too high (and maybe the result of collusion), and to supervise the work in progress, which he commonly thought was slower than it need be.[25] His chief aim was always to keep expenses down; so much so that he thought it hardly worth while to fill in the ravine sufficiently to bring White Hall on a level with Morrill—a decision that outraged Mr. White's sense of architectural fitness, and would, moreover, have given to the quadrangle something of the aspect of a shoot-the-chutes. "Now I beg of you," Mr. White writes in great distress, *"asking it as a favor,* that the water tables be put absolutely on the same line. . . . We are building for centuries and should not subject ourselves to the charge of stupidity from those who come after. . . . You had your way about the site— yield to the majority in regard to this slight matter of the level." [26] Mr. Cornell must have yielded—a good deal at least; for although the water tables of Morrill and White are not, judging by the naked eye, absolutely on the same line, the "stupidity," that is the difference, is not glaring. So the work was pushed on; but as late as February, 1868, although Morrill was virtually finished, White Hall had as yet been raised only to the first storey.[27]

With the buildings unfinished and the faculty still far from complete, Mr. White was preparing, late in 1867, to spend three months in Europe for the purchase of books and apparatus, when suddenly, to his excited imagination, disaster loomed on the horizon. A constitutional convention was then sitting at Albany, and an amendment to the report of the educational committee had been moved, to the effect that the revenues of the College Land Scrip Fund should be given to Cornell University each year only if specifically appropriated by the legislature—the implication of the amendment and the intention of its movers being that the legislature might, at any annual session, for good reason, refuse to appropriate it to the university. The amendment was supported by the friends of the People's and Genesee colleges and of Rochester University, the leader being Mr. Angus McDonald, former attorney for Genesee College. In the debates the history of the struggle for the Cornell charter in 1865 was reviewed, and the Rochester *Daily Union and Advertiser,* and other newspapers hostile to Cornell University, made this the occasion to exhibit Mr. Cornell once more as an unscrupulous land-grabber whose chief aim was to rob the state for the enrichment of the Cornell family. Mr. White, much alarmed, sent telegrams and wrote letters to many people, and interviewed many more, convincing some but finding others "shaky," or entirely "ignorant of the issues involved." The "malignant," as he said, was McDonald, whom "no argument could reach for the reason that he kept raising new questions and befogging the whole matter." [28] Fortunately, the cause of the university was ably defended in the convention, especially by Judge Folger, who offered a substitute to the amendment to the effect that the revenues of the College Land Scrip Fund should be appropriated to Cornell University "so long as said university shall fully . . . perform the conditions of the act of the legislature establishing said institution." The substitute amendment was adopted, the storm subsided, and in April, 1868, Mr. White left for Europe.

In Europe Mr. White had—there is no other word for it—the time of his life. His long and frequent letters to Mr. Cornell, written in such a rush as to be scarcely legible and barely literate, have something of the quality of breathless lyrics. "Have tried," he writes, "to shake off thoughts of the university, but 'distance lends enchantment to the view,' and I can think of nothing else." He was hardly settled in Paris before reporting: "Have begun my book purchases, and am postponing as to apparatus"; expect soon to investigate agricultural and technical schools; "will have an interview with the Minister of Public Instruction and some of the professors here"; have written to Professor Russel and Mr.

Fiske for a meeting; also to arrange for an interview with young Sibley, and "if he is at all the man for any of our professorships I shall 'gobble him up' "; have decided to "go personally and make the purchases of apparatus and chemicals at Heidelberg, Darmstadt, Erfurt, and Berlin." [29] All in one letter. And so with every letter—a dozen things done or to be done. And he does it all, and from time to time sends home great packing cases filled with books or apparatus (for which there is, of course, not enough money, more of which, of course, he accordingly asks for and obtains from Mr. Cornell). Not the least of his triumphs was that, in England, he managed to "gobble up" Professor Goldwin Smith, and Dr. James Law, a highly recommended young man in veterinary science. And so he returns, flushed with success, and pleased more than a little when it was jocosely said that he had brought back, as part of his European spoils, "an Oxford professor and a Scotch horse doctor."

When Mr. White returned from Europe there were less than three months to run before the great event for which three years of unremitting effort had been a preparation—the opening of the university in October, 1868. It was a time of belated reminders of last things to be done, of last-minute activities, conveying an impression of every one so rushing about that nothing seemed to be accomplished. When the students began to arrive, at all events, it could not be said that anything was really ready. White Hall had been raised only to the second storey; the shops and laboratory, although usable, were not finished; and even Morrill Hall still lacked doors to some of the rooms, and such like convenient accessories. Of the twenty-six professors, a number were not officially appointed until the day before the opening, and accordingly were not in Ithaca. Those who were on the ground were busy unpacking the cases of books and apparatus that had arrived, and wondering where others that should have arrived had got to. But more than anything else they were wondering what

THE MAIN QUADRANGLE IN 1872

The buildings (*left to right*) are Morrill, McGraw, and White Halls, Sibley College (west section), and the Laboratory. This photograph shows McGraw Hall nearly finished. The Laboratory, a frame building containing "the shops," housed Chemistry and Physics until Franklin Hall was built for those departments in 1883; and Civil Engineering until Lincoln Hall was ready for that school in 1889.

they could do with the quite unexpected number of students that had suddenly descended upon them.[30]

They had wanted students, of course, and had taken care to make known the advantages of the new university. Mr. Cornell had sent the first General Announcement to some three hundred prominent persons, and to more than a thousand newspapers; had also, much to Mr. White's dismay, published an article in the New York *Tribune* stating that students desiring to pay for their education while getting it could do so by giving half of their time to manual labor for the university.[31] But what no one quite realized was that the university had been advertised in other and more effective ways than these. For three years it had been heralded or denounced throughout the country as a novel and somewhat questionable "experiment," as "the Cornell idea"—an institution in which any person could find instruction in any subject, and in which professors would be appointed and students welcomed whatever religion they might profess, or even if they professed no religion at all. The university had become well known for the friends, and still better known for the enemies it had made; had become, in short, famous or infamous as the case might be for its "radicalism"—its frank and publicly announced departure from conventional academic and religious ideas.

For these reasons the professors on the ground found themselves, at the end of September, saddled with the largest entering class ever admitted to any American college up to that time—412 students: more than twice as many as could be provided with lodgings, together with the professors themselves, in the dormitory known as Cascadilla Place; and more than three times as many as could be conveniently taught in the class rooms available. Nevertheless, the professors on the ground, all sold on the "Cornell idea," got down to it with good will and determination. Entrance examinations were held in the dimly lighted basement of the Cornell Library. One professor made a brave show of teaching the French language to a class of two hundred; the department of geology was confined to a single room adjoining one of the coal cellars; and demonstrations in natural history were conducted in the vacant space next to a furnace. The library, in Morrill Hall, could not be used as a library, being in constant demand for holding recitations; and in any case, whatever it might be used for, it suffered the disadvantage of being always permeated with the variegated odors that seeped up from the basement, where the chemists prepared their instructive stenches.[32]

Whether, for the students, the promise of the "Cornell idea" was sufficiently attractive to outweigh its present inconveniences, I cannot say. One student at least—Mr. J. Y. Davis from Auburn —liked it well enough. He liked his room, nine by twelve feet, in Cascadilla Place, because it gave him a magnificent view, because it was exactly opposite the lift where he got his coal, and nearly opposite the elegant dining room where excellent meals were served—four kinds of meat with fish, and pie for dessert; he liked marching in military order to and from the campus; liked the chimes, the largest bell reminding him of the one on the big factory at Auburn; he liked the reception given on inauguration day in the Cornell Library, where the ladies appeared "in full dress costume with the Grecian bend"—it was "like the Bazaar except for the booths." Mr. Davis liked it all very much, but admitted that "as yet everything is in an uproar and confusion." [33] Maybe he liked it for that reason. Maybe students like uproar and confusion when there is a chance that something new and interesting may come out of it.

The uproar and confusion probably died down a little on Wednesday, October 7—the day set for the inaugural ceremonies, for which elaborate preparations had been made by the faculty and the citizens of Ithaca. The citizens, for their part and for the evening, had arranged a "Jubilee" in the streets and a grand reception in the Cornell Library assembly room. The faculty had arranged for the inaugural ceremonies in the assembly room in the morning, and in the afternoon for the formal presentation of the chime of bells donated to the university by Miss Jenny Mc-Graw. The weather, no doubt by some special dispensation of Providence, was fine, although a high wind was blowing.[34] At ten in the morning the assembly room, gaily decorated, was filled with students and faculty, citizens of the town, and distinguished visitors invited for the occasion. The ceremonies began with an address by Mr. Cornell—a very brief address, as we might guess; brief, but still the most pregnant address of the day, since it developed in simple terms the thesis: "The individual is better, society is better, and the state is better, for the culture of its citizens; therefore we desire to extend the means for the culture of all." Following Mr. Cornell's address, the Lieutenant-Governor, Stewart L. Woodford, administered the oath of office to Mr. White as President of the University, and then placed in his hands a casket of carved oak containing the charter and the seal of the university and the keys of the buildings.

Mr. White's address, carefully prepared, was a good one, but inevitably lacked the virtue of brevity. Fortunately, following the practice of old-fashioned divines, he itemized and italicized his main points, which were comprised under five heads: Foundation Ideas, Formative Ideas, Governmental Ideas, Permeating and Crowning Ideas, and Eliminated Ideas. Under these heads he set forth, with a wealth of illustrative comment, the aims of the university—the union of practical and liberal education, special emphasis on science, the close relation between the university and the school system of the state, the promotion of advanced graduate studies, the establishment of a variety of courses of study, and a greater freedom for the students, in respect to conduct and choice of studies, than had been customary hitherto. The Permeating and Crowning Idea was "to develop the individual man, . . . as a being intellectual, moral, and religious; and to bring the force of the individual to bear on society." The ideas to be eliminated were, first, the idea of the pedants—the gerund-grinders who "teach young men by text book to parse"; and, second, the idea of the Philistines—the men for whom "Greed is God, and Money-bags his prophet." The exercises were closed by an address, on behalf of the faculty, by Professor W. C. Russel; and another, on behalf of the Regents, by Chancellor V. L. Pruyn. The audience must have sat there—I have counted the words—for three and a half mortal hours.[35]

In the afternoon "an immense crowd," still unappeased, assembled on the hill for the formal presentation of the chime of bells, then housed in a wooden tower erected somewhere near the entrance to the present library.[36] To reach this spot one could drive up past the cemetery to Mr. Cornell's house, and from there climb the steep ascent; or one could drive from the corner of State and Aurora up the Catskill Turnpike, turning left on Eddy Road, to Cascadilla Place, and from there walk across the new wooden bridge over the gorge, climb the sharp rise where the present gymnasium is, clamber down and up the unbridged ravine just north of the present law building, and follow the path along a rail fence, enclosing a cornfield to the right, to the bell tower. From the bell tower one could see Morrill Hall, rising stark and garish on the hillside, and beyond it the half-finished walls of White Hall, and to the right of that the wooden building called the shops. Between these two buildings and Morrill Hall one could see a ravine six or eight feet deep, bridged by two dirt causeways—one leading from Morrill to White, the other from Morrill to the shops. Just beyond the shops were some rickety cow barns. Such was the outward, visible aspect of the Cornell University in October, 1868.[37]

The bells were formally presented, on behalf of Jenny McGraw, by Francis M. Finch, but the principal address was delivered by George William Curtis. It was what in those days people loved to hear, an oration—what was called a "notable effort," the requirement in all such displays being that the phrasing should be studied and rehearsed, and that the sentiments

134

should be edifying. Mr. Curtis met these requirements admirably, especially in his peroration, which was notable for nothing so much as for the brilliance of its imagery, unless it might be the irrelevance of its ideas. "Here is our university, our Cornell, like the man-of-war, all its sails set, its rigging full and complete from stem to stern, its crew embarked, its passengers all ready and aboard; and even as I speak to you, even as the autumn sun sets in the west, it begins to glide over the waves as it goes forth rejoicing, every stitch of canvas spread, all its colors flying, its musical bells ringing, its heartstrings beating with hope and joy." [38]

Mr. White, listening to this notable effort, looking out over the ragged cornfield and the rough pasture land and noting the unfinished buildings and the piled-up rubbish, experienced a momentary and unaccustomed sense of depression. No words, he felt, could fail more completely to express the reality.[39] The reality had been expressed by Mr. Cornell, in his address in the morning, with blunt brevity. A friend of his, he said, had recently come to Ithaca, had looked over the university, and had reported: "I did not find a single thing finished." But, said Mr. Cornell, "such is not the entertainment we invited you to. We did not expect to have a single thing finished. . . . It is the commencement that we have now in hand."

Not a single thing finished! It was indeed true, if we have in mind only the outward, material properties of the university. The "lofty clock-tower, looking proudly down," the "quadrangles as beautiful as those of Jesus and St. John," any building as satisfactory as Goldwin Smith Hall, even one as formidably impressive and curiously pinnacled as Sage College—all of these, so long dreamed of by Mr. White, were indeed unfinished, were as yet not even begun. Nevertheless, on that seventh of October, 1868, something was finished. The idea of Cornell University was finished, and Mr. Cornell had himself, in his address in the morning, expressed it with admirable precision.

135

I hope we have laid the foundation of an institution which shall combine practical with liberal education, which shall fit the youth of our country for the professions, the farms, the mines, the manufactories, for the investigations of science, and for mastering all the practical questions of life with success and honor.

This was what was finished on October 7, 1868—this idea of Cornell University. Seventy-five years later there is nothing we could wish to add to it, or anything we could wish to take away. And it is after all the idea that was then, as it is now, the important thing, since it was and is the source of all the rest. In response to this idea the first crude buildings were erected, the first books and apparatus were collected, and the first faculty was assembled. In response to this idea the first students came to be enrolled. And on this seventy-fifth anniversary we shall do well to remember that it is not the buildings however splendid, or the quadrangles however beautiful, but this idea conceived and brought to birth by Ezra Cornell and Andrew Dickson White— the idea of an institution freed from obligation to religious or political or social prejudice, and devoted to the advancement of knowledge in all fruitful fields of inquiry—it was this idea that then gave and still gives to Cornell University whatever high significance and enduring value it may have for learning and for the life of man.

DOCUMENTS

DOCUMENTS

1. Letters from Ezra Cornell to His Father, 1831, 1833

[The following letters, written by Mr. Cornell at the ages of twenty-four and twenty-six, are printed here chiefly because, by comparing them with letters written later (see below, Nos. 2 and 11), one can see the remarkable improvement which Mr. Cornell made, after he had reached a mature age, in his command of English. The originals of these letters are in the Cornell University Library; the first one is in the collection catalogued under MSS + Kc 8; the second is, with some other loose papers, in Mr. Cornell's *Memorandum Book*, Vol. III. The first letter has, along the edge in some places, rotted away, so that some words are missing.]

March 8, 1831.

HONORED FATHER,

I have expected to see thee out here ever since I was at home but I was disappointed. I learned that you were all well by a line that Elijah recd. from the[e]—my health is remarkably good & has been since I left home. Ower business moves on in good order. I have sold 200 tons of plaster and I think I shall sell the remainder this spring as ower home customers has not bot any yet. I shall go to work to finish the tunel as soon as the weather will admit. I expect we will cut it loer but it is not decided yet which will be the most prudent method. I have hired J. T. Irish for a year give him $222.00 or $18.50 per mo. and he boards himself. I presume you will expect to hear that I have made a wife of Miss Byngton but that ant the case and I never intended that it should be but I am happy to inform you that I am about to form a matrimonial connection with Miss Mary Ann Wood, and I presume you wont advance any objections to mar ower [happiness] I have the consent of her parents and [   ]e that every individual of the family is [pleased?] with the prospects of my becoming a member of the family her friends compliment her for the [allian]ce she has made as they are pleased to call it—the [19] March is fixt upon for the celebration [   ] I would be glad if it was so that thee & mother [   ] but the going is so bad that I shant look [   ] says wenever thee comes out the way he [comes?] the road by his house is the nearest [   ] cant and I must conclude pleas give [   ] of my connections and freinds [   ] of course.   EZRA CORNELL

Documents

Ithaca, Feb. 17, 1833.

The[e] will learn by Benjamin that we are all well & we were very glad to hear that you are injoying the same blessing — We are so buisy here at present that I have had but little time to spare with Banjamin. I have not engaged any longer than 1ˢᵗ May, but I am wanted here and I think it is possible that I shall stay and if I do I shall want the assist-ance of $800 or a $1000 to doo business with for I shant continue in the business that I have been in without a share in it Consequently I shall want the money thee owes me & I shall want the to [try?] to raise $500 for me wih what thee owes me if the[e] can have it for any length of time. Thee need not hesitate to borrow the money on account of meet-ing the payments for I shall be able to doo that part of it punctually the balance I can raise here.

I remain with much respect, etc.,

To Elijah Cornell.   E. Cornell

P.S. Pleas inform me respecting this business as soon as possible that I shall be able to calculate my business.   E. C.

2. Letter from Ezra Cornell to Amos Kendall, 1851

[The following letter is important because it indicates that as early as 1851 Mr. Cornell's financial situation was becoming desperate. It should be read in connec-tion with the Cyphering Book (Document No. 5), in which he says that in 1854 he was in debt $50,000, and also in connection with the letters from J. H. Wade and W. P. Pew (Documents Nos. 3 and 4). The letter is the first draft of the one pre-sumably sent to Amos Kendall, and is in *Cornell Papers,* Cardboard Box.]

New York, Sept 16, 1851

Dear Sir

My courage is fast failing. I have worked hard and incessantly for the past nine years at this Telegraph business, practicing the most rigid economy, and I am now worse off than when I began — At the time I first embarked in the business I was worth five thousand dollars in real estate, which rented for enough to support my family. Now that same real estate is encumbered with a mortgage for money invested in the Telegraph business, and I am in debt some $15,000 besides, for cost of construction of the various lines, and I cannot get the first cent from any of them towards paying interest on what I owe. Aside from this is the various claims of Patentees for account of patent.

For the last two years I have not recᵈ the first dollar for my own services, and have not been able to contribute the first cent towards the support of my family, they are wholly dependent on the charity of friends, and every line of telegraph that I have any interest in, as far as I know are [is] running in debt for expence of working, and I can see no prospect of any favorable change.

Under such circumstances what is to be done? for my part, I cannot answer the question. My wife well knows my ability to support my family by my labour if properly directed. She feels that I have followed the Telegraph quite long enough, and that it would be for our interest to abandon it in toto and all claims upon it and direct my energies in some more productive channel.

But there are difficulties in the way of this. I am in debt, my Telegraph interest is not sailable [?] for the reason that it is unproductive and even unable to sustain itself. It will not therefore pay my debts. There is still another difficulty if it possessed even a small value it could not be made available owing to the unsettled state of the Patent question.

I have paid Smith something near four thousand dollars in cash on a/c of patent for Erie line, and if I had the money in my pocket and the ground unoccupied, with my present knowledge on the subject I would not pay one quarter of that sum for the patent for the entire line. The Erie & Michigan line is in debt for expence of working & repairs—and it cannot be kept up another year without a large outlay for poles. Every gale we have blows more or less of it down now. If we could have had the undivided business for that rout[e], the line would have sustained itself. We had the Patentees guarenty that we should have it, but still every inch of the distance of the entire line is disputed by the O'Reilly troops who use the Morse instrument.

Smith is doing nothing to vindicate the rights of the Morse patent on this rout, and I cannot learn that he intends to do anything more. I have not seen nor heard from him this summer. In fact he has seemed to make an effort to injure me in every way and at every time an opportunity presented since I declined to surrender the [?] line and N Y & E line into his hands in payment for the patent. All business originating on his eastern lines for points on our western lines he has withdrawn from us.

I cannot hold on much longer something must be done by which I can get releaf [?] or I must give all up and fail.

It appears to me that under this state of affairs I have a right to appeal to Prof Morse for some degree of aid— It is true for all the days works I render[ed] him I received the stipulated price agreed upon— but I rendered him a service in the economy and perseverence on my management at a time when the success of his whole enterprise hung suspended by a brittle cord, tnat contributed largely to save the whole from destruction.

I believe that neither Prof Morse nor Smith believed there would be money enough to build the line from Wash to Baltimore at the time I took hold of it. I know that they talked much about getting a new appropriation from congress to enable them to complete the line so far as to test the practicability of the Telegraph as an agent for transmitting news.

Prof Morse said to me that if he could get a line in operation from the Capital to Baltimore even by laying the wire along on the fence, it would enable him to prove its practicability to congress & he then thought he could get a new appropriation. I enquired of him how much of the old appropriation was unexpended, and he informed me between seven & eight thousand dollars. I told him I could complete the whole line from Washington to Baltimore with that sum. He still doubted and only authorized the purchase of material to build half way from W to B. I went to work and put this half up, and at so small a cost that he see I was right, and then authorized me to go on and get material for the other half which was done and the line completed and put to work, and money enough left to pay the salary of Prof Morse and I think of Vail and Rogers for the year.

If I had been successful in the business I should not think of an appeal of this kind, but under the circumstances I think I have a claim. My devotion to the interest of Prof Morse and his great invention entitles me to some consideration in the settlement of this question of Patent.

As the agent of Prof Morse I wish you would consider this subject and also lay it before him, and if anything can be done let me know it at as early a day as possible. Our stockholders meeting takes place the first of Oct, and I want to get the question of patent settled by that time if possible, so there will be as few embarrassments as possible in the way of getting the line in a more successful condition.

Yours respectfully

Hon. Amos Kendall.   E. Cornell

3. Letter from Jeptha H. Wade to Ezra Cornell, 1853

[According to Otis E. Wood (see Document No. 14) J. H. Wade was "an artist from Seneca Falls." We are told that he gave up "both operating and painting, for a line from Cleveland to Cincinnati . . . which was called the 'Wade Line' " (J. D.

Documents

Reid, *The Telegraph in America*, 278). In 1853 he had a considerable interest in the Erie and Michigan, and had been for some time closely associated with Mr. Cornell in the management of that and other Cornell lines. In 1855 he and J. J. Speed, Jr., against Mr. Cornell's wishes, sold their stock in the Erie and Michigan to the rival New York and Mississippi Valley Printing Telegraph Company, of which Hiram Sibley was one of the principal owners; and in the same year, when Sibley and his associates forced Mr. Cornell to consolidate his interests with theirs to form the Western Union Telegraph Company, Wade was one of the twenty-two men who signed the agreement on behalf of the Sibley interests (*ibid.*, 281).

The following letter was in reply to a letter in which Mr. Cornell had evidently complained of inefficiency on the part of Wade. It indicates that Wade had long been exasperated by what he regarded as Mr. Cornell's assumption of "infallibility" as a manager of telegraph lines, and had decided for once to speak his mind without reserve. The letter should be taken with qualifications because it picks out the less admirable qualities of Mr. Cornell and, like a vicious cartoon, exaggerates and distorts them; and it may be read with advantage in connection with the letter from W. P. Pew (Document No. 4), who apparently had as much reason as Wade to be dissatisfied with Mr. Cornell but remained, nevertheless, his admiring friend. But the letter has a high value for all that because it does bring into sharp relief some of Mr. Cornell's limitations as a manager of complicated enterprises, and some of the personal qualities that tended to alienate his associates and subordinates. The letter is in the De Witt Historical Society Library, in a box marked "Cornell Telegraph Letters."]

COLUMBUS, NOV. 27, 1853.

DEAR SIR,

I improve the first leisure since my return home to answer your long and laboured letter of Oct. 29. . . . It is another striking evidence of what we understood pretty well before that it is easier to find fault with others than to do right ourselves. . . .

I cannot say I was disappointed at the tone of your letter. To admit that would be denying I ever heard you speak [well] of any other persons management of the telegraph in comparison to yourself.

You *playfully* speak of your letter as a *task* you would willingly have avoided. I say "playfully" because it certainly could have cost you very little thought or labor, being principally made up of "Erie Line" recollections, a sort of material for correspondence and conversation, which you have, you know, always on hand, ready cut and dried, for *all possible* occasions.

You must excuse me for laughing at this, as it makes you seem as if you were not *conscious* that your *past experience* in managing Telegraph affairs, is rather a *warning* than an example to anybody.

You have frequently said that if you did the amount of business which Speed or I have done, you could make large dividends, and are forever growling like a dog with a sore head that we do not apply *your economy,* and your course throughout. Now there is no *better friend to economy than I am.* But I have not forgotten the old adage *"penny* wise and *pound* foolish," and "that there is a withholding that tendeth to poverty." Those who have forgotten will find it strikingly illustrated in your past history.

I am sorry to say I have not had much experience in making dividends. But it seems to me in order to make dividends there is *one other* thing necessary, that is get the money to divide. You say in your letter:

"I managed the N. York and Erie Line 3 years with receipts arranging [averaging?] under $8,000 per an., and *still* came *within $5,000* per an. of *making it pay expences.* If I could have realized $10,000 per an. I should *have been above board.* These facts naturally lead me to the conclusion that there is a screw loose somewhere."

What an astonishing mathematical result you have here discovered, that if you had received ten and paid out eight, you would have had 2 left. Now for you to have continued these comparisons might have been construed by some wicked persons into *egotism,* and in stopping where you did, your modesty bespeaks your merit, and that you need not suffer by your extreme modesty I will volunteer for your benefit to carry the comparison a little farther.

Your *new* line 460 miles long, better located for business than any line west of N. York, received "less than $8,000 per an," ours, 50 miles shorter, an old line, along the worst of mud roads through the woods of Ia and Ill, paid about $17,000 per an. Your whole line, including N York office rec'd less than $8,000 per an. The receipts of our Cin. office for the past year [were] was $14,239.47. . . .

Your line was sold by the sheriff in less than 3 years, and ours wasn't. Now if you wish me to profit by your experience, please explain why it was, that your strenuous efforts and undisturbed devotion to its interests never got the total receipts of the "Erie Line" up to $8,000. A line 460 miles long, one end in Wall Str. and the other fed by thousands of miles of line extending all over the western country, and passing as it did through a large number of towns and cities of from 8,000 to 16,000 inhabitants, where the *local* business alone ought to have made it a good paying line. Now may I say with as much propriety as you, "there must have been a screw loose somewhere," though now the machine having gone to pieces we can't tell exactly in what part of the machine to look for the trouble. But why do *you,* and why need *I* dwell so long on *one line.* Why such partiality? Why cherish so fondly the memory of your darling "Erie Line." Why not gather in *mournful grasp* all the lines you ever undertook to manage and sing a *funeral requiem* to the whole family at once?

What about your "Troy and Montreal line?" I think a eulogy upon that would be quite as good a warning to telegraphers or stock holders as your pet "Erie Line."

And why not say something about your "Ithaca, Auburn and Palmyra Line." That with the benefit of your long experience, *personal* attention and *rigid economy* lingered excruciatingly with *fits* and *sinking turns* and *jeers* and *curses* nearly *six long months,* and then gave up the ghost.

And your "Connecticut Line," that never worked at all. Your "Albany and Newburg" line, Ditto, all of which are long since dissolved into their original elements, and are heard of no more, except an occasional murmur from the stock holders and laborers along the lines, the one because he paid so much money *in,* the other because he got so little *out. You say,* "You will excuse me when I inform you *I do not* understand it." *I say,* you will excuse me when I inform you *I do* understand it.

Some other lines I believe you projected and built, by utterly refusing ever to work an inch saved themselves from the lingering fate of the "Erie Line." And what is worse from being constantly brought forward like it as precedents, in support of your peculiar views as to what is expedient and proper in working telegraph lines.

Now your mathematical discovery comes into my mind again, that if you had received 10 and paid out 8, you would have had 2 left. But it's true, nevertheless, and it suggests another fact, that if you had received $15,000 and paid out $8,000, you would have had $7,000 left, and even [?] the $7,000 you *did* get, if you had carried your economy a little farther and paid nothing out you would have had it all left, and that amount would have just paid for the whole line when you bid it off at sheriff sale, instead of your friends having to advance it. . . .

Now if you only had to increase the business of your "Erie Line" in such small proportions to make it sustain itself *why the devil didn't you do it?*

Now I wish to look at this matter from all points and get a favorable view if there *is* one, and if you will be so good as to name any *one line* that you ever had the management of, that has not been affected by your person, as the Upas tree affects the surrounding atmosphere, or that has not been withered and blasted by your magic touch—I will agree to

Documents

adopt your policy forever after. I confess my ignorance of any such exception to your invariable rule.

You say the Indiana line has fully met your expectations. I frankly confess it also has mine, upon comparing the receipts of corresponding months, for 1852 and 1853, that is, before your administration and since. While the receipts of other lines have increased, we find the following figures for Daton [Dayton] office.

	1852	1853
Sept.	$476.84	$285.15
Oct.	486.89	341.35
Nov.	315.58	216.73
	1275.31	843.23

Other offices of which I have the statistics show a like result, a falling off of more than 33 percent, so that you will succeed in finishing its earthly career in about the same time that did the business for the "Erie Line"—3 years.

Never mind when it is defunct if you write for it as good an epitaph as you are constantly singing over the *Erie* its character will gain by its speedy dissolution.

After all this however much evil minded persons may be inclined to dispute your claims to being the only *infallible* telegrapher living—do not understand me as wishing to pluck a single laurel from your hard wrought [w]reath. My motto has ever been to "give the Devil his due."

I have great respect for your experience. You have been a *Martyr* in the cause. You have been long in the field and worked hard. You have sacrificed your "fortune and your sacred honor." You have stood in the vestibule, like a faithful watch dog, and growled at everbodys course but your own. You have then faced a *frowning world,* and found fault admirably with everything, right or wrong. You have fought more telegraph men—have fought and conquered even to extermination more telegraph lines, than all the rest of the men in the world put together.

You showed your ingenuity by claiming to be the inventor of the Brimstone Insulators—and showed your firmness by sticking to them manfully 2 years after every body else had found them a failure and thrown them away. You did not allow *their* opinions to change your infallible course, but continued nobly, to advocate their superiority and to use them, and would have done so till this time had not your lines brimstone and all, gone long ago to that place where brimstone was

146

made to go, and then you like a Christian repented, and denied you was the inventor.

You assisted in building the *first line,* and claimed to have originated the idea of running it on posts—and whether that be true or not, no one will for a moment withhold from you, the honor, of having invented and demonstrated a singularly expeditious but invariably successful way of "running a line into the ground.". . .

We are commanded to "have one God." This you have kept religiously. Your God is "Economy," but you make a slight mistake and worship "Parsimony" (at a ruinous sacrifice to yourself and everything you are able to influence). You have worn it in your bosom, and pressed it to your lips, oftener than ever a Heathen did his Idol. Neither has it seemed to make any difference how great the sacrifice. While receiving a heavy salary as President, Superintendant and only managing officer of that model "Erie Line," with a capital of $116,000, I have known you to *economise* by leaving your official chair without even a substitute, for two months at a time, and travel on foot, and alone knee deep in mud, from N York to Dunkirk and carry on your shoulder the whole distance a 24 foot ladder—when some *foolish, extravagent* President would have paid an Irishman $12 a month for doing the same thing— while he was staying in his office and attending to his own business.

I have known you to leave the Indiana line down 3 weeks at a time, between Dayton and Indianapolis, rather than squander $1.75 to pay for mending the break.

Now who does not envy you your position as telegrapher? We read— "Cursed is he that every one speaks well of." Now certainly you are in less danger from this source than any gentleman I ever had the pleasure of an acquaintance with. . . .

But enough of this. I never should have referred to these disagreeable *facts,* except, that we have got tired of being referred to the mortifying history of the "Decline and Fall" of a line which on account of its location and connections, should have been eminently successful and was, to say the least, used up by a series of blunders below suspicion.

Nor would I care anything about it had not your course affected us all, to considerable extent, and brought about the very state of things for which you are continually finding fault with Speed and me, when our principal misfortune is, in being found on board the same craft with you.

The only thing in your letter having any relation to the proposed subject is the proposition to call a meeting of Stockholders which it seems to me, would be entirely idle, in as much as the only things requiring adjustment, are those of which the stockholders generally know and can know nothing, viz. The settlement of Speeds, Cornells, Lees, and my interests, both as to what has been done and is to be done, to secure the existence of the line and make it even worth disputing about.

That part of the line which Lee put up, had stood so long when I took the matter in hand (being in the first place badly constructed) that portions of it badly needed resetting, 150 miles of it had been down several months, the wire was torn off, kinked up, frozen into the ice, and about 10 miles gone entirely, so that myself and 40 other men and a team repaired 4 to 5 mile a day—the thermometer 10 degrees below zero at that, the part that was up had to be taken down and the joints made over before it would work. The line was badly in debt and disgraced from one end to the other, and at both ends. In short it had been doced a little too much with that panacea that physiced all your lines to death. When I got it repaired, extended to St. Louis and the cable down across the River it worked well. The business increased and debts decreased, and continued to, till prevented by a series of circumstances beyond my control, viz. the line is getting old, and requires increased repairs, and will till it is rebuilt, taking now nearly or quite all the receipts to keep the line in working order. And further, myself and others had united with you, to get control of the Ia lines and the lines from St. Louis to Chicago, in order to connect with ours and make them more profitable, and by hard work and much time and money, succeeded in getting them, and at your earnest request left it for you to connect them. You have not done it, and "you will excuse me" for thinking you never intended to do it. You, in violation of all good faith, took the lease in your own name and for your own benefit, and have used it to benefit our rivals at our expense, and the result has been, a heavy falling off in our receipts at St. Louis and Cin'ty, where we look for our principal profits.

This explains the mistery with which you affect to be so sorely puzzled. It is the answer in few words to all your ineuendos. Now I see no immediate need of a meeting—called with imposing ceremonies, but simply a sensible business like consideration of what is most expedient for the future. As for the past, I for one, am prepared to show what I have done in detail, both recd and paid out. Require Lee to do the same. You and Speed do the same, and the business of the past is settled. Then show what each will do, and what is best for us *to unite in doing* and something may be accomplished.

Enclosed I send you such abstracts of money, recd and paid out, as will give you a starting point in looking for the *loose screw,* for the details, you or any other stockholder can have access to the books at all times.

Very respectfully

E. *Cornell esq.*   Your Obt Servt

Indianapolis.   J. H. WADE

4. Letter from W. P. Pew to Ezra Cornell, 1854

[W. P. Pew, originally from Ithaca, was an old friend of Mr. Cornell, and in 1854 was employed in the Pittsburg office of the Ohio, Indiana and Illinois Telegraph Company, which had been acquired by the Cornell interests in 1853 (J. D. Reid, *The Telegraph in America,* 252). The letter is significant for two reasons. First, because it shows, even more clearly than the letter from J. H. Wade, the deplorable condition of Mr. Cornell's telegraph lines; and, second, because, unlike the letter from Wade, it presents Mr. Cornell as he appeared to a friend and admirer. The original letter is in the De Witt Historical Society Library, in Ithaca.]

PITTSBURG, Dec. 14, 1854.

DEAR FRIEND,

I am aware that in writing you at this juncture, I but add perplexity to perplexity to an already overburdened mind, but necessity compels it. Mr. Wood and others have given me information of your difficulties and of the trickery and baseness of those you have so long befriended and made, towards you, and you must have troubles enough of your own, but I am so immediately connected with you and dependent on you that I can not do anything without your assistance, situated as I am at present. I am completely done over [for?], unable to move a peg, with no prospect of being in a better condition and daily and hourly growing worse. I have put off my creditors with encouraging statements, until they begin to think me trifling with them. I want to hear of no Being, being in a worse hell than I am in. I cannot endure it longer, and yet I have spent so much time and money in this business that I feel as if I ought to get something out of it—at least to pay the debts the line has got me in. To continue on in this way, would be worse than madness, and I am liable every day to have everything taken from me by the sheriff. I talked similarly with A&E folks, and told them I thought they ought to give me the stock in judgment that I might take the line and prevent others from getting it. They kept putting off, until they found my word coming true and about 56 miles of the wire was sold and much of the balance stolen and no body that deserved it got any of it. They told me to come on and get what I could—which I did. Now for a few moments let me give you a faint idea. I am here without one red cent, have had to borrow to pay toll on bridge. My messenger boy will leave this week if I dont pay him, about $15, dollars. My old messenger boys daily dunning me for what I owe them. My operator will leave very soon if I dont get something for him. Old operators pressing me for what is due them. The city water man just in office and been in every day this week. The gas bill due this week and must be paid. A horse I purchased in pretending it for the E&M, but gave my note for $50, which is past due. They want immediate pay. My clothes on my back getting quite ragged and have not paid for them yet, man who did pay for them is hard up and wants me to pay him. My wife but little better off, and visiting now cause we have not means to pay board. My Ithaca creditors pressing me hard, in Feb next I will have to pay life insurance and House do.—about $100, and yet I owe for the money I borrowed to pay it last year, $200, and upwards. My endorsers have paid for me, they are getting every dollar they can towards it from offices and otherwise. The $600 I borrowed to rebuild and repair line, due and I pressed to pay. My Pittsburg indebtedness about $800, N C about $250, Erie about the same, and Cleveland in all borrowed money included, about $500, and I not in a way of earning 1 dollar, and you not in a situation to help me. Mr. Breen the man I sent off in Pittsburg urging payment wondering why you dont answer his letters. The National not likely to make connection so long talked of. The House folks, with a heavy capital, like the fiends out of hell, bent on your destruction, who together with your treacherous clerks and assistants getting your lines business away from you. Mr. Reid tells me, they have applied for injunction on E&M and are likely to get it. From various sources I learn they have got the Southern Michigan line from you and [Catin's?] business etc., to the amount of $100 dollars a day from you. Now with these facts, how can we sustain our Cleveland line? I find the National have the Sandusky line and will send all their Michigan and Illinois business that way, that if they don't connect with the House and do with me, what will it amount to, we will get nothing but Cleveland and Buffalo business from the National and what little business you send me, which we cannot ever have answers for. Our poles all rotten and expence of repairing far exceeds the income of intermediate receipts, where is our hopes. You have been a friend to me, and helped me some, not what I expected, but all you could I suppose. I feel in honor bound to you.

I have had proposals made to me that would help me materially, by 4 different persons for different interests, not a great while ago. The House folks would have taken me in and done pretty well by me, now I dont spose they would. Notwithstanding my soul harrowing perfect torturing condition, I have refused any proposals thinking I could not leave you and yet if I get nothing for my lines, how can I pay you and others. I owe $9,000.00 most on line account—I could have made recently such a disposition of lines as to enable me to pay you and many more of my debts and a good situation permanent. I could not make up my mind to leave you, and I know you cant make up to me my loss, however well you may be disposed towards me. I have tried to see you, telegraphed and telegraphed you, to no effect. I suppose the dispatches did not reach you, or you have no line reaching to Indianapolis. I have asked if you had received them got no answers. I do sincerely think that the Cleveland line cannot be sustained with the competition we have and the business we are likely to get, we have much less than usual now, and we have been running in debt, largely, for long time. Even the little hopes I had of getting reports from your E&M has gone to the shades. I was about commencing to furnish the Pittsburg Press with reports, but the House folks got them from you. It does seem to me that you cannot withstand the powerful opposition they will bring to bear upon you, even if you retain the E&M. Besides they are like the fiends out of hell, bent on your destruction. Were I out of debt, I would volunteer to aid you and help you in this your time of need, but I am worth but little, and the duty I owe my creditors and friends and family call me to do something towards making payments and gaining a livelihood. In three different ways I have had strong inducements to leave you recently, but a feeling of honor and remembrance of friendship prevented me, and I am still working on the cow tail principal [*sic*], going down hill with not a shadow of hope that by sticking with you we will either of us be benefitted. Now will you write me back and say, what are you making all of this adieu [*sic*] about. Your line is only an incumbrance to me and not worth the time spent in reading your letter. If you do, you will but be doing what every man I ever dealt with yet, has done, before you.

Had you not better compromise or sell out entire and go home and take some comfort the remainder of your days. Sell at a sacrifice, better go home and engage in a quiet and easy business. You can at least get enough to pay your debts and retire with ten thousand and perhaps more. Your life as at present is anything but happiness to you. Indeed if you keep on, I doubt whether with the energy and perseverance you have, and the fiendish opposition, that you can retain your rationality. An honest man cannot endure the treatment he meets with on every hand. You must make yourself a damned rascal first, and that is not a pleasing thought. You have done enough in your day, to enjoy the few years left you. Sell out and go home to your family and be a comfort to them. *Now* for your present situation, I feel that you are almost friendless. You have scarcely one in your employ, who is working for your interest. They all talk that you are running under and going to the devil fast, or at least many of them so far as I can learn—and your clerks and operators are very inefficient and indolent. For instance, on examining the books to see how it is that we are sinking so fast and not getting ¼ the expence in Pittsburg and Cleveland I find by the booked messages here, that this office has been paying out from 3 to 25 cents, on thorough business to the National, more than we had checked us at Cleveland, although I had tariff list made out and charged both operators to see to it. On very few instances messages are ever checked largely and not a day but messages are [bulled?], sadly so. Often, the number of words in check are more than in message. These things should be stopped and corrected. In this I enjoin perfect secrecy. Examine for yourself. If not too much of a task I would send you copy of all the business for the last few months that you might see for yourself. Once or twice I attempted to send back errors but found I had too much to do, and [name undecipherable] unwilling to attend to it. I presume it was useless, for I don't suppose any attention was paid to it by any one. You have too much to do yourself, and have not faithful and trusty assistants and those willing to trouble themselves sufficiently. I have tried to see, spose I cant. What to do I dont know. If you care but little for me and my lines, let me dispose of them and pay you and pay some of my creditors. Is not that my duty. I cant decide myself. My lines can be of but little use to you and I may possibly dispose of them so as to realize something. I dont know as I can now. Spose it is too late. In answering me, dispossess yourself, of self, and do by me as you would be done by. If you were in my situation would you have stuck to me as I do to you, against all good judgment and merely as a matter of feeling and honor and lose as much as I have. Can I see you? When and where. If I dont get some money immediately I will have to close here. I will be closed up by sheriff and I left alone to operate here if not closed. Do answer me quickly, that I may know what to do. I am completely done over.

Truly and Respectfully,

E. Cornell esq.   Yrs   W. P. Pew.

Documents

5. Ezra Cornell's Cyphering Book

[In 1823, at the age of sixteen, Ezra Cornell got eighty-five folio sheets of hand-made paper and bound them together within flexible cardboard covers. On the first page he wrote, with as much ornamental skill as he could: "Ezra Cornell's Cyphering Book, December 23, 1823." Page 2 contains a "Numeration Table" and a "Multiplication Table." The first is arranged as follows:

1 One
21 Twenty one

and so on up to the number 987654321. The multiplication table was no doubt the one in use at the time, namely:

1	2	3	4	5	6	7	8	9	10	11	12
2	4	6	8	10	12	14	16	18	20	22	24

and so on to the last line, which is

12	24	36	48	60	72	84	96	108	120	132	144

The following pages, up to page 122, are filled with practical rules and exercises in arithmetic, beginning with simple addition and subtraction and going on to fractions, compound interest, weights and measures, the equation of payments in state and federal, American and British money, annuities, and barter. His practice was to set down the rule under the proper heading, and then work out problems illustrating the rule. On page 56, in one of the vacant spaces, he wrote: "February the 13, 1824. I have got just 503 sums to this date. Ezra Cornell." The last numbered page is 76, but on what would be page 122 there is a new heading: "Loss and Gain." Here the book ends, so far as rules and practical exercises are concerned (except that on the last page of all, which would be page 170, there is an exercise under the "Rule for Raising the Dominical Letter"). No exercises were ever done under the heading "Loss and Gain"—probably because at that time (1825) Ezra left home. But thirty-five years later, at the age of fifty-three, Mr. Cornell for some reason or other turned up this old Cyphering Book, and seeing the heading "Loss and Gain" was impelled to make an entry under it. Other brief entries were made in 1864, 1865, and 1866. These entries, being of considerable interest, are printed below. The Cyphering Book is in the Cornell University Library.]

Loss and Gain

The above, or the examples in the above rules, though not entered in this book I have been practicing ever since the above was written, and it has been a life long struggle to see which would preponderate. In 1844, there was a balance perhaps of a couple thousand dollars on the credit side. In 1854 the contest was a doubtful one, and a debt with which I was then encumbered amounting to $50,000 would probably have swept the board if the game had been stoped at that period, but the contest has been continued, with increasing success for the side of gain and at the present period Feb. 1, 1860, that mountain of debt has mostly been paid at the rate of 100 cents on a dollar with 7 per ct interest added,

and a yearly income of $15,000, seems to be a reliable guarenty that the cr side has won the victory.   EZRA CORNELL
   FOREST PARK, ITHACA, TOMPKINS CO. N. Y.
     February 1, 1860

                                                      ITHACA Aug. 29, 1864
   The favorable change indicated above which promised to give a favorable turn to the life long, Loss and Gain a/c continues. The yearly income which I realize this year will exceed One Hundred Thousand dollars — My last quarterly dividend on stock in the Western Union Telegraph Co was $35,000, July 20, 64. The Div for Oct quarter will be as large.
   My greatest care now is how to spend this large income, to do the most good to those who are properly dependent on [me], to the poor and to posterity.   EZRA CORNELL

                                                      ITHACA Nov 1865
   I have just endowed the Cornell University with the sum of $500,000, and paid to the Genesee College $25,000 for the privilege of endowing the University as above. Such is the influence of corrupt legislation.
                                                      EZRA CORNELL

                                                      ITHACA Decr 20, 1866
   This evening the Cornell Library was dedicated. The cost of the Library and books at this time has been about $65,000, all paid for by me, and the Deed of the Property & Keyes of the Edifice delivered to the Trustees this evening in the presence of an audience of 1000 of my fellow citizens assembled in the Lecture room of the Library.
   Everything passed off pleasant and agreeable   E. CORNELL

6. Letter from Andrew D. White to Gerrit Smith, 1862

[The following letter reveals the very genuine desire of Mr. White to help in founding a new type of university in New York State, even to the extent of contributing a considerable part of his fortune to it. The first draft of the letter, in Mr. White's handwriting, and a photostat of the letter as finally sent, are in the Cornell University Library. *White Papers*, Tin Box.]

                                                      SYRACUSE Sept. 1st 1862
Hon. Gerrit Smith
DEAR SIR
   I write you on a subject wh. occupied your thoughts in days gone by,

with which I was then encumbered amounting to $50.000 would probably have swept the board if the game had been stoped at that period, but the contest has been continued, with increasing succefs for the side of gain and at the present period. Feb. 1. 1860 that mountain of debt has mostly been paid at the rate of 100 cents on a dollar. with 7 per ct interest added, and a yearly income of $15,000, seem to be a reliable quaranty that the cr side, has won the victory.

Forest Park Ithaca. Tompkins Co
N.Y.
February. 1. 1860

Ezra Cornell

Ithaca Aug 29, 1864.

The favorable change indicated above which promised to give a favorable turn to the life long, Lofs and Gain a/c continues, The yearly income which I realize this year will exceed One Hundred Thousand dollars.

My Last quarterly dividend on Stock in the Western Union Tel Co _ was _ $35,000, July 20. 64, The div for Oct quarter will be as large =

My greatest care now is how to Spend this large income, to do the most good to those who are properly dependent on _ to the poor, and to posterity _

Ezra Cornell

A PAGE FROM THE "CYPHERING BOOK" (REDUCED)

and to wh., I hope, you may be turned again—the subject of a new university, worthy of our land and time.

To this my own earnest thinking and planning have been given for years.

As a student at two American Colleges and at two European Universities, and as Professor at a third American College my main aim has been to fit myself to help in founding and building a worthy American University.

And I have aimed not merely to urge others to work and give;—let me state to you, in confidence, what I am prepared to give and do myself.

Within eighteen months from this date I expect that, by the settlement of my father's estate, I shall be put in possession of about three hundred thousand dollars of which over two hundred thousand are productively invested.

The greater part of this I am anxious to devote to the work above suggested; but the whole sum would not be enough—nor half enough.

It would suffice to build and fill a magnificent University Library— or to build and equip one of the finest observatories or laboratories in the world; but; expended on a whole university;—spread out to cover all the needs of all its departments, it would but give the country one more petty begging institution—and of such there are too many already.

There is needed a truly great university.

First, to secure a place where the most highly prized instruction may be afforded to *all*—regardless of sex or color.

Secondly to turn the current of mercantile morality wh. has so long swept through this land.

Thirdly to temper & restrain the current of military passion wh. is to sweep thro. the land hereafter.

Fourthly, to afford an asylum for Science—where truth shall be sought for for truth's sake, where it shall not be the main purpose of the Faculty to stretch or cut science exactly to fit "Revealed Religion."

Fifthly—to afford a center and school for a new Literature—not graceful and indifferent to wrong but earnest;—nerved and armed to battle for the right.

Sixthly to give a chance for instruction in moral Philosophy, History and Political Economy unwarped to suit present abuses in Politics and Religion.

Seventhly—to secure the rudiments, at least, of a legal training in which Legality shall not crush Humanity.

Eighthly—to modify the existing plan of education in matters of de-

Documents

tail where it is in vain to hope improvement from the existing universities.

Ninthly—to afford a nucleus around which liberally-minded men of learning,—men scattered throughout the land—comparatively purposeless and powerless,—could cluster,—making this institution a center from wh. ideas and men shall go forth to bless the nation during ages.

But, sir, an institution to do these things must be splendidly endowed. It must have the best of Libraries—collections in different departments— Laboratory—Observatory—Botanical Garden perhaps—Professorships —Lectureships.

If the institution is to be effective in reform it must be on such a scale as to *force* the public to respect it—and it must present such decidedly superior attractions that students will flock to it—despite the pulpits.

To admit women and colored persons into a *petty* college would do good to the individuals concerned; but to admit them to a great university would be a blessing to the whole colored race and the whole female sex,—for the weaker colleges would be finally compelled to adopt the system.

To support pure science by a struggling college with small endowment against the pressure of the existing colleges would be vain. Pure science must have a stronghold and therein can we place Agassiz and the young men whom he is training.

To support reforms in the existing modes of instruction a feeble college would be powerless; but a great university with such men as you could choose would be invincible.

My soul is in this. The offer of my fortune and life for it is not the result of any sudden whim—it is the result of years of thought and yearning for better things in our beloved country. No other bestowment seems to me to strike so deep or reach so far. None seems likely to be so long deferred if we cannot do something now.

Noble charities of the ordinary sort will always be cared for by Christians at large;—educational institutions of the ordinary sort are arising on all sides. Vassar's college endowed with 500,000 dollars for the Baptists—the Sheffield Scientific School at New Haven with 100,000 endowment for the Congregationalists—Geneva College with over 200,000 endowment from Mr. [?], Mr. Swift & my father for the Episcopalians.

But who shall give for the greater purpose?—who shall establish a center of education permeated with the true spirit of Christ;—yet unshackled. The men who are able, willing and well inspired come rarely. Probably no one whose ideas on religion and education are so correct as

157

Documents

yours, and whose power to give is so great as yours will stand in our state during the present century.

Were my fortune larger I should begrudge you the noble fame which would come by such a foundation,—as it is, I am ready to throw in the bulk of my property and to you shall be the glory.

May I ask then—if you encourage me to hope—even a little—for your leadership:—and if so may I ask for some of your thoughts and plans.

From some things wh. have been told me I am led to believe that, by independent processes of thinking, I have arrived at some theories and plans much like your own, and, should you encourage me, it would be the happiest duty of my life to exchange thoughts and to elaborate my own proposals in view of yours.

I write in one of the darkest periods of our national history; but I remember that the great university of Leyden was founded when Holland was lying in ruins.

In the hope of living to see a true liberal university in western New York—acting with power on a regenerate nation I am, Sir,

With great respect,
Heartily yours
AND. D. WHITE.

7. Letter from Francis M. Finch to Ezra Cornell, 1864

[The following letter indicates that Mr. Cornell did not at first intend to make any substantial gift for educational purposes during his lifetime. If this intention had been carried out it is likely either that there would have been no Cornell University, or that it would have been something quite different from the institution that was in fact established. So far as I know there is no reference to this letter, or to the intention mentioned in it, in any published account of Mr. Cornell's life or of the founding of the university. The original letter is in the De Witt Historical Society Library, in Ithaca.]

ITHACA, January 15, 1864.

. . . Your remarks with reference to a will have staggered me. . . . I had assumed that your general purpose was, after using freely for the public good your means, as I have seen you steadily do, to leave the remainder in equal portions to your heirs. I had not dreamed of any scheme of public beneficence or charity to be provided for by will. My thought was only this: to make a will appointing executors; to give to them the Library lot [this refers undoubtedly to the site of the Cornell Library at the corner of Seneca and Tioga Streets] and such an amount

158

as you would deem sufficient in Trust to be expended by them in completing your plans and then to convey the whole to the Library Trustees. That would remove one possible difficulty. Then to give to your executors a power to sell real estate and divide the proceeds. That would remove another. Then, if you so preferred, to give them your Telegraph Stock in Trust, either to hold the same together for a period of years or to divide it equally—thus avoiding a necessary sale. That removes a third difficulty. Then executors do not have to give security; that obviates a fourth difficulty; and finally a certified copy of such a will proves itself in any State so as to allow the executors to qualify and act there; and that removes a very serious trouble. It was some such will that I had in mind, one that left your property to descend just as it would if no will was made, and yet that went far enough to avoid the difficulties which, as a lawyer, I so often run against in the case of minor children and large estates and which would secure beyond the reach of accident or difficulty the completion of your Library. . . . So far, I thought it an act of duty and friendship to go with my suggestion. Beyond that I had no thought. Now you must excuse me if I hesitate to follow you into the field you have opened: and if, too, I suggest whether it is not best for the present to make some such formal will as that I have indicated, leaving the question whether you should hereafter allot so large a portion of your property to beneficent and public purposes for a very deliberate and mature consideration. If you should determine upon such an allotment no aid, advice or assistance within the scope of my ability should be wanting and yet I should feel horribly incompetent to do more than merely follow your lead. I like better, *much* better the plan you are now acting on of doing good as you go along—while you are present to execute your own plans—while it is possible to see and detect and correct mistakes if they occur—than that of reserving such things for Executors or Trustees. It is worthy of consideration, too, whether the example of the father might not be followed by the children and if so whether something beyond a liberal independence might not wisely be confided to them. Considerations like these must be weighed by you and by you alone: no third person can ever help you to decide them for they depend very much upon facts and opinions known only to yourself in their full extent. If after such reflection as I am sure you will give the subject you should in the end conclude [to] devote by will some portion of your property to beneficent or public purposes beyond what we all know you will do in your life time and should fix and determine the amount or proportions then I should freely discuss

Documents

with you the objects and purposes to be accomplished and the best means of doing so. But I could not do that without some serious reflection where as yet I have indulged in none. . . . Whenever the time comes that your own *preliminary* intentions are settled and fixed I will "shell out" at your command all the ideas or plans that I think may be of any use to you. But I should have to get them together, sift them, and label them first.

I have written you very frankly, thinking seriously while doing so; but the whole subject is of such magnitude—takes me so much by surprise—that I ought, really, to have reflected more before writing at all. But you have my first impressions drawn out by your letter.

Of course your letter shall be thoroughly confidential. . . .

8. Proposal Made by Ezra Cornell to the Trustees of the Agricultural College in September, 1864

[According to Mr. White (*Autobiography*, I, 296) Mr. Cornell offered to give the Agricultural College $300,000 provided the legislature would give to it one half of the Land Grant Fund, which the Comptroller estimated at approximately the same sum. An account of the offer, based on an interview with Mr. Cornell, published in the New York *Evening Post,* October 2, 1868, also says that the condition was one half of the Land Grant Fund. But shortly after the September meeting of the trustees in Rochester, at which the offer was made, Mr. Cornell sent to the trustees, in a letter to President King, a copy of the proposal which he says he made at the meeting; and in this copy the condition of his offer was that the legislature should appropriate to the College $30,000 annually, which would be a good deal more than the interest, even at the normal rate of seven per cent, on $300,000. A copy of the letter to President King, in Mr. Cornell's handwriting, is in *Cornell Papers,* Memorandum Book, II. It is of this copy that the following is a transcription.]

ITHACA Oct 4, 1864

Hon John A. King
President

DEAR SIR
I herewith place at your disposal a copy of the proposition which I had the honor to submit to the Trustees of the New York State Agricultural College, at their recent meeting at Rochester.

To the Trustees of the New York State Agricultural College:
MR. PRESIDENT AND GENTLEMEN,
I have listened patiently to the discussion which has so fully developed the present helpless situation of the College, and shown so little encour-

agement in its future prospects, untill I have come to the conclusion that the Trustees would be justifiable in changing the location of the College if it can be done with the approval of the citizens of Ovid, and an adequate endowment thereby be secured for the College in some other proper locality

Therefore I submit for your consideration the following proposition.

If you will locate the College at Ithaca I will give you for that object a farm of three hundred acres of first quality of land desirably located, overlooking the village of Ithaca, and Cayuga Lake, and within ten minutes walk of the Post Office, the Cornell Library, the Churches, the Railroad Station and Steam Boat landing. I will also erect on the farm suitable buildings for the use of the College, and give an additional sum of money to make up an aggregate of three hundred thousand dollars, on condition that the Legislature will endow the College with thirty thousand dollars per annum from the Congressional Agricultural College fund, and thus place the College upon a firm and substantial basis, which shall be a guarantee of its future prosperity and usefulness, and give to the farmers sons of New York an institution worthy the Empire State.

Respectfully
E. CORNELL

Hoping that the above proposition may lead to the solution of the question which has so long perplexed the minds of the board of Trustees in relation to a prosperous Agricultural College

I remain
Yours respectfully
E. CORNELL.

9. Act to Establish the Cornell University, 1865

[The printed form of the bill introduced by Mr. White February 7, 1865, has the following caption: "State of New York, No. 145. February 7, 1865. Introduced on notice by Mr. White—read twice, and referred to the committees of literature and agriculture." The rest of the bill is printed below in roman type. Parts omitted before the bill was signed by the Governor are bracketed; additions made are printed in italics. The essential changes, made in the form of amendments, one in the Senate in favor of the People's College, the other in the Assembly in favor of Genesee College, are in Section 6. The other changes, designed to improve the form, or to avoid repetition, or to make the act more watertight from the legal point of view, were made, as I suppose, in the Judiciary Committee, and probably by Judge Folger (see Mr. White's *Autobiography*, I, 299), when the bill was referred to that committee to be put in final form. There are three copies of the printed bill in the Cor-

Documents

nell University Library, one of which has some of the minor changes and the two
amendments interlined or written out on attached sheets in Mr. Cornell's handwriting. An exact reproduction of the engrossed act, with the signature of the Governor, Lieutenant-Governor, and Speaker of the Assembly, is in the Cornell University Library, catalogued as MSS++ Kc 1. The act is in *Laws of New York, 1865*,
Chapter 586; and *Laws and Documents Relating to Cornell University,* 21. In the
latter collection there is a slight error in Section 6: ". . . restriction or condition
whatsoever, save as [is] in accordance with the provisions of this act."]

AN ACT to establish the Cornell University, and to appropriate to it
the income of the sale of public lands granted to this State by Congress, on the second day of July, eighteen hundred and sixty two[.];
also to restrict the operation of chapter five hundred and eleven of
the laws of eighteen hundred and sixty three.
Passed April 27, 1865; three-fifths being present.
The People of the State of New York, represented in Senate and Assembly, do enact as follows:
   Section 1. Ezra Cornell, William Kelly, Horace Greeley, Josiah B.
Williams, William Andrus, John McGraw, George W. Schuyler, Hiram
Sibley, J. Meredith Read, John M. Parker, and such other persons as
may be associated with them for that purpose, are hereby created a
body politic and corporate, to be known as the Cornell University,
which university shall be located in the town of Ithaca[.], *in the County*
of Tompkins, in this State. The [object of the] corporation hereby created
[is the cultivation of the arts and sciences and of literature, and the instruction in agriculture and the mechanic arts and military tactics, and
in all knowledge; and it] shall have [all] the rights and privileges necessary to the accomplishment of the object[s] of its creation as [it is herein]
declared[,] *in this act,* and in the performance of its duties shall be subject to the provisions and may exercise the powers enumerated and
set forth in the second article of the fifteenth chapter, title one, of the
Revised Statutes of the State of New York.
   § 2. The *first board of trustees of said corporation shall consist of the*
persons named in the first section of this act, [shall be the first board of
trustees of said corporation,] together with the governor and lieutenant
governor, the speaker of the house of assembly, the superintendant of
public instruction, the president of the state agricultural society, the
librarian of the Cornell Library, and the eldest male lineal descendant
of Ezra Cornell, who shall be ex-officio members thereof. [and there]
There shall be [eighteen] *seventeen* trustees, exclusive of the ex-officio
trustees[.]; [The said board of trustees shall be so constituted, by election

Documents

from time to time as the by laws shall direct, as that] *and, to make up the said number of seventeen, the ten persons who are named in the first section of this act, and the said ex-officio trustees, or a quorum of all of them, shall, at their first meeting, in pursuance of this act, elect seven other persons to act with themselves as members of said board of trustees. But* at no time shall a majority of the board be of one religious sect, or of no religious sect.

§ 3. The farm and grounds to be occupied by said corporation, whereupon its buildings shall be erected, in such [number] *manner* and to such extent as the trustees may from time to time direct and provide for, [shall be situated in the town of Ithaca, county of Tompkins, and] shall consist of not less than two hundred acres.

§ 4. The leading object [as to plan of instruction in] *of* [said] *the* corporation *hereby created* shall be to teach such branches of learning as [relate] *are related* to agriculture and the mechanic arts, including military tactics[.]; *in order to promote the liberal and practical education of the industrial classes in the several pursuits and professions of life.* But such other branches of science and knowledge may be embraced in [this] *the* plan *of instruction and investigation pertaining to the university* as the trustees may deem useful and proper. And persons of every *religious denomination,* or of no religious denomination, shall be equally eligible to all offices and appointments.

§ 5. The corporation hereby created may hold real and personal property not exceeding three millions of dollars in the aggregate.

§ 6. The income, [and] revenue *and avails* which shall be received from the investment of the proceeds of the sale of the land, *or of the scrip therefor,* or [of] any part *thereof* [of them,] granted to this [s] *S*tate by the act of [c] *C*ongress, "An act donating public lands to the several [s] *S*tates and [t] *T*erritories which may provide colleges for the benefit of agriculture and the mechanic arts", approved July second, eighteen hundred and sixty two, are hereby appropriated to, and shall, from time to time as the same shall be received, be paid over to the trustees of the corporation hereby created, for its use and behoof[,] in the mode and for the purposes in said act of [c] *C*ongress defined[;], provided, however, that no part of such payment shall be made [until] *unless* the said trustees shall prove to the satisfaction of the [c] *C*omptroller, within six months after the passage of this act that the said corporation possesses a fund of five hundred thousand dollars at least, given by [the honorable] Ezra Cornell, of Ithaca, *aforesaid, which last named fund shall be given absolutely and without any limitation, restriction or condition whatsoever,*

163

*save such as is in accordance with this act, nor shall the same be in any
manner repaid or returned to the said Cornell, his representatives or assigns, except as in this act provided, and any vote or resolution, or act or
proceeding to return or repay the same, except as in accordance with this
act, shall be void; and provided, further, that no such payment shall be
made unless within six months from the passage of this act said Ezra
Cornell, of Ithaca, shall pay over to the trustees of Genesee college,
located at Lima, in this State, the sum of twenty five thousand dollars,
for the purpose of establishing in said Genesee college a professorship
of agricultural chemistry. Provided, further, that the trustees of the
People's College at Havana may, in place of strict compliance with the
conditions of the act, chapter five hundred and eleven of the laws of
eighteen hundred and sixty three, in the details thereof, within three
months from the passage of this act, deposit such a sum of money as, in
addition to the amount already expended by them upon or for the purposes of their corporation, shall, in the opinion of the regents of the
university of New York, be sufficient to enable the said trustees fully to
comply with the conditions of the said chapter five hundred and eleven
of the laws of eighteen hundred and sixty three. Such deposit, if made,
shall be made in such place, and on such terms as shall be satisfactory
to the said regents of the university. And the said deposit shall not be
withdrawn or removed, or in any way affected or impaired, except to
be applied under the directions of the said regents, for the purposes of
the said People's College, or upon the trustees thereof relinquishing any
claim to the benefit of the said act of eighteen hundred and sixty three.
But nothing contained in this provision shall release the said trustees of
the People's College from the conditions and obligations imposed or
contained in section three of said act. They shall, on the contrary,
in addition to the making and continuing such deposit as aforesaid,
within the said three months, show to the satisfaction of the said regents
that they have complied with the requirements of the said section three,
and that the college grounds, farm, work shops, fixtures, machinery,
apparatus, cabinets and library occupied or owned by them, are not encumbered, aliened or otherwise disposed of. And nothing contained in
this provision shall release the said trustees of the People's College from
a full and perfect performance of the terms and conditions of the said
act, chapter five hundred and eleven of the laws of eighteen hundred
and sixty three, in all its details and within the time therein limited
therefor. Nor shall the trustees of the said People's College receive from
the Comptroller any portion of the income and avails of the said lands*

*until they have complied with and performed the terms and conditions
of the said act, chapter five hundred and eleven of the laws of eighteen
hundred and sixty three, to the satisfaction of the said regents; nor shall
they receive any portion of the said avails and income or revenue, unless
they comply with the conditions of this act, by making and continuing
the said deposit. If the trustees of the People's College shall not, within
the term mentioned in the said act, chapter five hundred and eleven,
have complied therewith, to the satisfaction of the said regents, or if,
within the said term of three months, they shall not have made the said
deposit, in accordance with and upon the terms fixed by this act, then
the avails, income and revenue which shall be received from the invest-
ments of the proceeds of the sales of the said lands or of the scrip therefor, shall be disposed of to the corporation hereby created in the manner
provided for in this section, and not before. If, on the other hand, the
said trustees of the People's College shall, within the time provided for
in the act, chapter five hundred and eleven of the laws of eighteen hundred and sixty three, and as herein provided, to the satisfaction of the
regents, comply with the obligations thereof and hereof, so that they
shall be entitled to receive and enjoy the benefits thereof and hereof,
then the said fund of five hundred thousand dollars, given by Ezra
Cornell, shall, in his option or that of his personal representatives or
assigns, revert to him or to them. Moreover, the trustees of the People's
College may at any time, upon written notice to the said regents, withdraw and remove the aforesaid deposit; but such notice and withdrawal,
or either of them, shall be deemed a relinquishment and forfeiture by
them of the benefit to them of the said chapter five hundred and eleven,
and of the benefit of this act, and thereupon, upon the performance of the
said Ezra Cornell, or of his heirs and of the corporation hereby created
of the conditions and obligations of this act, the said income, avails and
revenue shall be disposed of to the said Cornell University, as is herein-
before provided.*

§ 7. The trustees of said university, *if they shall become entitled to the
benefits of this act,* shall make provision to the satisfaction of the
regents, in respect to buildings, fixtures and arrangements generally,
within two years of the passage [of this act] *thereof,* to fulfil*l* the provisions of the aforesaid act of [c] *C*ongress[,]. [and they] *They* shall *also*
make all reports, and perform such other acts as may be necessary to conform to the act of [c] *C*ongress aforesaid. The said university shall [also]
be subject to the visitation of the regents of the university of New York.

§ 8. From and after the time the said corporation shall have become entitled to the benefits of this act as aforesaid, the said university grounds, farm, work shops, fixtures, machinery, apparatus, cabinets and library shall not be encumbered, aliened, or otherwise disposed of by the said trustees, *or by any other person,* except on terms such as the legislature of the [s] State of New York shall have approved[.], *and any act of the said trustees, or that of any other person which shall have that effect, shall be void.*

§ 9. *The several departments of study in the said university shall be open to applicants for admission thereto at the lowest rates of expense consistent with its welfare and efficiency, and without distinction as to rank, previous occupation or locality. But with a view to equalize its advantages of all parts of the State,* [The corporation hereby created] *the institution* shall [receive] annually *receive* [one student] *students, one* from each assembly district of the [s] State, to be selected as hereinafter provided, and shall give them instruction in any[,] or in all the prescribed branches of study in any department of said institution, free of any tuition fee, or of any incidental charges to be paid to said university, unless such incidental charges shall have been made to compensate for damages heedlessly or purposely done by [said] *the* students to the property of said university. The said free instruction shall, *moreover,* be accorded to said students in consideration of their superior [physical and mental] ability, and as a reward for superior scholarship in the academies and public schools of this [s] State, [. and] And [the] *said* students shall be selected as *the legislature may from time to time direct, and until otherwise ordered as* follows: The school *commissioner or* commissioners of each county, *and the* board of education of each city, or those performing the duties of such a board, shall select annually the best scholars from each academy and each public school of their respective counties or cities as candidates for the [u] University scholarship. The candidates thus selected in each county or city, shall meet at such time and place in [each] *the* year as the board of supervisors of the county shall appoint, to be examined by a board consisting of the school commissioner or commissioners of the county, or *by the said* board of [public instruction] *education* of the cities, with such other persons as the supervisors shall appoint, who shall examine said candidates, *and determine which of them are the best scholars,* and the board of supervisors shall then select therefrom [the best scholars] to the number of one for each assembly district in said county or city, and furnish the candidate thus selected with a certificate of such selection, which certificate shall entitle said student to admission to said [u] University, subject to the examination

Documents

and approval of the [f] Faculty of said [u] University. In making the*se* selections [above referred to] preference shall be given (where other qualifications are equal) to the sons of those who have died in the military or naval service of the United States[.]*; consideration shall be had also to the physical ability of the candidate. Whenever any student selected as above described shall have been from any cause removed from the University before the expiration of the time for which he was selected, then one of the competitors to his place in the University from his district may be elected to succeed him therein, as the school commissioner or commissioners of the county of his residence, or the board of education of the city of his residence, may direct.*

§ 10. All payments made under this act, *out of the treasury of the State,* shall be made by the treasurer on the warrant of the [c] Comptroller, out of the special fund on deposit with the treasurer, arising from the receipt of the income and revenue *and avails* mentioned in the sixth section of this act.

§ 11. Chapter five hundred and eleven of the laws of [1863] *eighteen hundred and sixty three,* entitled "An act to appropriate the income and revenue which may be received from the investment of the proceeds of the sales of the lands granted to the [s] State by the act of [c] Congress, entitled 'An act donating public lands of the several [s] States and [t] Territories which may provide colleges for the benefit of agriculture and the mechanic arts', approved July second, [1862] *eighteen hundred and sixty two,* passed May fourteenth, [1863] *eighteen hundred and sixty three",* [is hereby repealed.] *shall be read and construed subject to the provisions of this act, and wherever the provisions of the said act, chapter five hundred and eleven of the laws of eighteen hundred and sixty three, and the other provisions of this act shall conflict, the provisions of this act shall be deemed the law, and shall prevail.*

§*12. The Legislature may at any time alter, or repeal this act.*

§[12] *13.* This act shall take effect immediately.

10. Agreement in the Senate in Respect to the People's College Amendment of the Cornell University Bill, 1865

[The following document sets forth the terms of the agreement which induced Mr. White and his friends to vote for the amendment in favor of the People's College. The document, without date or heading and written in a clerkly hand, is in *Cornell Papers,* Cornell University Library, MSS+Kc 8.]

Documents

The undersigned declare that while the Cornell University Bill was under discussion in committee of the whole Senate, the Hon. Mr. Webber member of the Assembly from Schuyler Co and Downs also of Schuyler Co the brother in law we understand of Hon. Charles Cook and an authorized agent of the Peoples College in Albany agreed in our presence that if the amendment giving to the Peoples College three months more in which to comply with the requirements of the act of 1863 should be adopted they would withdraw all opposition to the Bill in all its stages through the assembly and elsewhere and we declare that upon the faith of such agreement fully and openly made we and other Senators voted for the amendment.

A. H. Bailey

James A. Bell

Andrew D. White

11. Ezra Cornell's Defense Against the Charge of Being the Founder of an "Aristocratic" University, 1865

[The following document, in Mr. Cornell's handwriting, has no heading; but after the document was folded the following words, in another hand, were written along the margin: "Hon. Ezra Cornell's Statement," under which Mr. Cornell added the words: "made while the C U Bill or charter was pending before the committee of the Assembly 1865." For the occasion on which the charges were "made by the Attorney of Charles Cook" see above, p. 101. The document is in *Cornell Papers*, MSS+ Kc 8.]

1865

The great effort made by the Attorney of Charles Cook to prejudice the minds of the Ass^y Com. against the bill chartering the "Cornell University" in his speeches of thursday & friday last—on the assumption of the aristocratic character of the proposed institution, or of myself as its patron, has led me to examine my own position to ascertain if it was obnoxious [?] to the charge of aristocracy. My parents were quakers, and I was brought up in that faith and have only deviated from the direct line by marrying a lady who was not a member of the society, and by falling into the popular form of dress and speech. My grand parents & great grand parents on the side of both father and mother were of the same religious denomination. I am a mechanic and farmer and my wealth is the legitimate fruit of those pursuits, I have never speculated, in any kind of property, stocks or securities. My wealth has

168

Documents

arisen from carefully investing my surplus earnings in a business which has grown with the growth of the country (the Telegraph). I have not even speculated in the stock of telegraph companies. When I could sell stock to make money, I have been content with the belief that I could make more by holding the stock and profiting by the increase in its value from the growing increase in the business. My father was a mechanic and depended on his trade to support his family—his brothers were all mechanics or farmers, as were my mothers brothers. My father's father was a farmer, my mothers father was a mechanic — My brothers and my sisters husbands, are all either farmers or mechanics — My wife's father & grand father were mechanics, her brothers and her sisters husbands are mechanics, farmers, manufacturers & engineers.

I have no relation of any degree within my knowledge who is or has been a lawyer, physician, Minister of the Gospel, merchant, politician, office holder, gentleman loafer or common idler — None who have been drunkards or recipiants of charity. All have procured an honest and compleat support for their families by *productive labor,* none but myself have acquired anything like a fortune, and mine is placed at the disposal of the industrial classes. I cannot conceive it to be possible that any man can be more thoroughly identified with the industrial, laboring, and productive classes, than I am, and my ruling desire is to dispose of so much of my property as is not required for the reasonable wants of my family, in a manner that shall do the greatest good to the greatest number of the industrial classes of my native state, and at the same time to do the greatest good to the state itself, by elevating the character and standard of knowledge of the industrial and productive classes. I tender the sum of $500,000 to the State to be added to the donation of congress, for the sole object contemplated by congress, for the education of the Agricultural & Mechanical classes. In the Organization of such an institution, I am controlled to a great extent by circumstances. I find the only two institutions in the state which were organized on the basis of educating the industrial classes, failures, from the want of adequate means, and from other causes, which in my judgment render it unwise to attempt to rear the desired edifice on their foundation.

Therefore after a consultation with the best and most influential trustees of both the State Agricultural College at Ovid—and the Peoples College at Havana, they advised the new organization—for the new institution and tendered the name of "Cornell University." The name I demurred to, fearing it would be charged that I have an undue ambition in that particular. I was met with assurances that it was eminently proper that the institution should bear my name, and I made no further objection.

The trustees were thus selected from the trustees of the two old boards, and from persons outside both boards.

The ten persons named, represents, three mechanics,—three farmers— one manufacturer—one merchant—one lawyer, one engineer—and one literary gentleman. The ex-officio trustees represent the State government, the common school interest of the state, the State Agricultural Society, the County of Tompkins through its public librarian—and the Cornell family. Can the industrial classes of the State select a board of trustees more likely to protect and foster its interest than the one here selected? I think not.

As to the manner of my using money, I may be permitted to say that I never in any instance exacted or accepted in any form more than seven percent [this was the usual rate at that time] for money loaned, and the only loans which I have made to individuals have been to persons who were unable to furnish such securities as capitalists or bankers exact, and who required the money to protect their business and property from the grasp of the usurer, or from some misfortune in business—to young men to purchase farms—to widows of soldiers to purchase a small house [or, perhaps, home] and for like objects—I have $100,000 thus invested, on what bankers call doubtful securities, but the loans are such as humanity demanded, and the security such as the parties could give.

Of donations, I will not speak other than to say, since the war commenced, they have been given for the support of soldiers families, supply substitutes for drafted men and kindred objects for the support of the government.

E. CORNELL

12. Letter from a Cornell Student, October, 1868

[A photostat of the following letter is in the Cornell University Library, catalogued as Cornell MSS+ Kc 276. It was written by Mr. John Yawger Davis to his brother Charles in Auburn, and is dated Ithaca, Oct. 9, 1868, two days after the formal opening of the university. The peculiarities in capitalization and punctuation were probably due to haste more than to ignorance.]

I have just got into my room. It is in the water cure building called Cascadilla building or Cascadilla place. In this building the students take their meals.

My room is No. 158 first floor south wing south side of the hall and second west of the main entrance.

My room is nine feet one way and twelve feet the other and twelve feet high.

I have one large window on the south side three feet wide and eight feet high. . . . My door opens opposite the dumb waiter room by which the coal is hoisted from the basement and where we will get our coal every morning and evening.

Nearly opposite is the dining room door. There is a large and elegant dining room sufficient to accommodate all the students the tables are large enough to accommodate twenty each the room is about thirty feet high. . . . there is a splendid table set for every meal for dinner we have three courses first soup then three or four kinds of meat including fish and one kind of pie for desert thus far we have had plenty of every thing and the best of it.

As yet every thing is in an uproar and confusion but when we get a full start I think we will like it very much. I wish you were here I would like it so much.

Yesterday morning at nine oclock according to notice given we all met at this building and formed in line in the hall first the Seniors or those that come from other colleges as seniors and next juniors sofomores and juniors [freshmen?] or those commence[ing] their first term in this college, the seniors going in first and the other classes next. They first drew rooms set apart for captains the next two classes drawing of commissioned officers and the rest drawing rooms for the whole school. . . . We then went and found our rooms. . . .

We are now under the command of Major Whitelsey [*sic*] who will require us to be in readiness for his orders and I believe he will require us to form in line immediately after breakfast and march over to the university chappel and at one oclock to march back again to dinner and at some time in the forenoon to drill a little there has been a requisition made on the governor for five hundred stands of arms.

Major Whitelsey will be our governing officer all that he will require is that we are here at meal times and at chappel and that we put out our lights by a certain hour and that we keep ourselves and rooms clean and in order and all that the other officers will require is that we are at recitations and that we have our lessons well the rest of the time we will have to ourselves to go where we please. there will be no smoking in recitations but it is required that we have our lessons. On the eighth [seventh] we all attended the inauguration exercises in the morning at

Documents

which president White and the faculty were sworn into office and the president gave his inaugeral address. . . . Mr. Cornell also spoke some in the afternoon we went upon the hill and listened to speeches by Professor Agassiz and George Wm. Curtiss and in [by] Mr. Weaver the superintendant of public instruction, . . . and also to a speech made by a person in behalf of Miss Jenny McGraw who gave the chime of bells to the University they are splendid bells the largest one being like the one on the big factory and eight smaller ones.

After the speaking the chimes were rung to play Old Hundred hail columbia and other tunes. it sounded nice in the evening the citizens had a reception and jubilio the reception for the students and the jubilio for the boys in the town the reception was in the library hall and the jubilio was in the streets the hall was cleared of seats and the ladies appeared in full dress costume with the Grecian bend in many cases it was like the bazaar excepting the booths and the citizens vied with [each] other in making it pleasant for the students. I got introductions to the Presbyterian minister and his wiffe and a great many ladies and gentlemen besides. We expect to have a sociable once every week in the reception room which is larger and [or] as big as the dining room hall.

Oh I forgot to say that among the other requirements we will have to learn dancing under the instruction of the cadetts so that we may invite ladies to our sociables and dance with them I expect we will have great times those times when things are more settled we will have a bathing room in each hall where we can take a shower bath either hot or cold or get water to wash ourselves whenever we wish

I can't think of anything more I am sitting on the corner of my bed and writing on my wash stand because we have no chairs yet

13. Letter from Andrew D. White to George L. Burr and Ernest W. Huffcut, 1893

[In the following letter Mr. White, for the very special reasons indicated in the letter itself, set forth in great detail his own part in the founding of Cornell University. If the letter is, as Mr. White acknowledged, somewhat egotistical and self-regarding in tone, his excuse was that he was writing in confidence to two very intimate friends, and desired the letter not to be made public at the time. He nevertheless wished it to be carefully preserved as a record of facts which some future historian might use. At this late date there can be, I think, no valid objection to publishing the essential parts of the letter, and there is at least one very good reason for doing so. Egotistical or not in tone, the letter does set forth, more explicitly

172

Documents

than any other document or printed record, the facts of the matter; and thereby confirms one in the conclusion, which is moreover supported by all the other evidence, that while Mr. Cornell was chiefly responsible for giving Cornell University a splendid endowment, Mr. White was chiefly responsible for making it the kind of university it became. A rough draft of the letter in Mr. White's handwriting, and a fair copy in another hand, are in the Cornell University Library. *White Papers, Tin Box.*]

Personal and confidential

9 BRUNS [?] PARK, HELSINGFORS, FINLAND

Sept. 8, 1893

To Professors George L. Burr, and Ernest W. Huffcut.

MY DEAR FRIENDS,

Permit me to write you in regard to a matter of much delicacy and in which I must put myself somewhat unreservedly into your hands, trusting to your kindness and discretion as to the result. At the inauguration of President Schurman he referred to me, no doubt with the most kindly feeling, stating in effect that "among those who had most to do with securing the original charter of Cornell University" was myself, but that I "had now returned to my first love."

I trust that you will not think me unduly egotistical when I say that this seems to me an inadequate statement.

It is simply unhistorical and absolutely misleading to those who shall hereafter look for the history of the University in documents issued under the highest sanction.

Both of you have to some extent acquainted yourselves with the University history, and I think that you will both allow that the statement above is either too little or too much.

This strikes me with all the more force in view of the approaching anniversary. I shall be content if at that time not one of the orators sees fit to mention my name; I should prefer infinitely to have it go unmentioned rather than that any statement should be made like that above referred to.

If my name is not mentioned at all no one will be misled, & perhaps some person hereafter looking into the matter will bring out something near the truth.

The main facts are simply these.

The first suggestion ever made having in view the keeping of the Land Grant Fund together for a *single* university came from me.

The one man who prevented in 1864 the division of the Land Grant Fund amounting then, according to the estimate of the Comptroller,

173

to about $600,000, between the twenty & more colleges, which sought to divide it, was myself, as chairman of the Senate "Committee on Literature."

The one man who prevented its division at a later date [this can only mean at a later date in this the same year, 1864] between the "People's College" at Havana, and the State Agricultural College at Ovid, was myself as chairman of the same committee.

During an entire winter in that capacity I opposed Mr. Cornell & the State Agricultural Society on this point. . . .

When, during the summer following . . . Mr. Cornell made his proposal to divide the fund, he to give three hundred thousand dollars ($300,000) to the State Agricultural College at Ovid, so that this added to half the Land Grant Fund . . . would make up a sum equal to the entire estimated proceeds of the Land Grant, and when this was applauded to the echo by the authorities of the State Agricultural Society at Rochester [this was in fact a meeting of the trustees of the Agricultural College], I, in their presence, still refused to accede to this division, but told Mr. Cornell that I would bring in a Bill to give the *entire* Land Grant Fund to a new institution provided he would make this same offer to it.

It was to me that during the following Session of the Legislature Mr. Cornell stated that he had five hundred thousand dollars ($500,000) more than he or his family needed, asking what I would suggest as to the disposal of it.

It was I who answered as follows; "as regards institutions of a charitable sort we can always rely on the kindly instincts of the people at large; as to primary education, we can rely upon the State; as to advanced education, but few & chosen men understand it & see the value of it, & for this we must rely on individual munificence."

I then told him in a general way what sort of an institution for advanced instruction was needed;—one which should be unsectarian, fully equipped for the highest instruction in the sciences & the arts, and in history & in modern literature as well as for the branches hitherto carried on in the Colleges of the State, an institution in which various courses should be maintained, carried on in the same buildings & estimated of equal dignity, & in which women might receive an education equal to that given to men.

I showed him that here was a chance which might never happen again.

I had many conversations with him on this subject & at last he made

Documents

his proposal to give half a million of dollars ($500,000) to a university to be established at Ithaca on the lines suggested by me.

It was I who suggested the name of *Cornell University;* he at first opposed it, but I conquered his scruples by showing him that this was simply in accordance with a time-honored custom in our own & other countries, citing the names Harvard, Yale, Brown, Williams & others.

I then made a rough draft of a charter, to which Mr. Cornell contributed parts relating to the Land Grant, and this was put into shape by Charles Folger, at that time Chairman of the Judiciary Committee of the Senate, afterwards Chief-Justice of the State and Secretary of the Treasury of the United States.

It was I who suggested both in the interest of the State & to secure the hearty co-operation of Judge Folger that the Willard Asylum—which had just been authorized—should be established on the Agricultural College property at Ovid, within Judge Folger's district, & this was done.

It was I, who, during the winter addressed small meetings of members of both houses in Mr. Cornell's rooms, explaining the plan to them, showing its necessity & various advantages.

It was I who, when a crisis came, in the Senate, & we found the lobby of the New York Central Railroad opposed to us, in order to secure the votes of the Anti-Cornell men in the Assembly, held the New York Central bill from passing the Senate & prevailed on a majority of the Senate not to take it up until justice was done us.

It was I who, at Mr. Cornell's request, nominated one half of the original Charter Trustees, he naming the other half.

It was I who, in the bitter struggle for our Charter against all the Colleges of the State, saw personally all the leading Editors of New York & enlisted them on our side by a full & fair presentation of the whole subject, inducing them to support us thoroughly, as they did in their papers. [An examination of the leading papers indicates that Manton Marble of the *World* was the only editor who had anything much (favorable or unfavorable) to say about the matter.]

I do not underrate Mr. Cornell's work—I set it far above my own.

That he, a man who had never had the advantage of a University or Collegiate education, should have been willing to make so munificent a gift & in so broad a spirit was the greatest thing of all; that I have always acknowledged, & in his scheme for the "location" of the lands he showed foresight equal to his devotion to the interests of his fellowmen. . . .

175

Documents

Nor do I depreciate in the slightest degree the admirable service rendered by Mr. Lord in the Assembly, nor do I underrate the suggestions made from time to time by Judge—then Mr. Finch.

But the facts are as above stated.

I may add another point; Mr. Cornell was then one of the oldest—if not the oldest—members of the Senate, austere, not communicative to his associates generally, in fact, so reserved in his intercourse with his fellow-senators that they hardly knew him personally, I was the youngest member of the Senate & in my enthusiasm made the interest of the proposed university a personal matter, laboring individually with the other members & obtaining thus the co-operation which could not otherwise have been secured.

The idea of founding a University worthy of the State of New York was an old dream of mine cherished even while I was at Geneva (now Hobart) College, strengthened at Yale, developed more & more during my student days abroad; whether I live to return or not you will find marked passages in my European diary showing this.

Among my old letters, too, will be found a correspondence with Gerrit Smith, in which I offered him one half of all that I possessed on condition that he should carry out a plan, which he at one time favored, of establishing a University in the State of New York.

It was this hope of contributing to the establishment of a university freed from the old shackles which led me to accept the Professorship at the University of Michigan, since I saw there an opportunity to make a beginning of such an institution as I had dreamed of.

It may be said that I published too little after the organization of the university on the general subject.

As to this, I had stated my views in my speech in the Senate on the University bill, had developed them in the "Plan of Organization" & in my Inaugural Address, had defended them in sundry newspaper articles, & afterwards presented them in my Address to the State Agricultural Society, & in various magazine articles, lectures, etc.; but after we had opened the University came my conviction that mere writing & talking about Universities was not what was wanted,—that to establish an institution of a general university character & on the lines I had suggested to Mr. Cornell was what was wanted; that if this succeeded there was no need of elaborate treatises on the subject, & that if it did not succeed such treatises would not accomplish the end which I had in view.

This is what led me to be silent under President Porter's attack; I could have answered him fully, but I left it to time to answer him & time has done it—Yale following our example in things which he declared preposterous—adopting them even during his presidency.

I think I may claim in this matter to have been free from any unworthy personal ambition; I had not the remotest expectation of being elected to any place in the institution, my election to its Presidency was a surprise to me and I accepted it only because the election was unanimously made by the Trustees & so earnestly pressed upon me by Mr. Cornell, but I accepted making a distinct statement that I should be regarded simply as a *locum tenens,* holding the place until some man more fit for it could be secured.

Such a man, indeed, I had endeavored to secure—President Martin Anderson of Rochester, & was only dissuaded when Mr. William Kelly, President of the State Agricultural Society informed Mr. Cornell & myself that, if we insisted on choosing Dr. Anderson, his duty would be to retire from his Cornell Trusteeship & devote himself to the interests of Rochester as against Cornell.

Whatever ambition I had, & in this I was strengthened by the counsels of my dear wife, was in the direction of accepting a Professorship which had been tendered me at Yale.

As to the period following the struggle for the Charter; it was I who visited the foremost technical institutions of England, Germany, France, & Italy, with reference to the best organization of similar departments at Cornell, & this was without any cost to the University—either for salary or expenses.

It was I who laid the foundations of the Library & the collections of various sorts by purchases in Europe & elsewhere, securing special donations from Mr. Cornell, Mr. Kelly, and others, & adding to them myself.

It was I who suggested at the very outset the plan of non-resident Professors, which I had thought out long before & to which I had called George William Curtis' attention years previous at Ann Arbor—as you will see by referring to his speech at the opening of the University in 1868. [There is in Mr. Curtis' speech no reference to the idea of non-resident professors.]

It was I who enlisted Agassiz, Lowell, Curtis, Goldwin Smith, Bayard Taylor, James Law, Froude, Freeman & others, who came and & gave a most valuable impulse to the new movement.

It was I who suggested and carried through the Legislature the

Amendment to our Charter providing for the election of Alumni Trustees, &, so far as I know, this was the first admission of Alumni to such privileges in the United States.

As to the admission of women my simple claim is that as I had advocated it some years before at the University of Michigan, so I urged it in my Inaugural Address, & pressed it later upon the Trustees, drawing up the Report to the Board in favor of it.

It was I who suggested the establishment of fully equipped mechanical laboratories & workshops in connection with the Department of Mechanical Engineering, purchasing the first power-lathe for that purpose with my own funds, since I hardly dared approach the Trustees at that time with a proposal to make such purchase of which they could hardly then see the advantage.

It was immediately following a suggestion of mine in an Annual Report that Mr. Sibley broached to me first of all his wish to erect a College Building for us & and it was in accordance with my suggestion, made at various times from Berlin as well as from Ithaca, that he made various additions to the Sibley Building & Equipment.

It was immediately after a conversation with me on the subject of the University, & especially the University Library, that Miss McGraw —afterwards Mrs Fiske—avowed to her father her wish to do something for the institution, &, receiving his permission, gave us the chimes as a beginning of gifts.

It was immediately after an Address of mine that John McGraw came to me and said, "I will stand by you", & in response to my suggestion gave us the building, which bears his name, & other things.

It was upon a suggestion of mine & for the purpose of anchoring Classical studies at the University that Mr. Cornell purchased The Anthon Library.

It was I who, as Professor Anthony will testify, suggested the establishment at Cornell of the first Department of Electrical Engineering ever erected in the United States, indeed, ever created anywhere, as far as I know, asking him to prepare a plan of instruction & to come before our Executive Committee with it, &, when Judge Boardman & others opposed it & seemed likely to defeat it, I pledged myself that it should not make any demands upon the University Treasury during its first year & that I would myself meet all the cost of it beyond the appropriations already made for that year.

What I had done for the development of historical studies at the University of Michigan & in the country at large Professor Herbert Adams

& President Adams have told you—what I did at Cornell to found a proper department you know.

As to the department of Political Science for practical training so far as I know I was the first to suggest it in any country;—in my Johns Hopkins address and in my Report as Commissioner to the Paris Exposition on Political Education in Europe—& was prompt to carry it into effect at Cornell—as far as our means allowed.

From me came the first successful plan for an Unsectarian University or College Chapel in the United States, & the establishment of a Christian but non sectarian pulpit. Mr. Dean Sage's proposal was for a Chaplaincy, with a suggestion that it be held by a resident Clergyman of some one denomination. This I declined to urge upon the Trustees, but presented my plan which he accepted and which other institutions have since imitated.

It was I who, by the aid of Mr. Schuyler against great opposition—which defeated the plan during several meetings, led the Trustees to establish the Scholarships and Fellowships out of the monies which had been advanced by various Trustees at an earlier day to pay the University debt.

And I may add one more fact, for your eyes alone;— I do it with reluctance, but I propose making a clean breast of the matter;— No other man, so far as I know, has given so large a proportion of his fortune to the University as I have, & I have given not showy things, but have scattered my gifts among many of the lesser things, which, while scarcely noted, have given a University tone & character to the institution.

There is also another thing of which I may justly remind you; in view of the great increase in the number of professors & of their high character, it should, I think, not be forgotten that in the early days it was with the utmost difficulty that men of ability & standing could be induced to cast in their lot with Cornell; it was an untried experiment, laughed at by conservative University men throughout the country, the surroundings on the hill at Ithaca were not at first attractive, much had to be done with very small means, &, as I look back, I feel surprised that I was able to secure & hold such admirable men as I induced to come into the College faculty & to remain in it.

And one thing more. The curse of American Colleges & Universities of the newer type had long been dissensions in Boards of Trustees & Faculties. The history of Union, Hamilton, Michigan, Wisconsin, & a multitude of others, showed promising institutions absolutely paralyzed by such dissensions. With all the difficulties at Cornell in the early days there were plenty of inducements to dislike & dissension. I have never ceased to congratulate myself that these were kept under & that I never had a quarrel with any person connected with the institution, & that my influence from the first was exercised effectively in favor of peace. . . .

The one thing in my life to which I look back with pride [with greatest pride, he must surely have meant] is my connection with the foundation of the institution.

You know, to some extent, the opposition which confronted me but you can hardly know how bitter & trying it was at times.

[There are three more pages of the letter, answering the statement that he had "now returned to his first love," and suggesting that perhaps some more adequate recognition of his part in the founding might be made in the coming anniversary celebration. The letter then closes as follows.]

Pardon me for writing you so long a letter.

It was mainly written at Upsala when there came to me a vivid idea of the value of work done in founding & maintaining a University; there is no statement in it which cannot be confirmed either by living witnesses or by documents.

I ask you to consider it, to preserve it, but for the present to keep it to yourselves.

I remain to both of you,

Most sincerely your friend,
Andrew D. White.

I prefer to have this remain in custody of Prof Burr at the White Library. A. D. W.

14. Recollections of Ezra Cornell by Otis E. Wood

[Otis E. Wood was the brother-in-law of Ezra Cornell, and for some years associated with him in the telegraph business. When Mr. Wood was an old man the late Professor Charles Henry Hull had a conversation with him about Mr. Cornell. What Mr. Wood said was taken down by Alice Durand, now Mrs. Henry Edgerton. The following document is a typewritten transcription of her notes. Attached to the document is a sheet on which Professor Hull wrote the following note:

Ezra Cornell's characteristics.

Notes by Alice Durand (Mrs. Henry Edgerton) of a conversation I had with Otis E. Wood, she being present as stenographer.

Charles H. Hull.

The document is one of many very generously given to me by Mary Hull. It is obvious that in respect to dates and specific events Mr. Wood's memory cannot be trusted. The value of the document is that it gives us an account of Ezra Cornell and certain of his activities by a man who knew him intimately and was himself highly intelligent.]

I never knew Mr. Cornell before he came courting my sister (Miss Wood). The first recollection I have of him was when he and my sister took their wedding journey to the Clinton House,—it was then just opened,—about 1831.

(The Governor Alonzo Cornell must have got together a good deal of material—have you any idea what became of it?)

No—Mr. Cornell himself was a man who always kept everything. He made statistics the rule of his life. At the time the University was founded, it happened that I was ill, and in that way came to know a good deal about the beginning of the University—when Mr. Cornell and President White were making arrangements for the largest University in the world on three millions of dollars—and with no idea how long it would take to realize that either!

Mr. Cornell was a peculiar man in that way. This impresses me as a better idea of the character of the man than anything else I can give you in a few words. He needed a great deal of money because he used a great deal of money, but he didn't want a dollar for himself. His life all the way through was a remarkable example of the "generous-to-a-fault" character.

The endowment of the City Library was his first emerging from a debt of fifty thousand dollars that he had got buried under in building the Pierpont and Dunkirk Telegraph line,[1]—now a part of the Western Union. He had made six thousand dollars,—the first money he had ever realized—in building a line of telegraph between New York and Albany. His next venture was in building a line from Bridgeport, Connecticut, up through the Housatonic valley to Pittsfield, I believe, and from Troy to Buffalo[2] and Montreal,—a sparsely settled country, you see; and with the building of lines through the still more poverty-stricken country in New York, he lost all that he had made and got buried under this fifty thousand dollars indebtedness. He never "dug out" of this load, as they say, until the late fifties. Shortly before the University was founded,[3] he made arrangements with the Morse patentees to go on and develop the business. It started slow and hard; people were incredulous. The arrangement was this: they told him to take this patent and organize it into companies as he could, and they

[1] The New York and Erie.
[2] From Troy to Montreal, but not through Buffalo.
[3] About eighteen years before.

Documents

would take their pay at the rate of one hundred dollars a mile in stock in any of the companies he might organize. He went all through the country and organized the two lines spoken of—profitless lines because they had no feeders and because the project was new and the country poor. He once said to me: "This served me just right. I always prided myself on being a bundle of statistics all through—I ought to have known better than to invest my money east of Buffalo, because I knew that the country was developing twice as fast west of Buffalo as east. I am going to drop all this business here and start in at Buffalo and build telegraph lines in the West." [4]

He did that. He built the first line that began to be prosperous at all [5] from Buffalo to Cleveland, Detroit, and Milwaukee—there wasn't much Chicago in those days,—it was a town of seventeen thousand and Buffalo had twenty-five thousand. That was about 1847, I should say. About that time two other lines, the Sibley line and the Electro-Chemical [6] started up a vigorous competition with the Morse lines. These two lines struck off south to Columbus, Louisville, and St. Louis, and the whole district was so poor that the competition ruined all three. The result was that the stocks ran down so that you could buy them up at any price, and Mr. Cornell went about buying all he could get hold of. — He was an original Whig, you know, and believed in borrowing all the money he could get. — Well, he bought stocks no matter what line they were in; he got a lot of them for ten cents on the dollar, and some even as low as three and five cents on the dollar.

His associates in the business were Colonel Speed and a Mr. Wade, an artist, from Seneca Falls, and the other two companies approached them on the subject of consolidation. Mr. Cornell was a man who was not easily approached, because he could live on less than any other man, and his way of doing business was to starve others out,—and he didn't mind the starving himself out at the same operation. Well, the other two companies knew that he was not to be approached on the question of consolidation,[7] but they did go to Speed and Wade. Speed and Wade had never gotten very much money out of it—neither had Mr. Cornell for that matter—and they were easily induced to believe that the putting together of all these rival interests would enhance the earning value.

[4] In fact the Erie and Michigan was built before the New York and Erie.
[5] The New York, Albany and Buffalo was more prosperous than the Erie and Michigan.
[6] What company this refers to I have no idea at all.
[7] As a matter of fact the Sibley company did "approach" Mr. Cornell, making him a definite offer of consolidation, which Mr. Cornell was finally forced to accept.

They were sure that it had a profitable earning capacity,—for example, the part of the Western Union between New York and Albany had divided 8%.

The general consolidation took place in '54—but it might have been '64,—I don't remember that point.[8] (It wasn't more than two years after the consolidation that the stocks were worth $2.20 on the dollar. This began to make the stock dividends—which simply means that they watered the stock,—and that was the way they pulled out.)

Mr. Cornell fought this consolidation with all his might. Sibley, who was the first president of the consolidated lines, I believe, was in favor of it. It was said that Mr. Cornell would fight in favor of a wrong thing with as much desperation as he would if it were right. He fought this consolidation, and they actually forced the wealth that it brought upon him.

To go back to Mr. Cornell's early life: Mr. Cornell's courtship of my sister was during the time that he lived as a boy at De Ruyter. He was a tall, slender, gaunt boy,—not altogether an attractive lad, and yet he had a rather forceful manner after all. He was raised in De Ruyter,— born there on Crum Hill.[9] You look up the main street and can see the old house that he himself built, as a boy of sixteen or eighteen, for his father's family. It was still standing twenty, maybe thirty years ago,— I don't know whether it is still there or not.

The old gentleman, Ezra's father, was a thoroughbred Quaker, a potter by trade. Ezra learned pottery first as a lad. The old gentleman was a sly Quaker,—they used to tell of him that once when he carried out a load of the rather fragile, unglazed pottery to the merchant to sell, Mr. Annas complained: "Elijah," he said, "thy ware is not as good as last year." The old gentleman was loaded for that: "Thee must remember that in the weakness of the ware lies the strength of the trade." Well, that was so shrewd that Mr. Annas forgot all about the discounts he was entitled to.

The old people wore the Quaker garb and spoke the "plain language." Mr. Cornell married "out of meeting," and did not wear the garb. In conversation with the family he always used the plain language, but not in talking with those outside. He had many Quaker ways. He liked the Sunday afternoon "visitation"—after meeting, you know, the Quakers have a visitation for a whole week.

[8] The agreement was reached in 1855, the company incorporated in 1856.

[9] Born at Westchester Landing on the Bronx River, moved to De Ruyter when he was twelve years old.

He had a little set-back which comes to some people, as a young man in his courtship—perhaps it hadn't gone as far as a courtship. There was a Wealthy Russell—"Aunt" Wealthy Russell, she was afterward called —who lived in Scipio, one of several Quaker colonies. She was much admired by Ben Smith, a boy of the neighborhood, and a rival of Mr. Cornell for Wealthy's affection. Mr. Cornell had been quite constant for two or three years, but Ben Smith had got ahead: he had done something very cunning in the way of inventing some small thing (it wasn't a University that he had built!) that Wealthy admired very much. So she switched off in the direction of Ben Smith. Mr. Cornell was chagrined, but he had lost Wealthy. She never married, however. Once in later life she met Mr. Cornell after the University had been founded, about 1870, perhaps, and had some pleasant conversation. Ezra said "Wealthy, does thee think that Ben Smith could do as well as this?" And Wealthy had to say that he could not.

He had a peculiarity in his early life in the way of entire forgetfulness of his own needs and those of his family. He did not even attend to their education.[10] And he was forgetful of himself. There was no selfishness in the man; he was unreasonably generous,—it would have been better for himself and for his family if he had been more selfish. He had no credit at home or abroad. He couldn't even buy a sack of flour for credit; and he was always forgetful in money matters—small accounts against him ran at the mill here for years.

After he fell in with the telegraph companies, he went in with Moore's double mould [board] plow, an Ithaca invention.[11] Being of an inventive mind himself, he was put in charge of introducing this and he took the states of Maine and Georgia to develop. That was one of his "bad guesses." Georgia was coming forward at that time as the great agricultural state of the South, but when he got there he found that the plow of the state was a darkey and a hoe. About 1843, on his return from the South, he came into Washington, and the telegraph was just being talked of.

During this trip to the South, the family lived at "The Nook," and they were poor enough! My father, who lived five or six miles out in the country, used to come to town with his lumber wagon loaded with things to carry the family along. And it is characteristic of the man that

[10] This probably means no more than that in early years he left the education of the children to Mary Ann.

[11] Before, not after, he became interested in the telegraph.

when he came home after a two or three years' trip,[12] instead of bringing at least a sack of flour or something practical, he brought a trunkful of gilt-edged books. But the old gentleman went on very cheerfully taking care of the family,—there were only eight or nine of them.[13] But it shows the bent of the man and his lack of forethought for the family; he was a visionary. He couldn't do anything on the same plan with ordinary people. He had great plans and made great out-puts,— but not for himself. He never would have built the fine stone house except for President White.[14]

White urged it as a matter of convenience. Mr. Cornell had a Quaker hospitality and generosity,—he always wanted people he was connected with to come and live with him. It happened about that time that William G. Fargo, of Wells-Fargo Company, had built a great mansion at Buffalo, and White said to Cornell: "You want to built a good house. There are so few men in the world who ever get ready to build a good house and live in it. You owe it to the future to live in a good house. Go and look at W. G. Fargo's house in Buffalo and see what you don't want to build a house like. That is a hotel—you don't want to entertain your friends like that, but you want to live in a good house." Mr. Cornell never lived in the new house himself—he wanted things for other people, not for himself. The chagrin of his life, I think, was that in the $625,000 judgment in the telegraph case a million dollars was so involved that he couldn't give it to the University, and it fell to his family.[15] He was a man who spent his energy and his life working for the good of somebody else,—giving his money in such shape that people couldn't get rid of it.

He came to be a trustee of the Agricultural College in Ovid. He was the leading man in this part of the country in his early life in pushing forward farming interests. He was very fond of raising short-horns, and there were great fables of the fierceness of this particular kind of cattle. Perhaps his interest in farming matters in his early life was a little because Miss Wood's father was a prominent farmer who had made a good thing of a poor farm, and Mr. Cornell's interest might perhaps

[12] The trip to Georgia took only three or four months, but it was followed almost immediately by the trip to Maine, and from then he was absent from Ithaca for some years.
[13] In 1843 there were only four children living.
[14] The house is now the Llenroc fraternity house.
[15] This must refer to the suit brought by F. O. J. Smith against Mr. Cornell, which dragged on for some twelve years, and never, so far as I can learn, came to a decision. I have found no other evidence that it interfered with Mr. Cornell's gifts to the university.

have been to please his father-in-law. He did a good deal in those days in improving the breed of stock,—back in the forties. Old Mr. Stevens (the father of Clement Stevens) a butcher, used to say: "The first animal that I ever hung up in my market that was good enough to sell was a four-year-old raised from Mr. Cornell's stock, brought in the early forties from the American Institute Fair in New York." He was interested in all kinds of agricultural work, and had a good deal of money in the mill.

Otis Eddy, who had a cotton factory where Cascadilla now stands, was a great friend of the family, and it was through his influence that Mr. Cornell came to Ithaca. He walked into town—that was his way to get anywhere—to walk. He started from De Ruyter to walk to Ithaca, having heard that great things were happening at Ithaca. That was just after the Canal boom, between 1828 and 1832, when Ithaca was to be another Chicago, located at the Inlet! He walked as far as was convenient for one day, and stopped at McLean over night. He got up early the next morning and set out before breakfast. He stopped at the first stump along the way to count his money—they tried to get a piece of that old stump to put into the new house, but they couldn't find it.

When he came to town he stopped at the old hotel that used to be [   ]. Now, this was one of his Quaker capers: he said to the landlord, "If a decent young man were to come along and say that he had had no breakfast and had no money to buy one, what would you do?" "I would tell him come in and have something to eat," the man told him. "Well," said Mr. Cornell, "here's your chance." When he came out after he had had his breakfast, he put down twenty-five cents. "I thought you didn't have any money," says the landlord. "No, I didn't say so. I just wanted to know what you would do if I didn't have any."

Thompson of the Clinton House used to say that in hard-luck times he met Mr. Cornell in New York one morning and asked him how he was getting on. Mr. Cornell took a twenty-five cent piece out of his pocket and said: "There, that will buy my dinner, but where the next is coming from, I don't know." Mrs. Cornell said she had known him when he was worse off than that. "He had nothing in his pocket, but as he was going down Broadway he found ten cents on the sidewalk and bought himself some breakfast."

The most remarkable thing in the inception of Cornell University was that it was located at Ithaca. We had no way then of getting to the New York Central Railroad without going to Owego and Binghamton and Syracuse.[16] So Mr. Cornell found himself with a university and 990,000 acres of public land and no railroad, and the only respectable thing he could do was to build a railroad to the New York Central. He put an astonishing amount of money into those railroads, one to the northeast and one to the northwest—about $1,900,000 altogether.

15. Letter from George S. Batchellor to E. W. Huffcut, 1894

[In 1865 Mr. Batchellor was Inspector General on the staff of Governor Fenton. The following letter was written for reasons given in the letter itself. Some parts of it are here printed because it gives some additional information about Mr. White's share in the founding of Cornell University. The letter is in the university library.]

PARIS, July, 1894

Professor E. W. Huffcut,
DEAR SIR,

While in America last September I was honored with an invitation to be present at the celebration of the twenty-fifth anniversary of the foundation of Cornell University but was obliged to decline, owing to my early departure for Europe. I felt particularly desirous of being present . . . as I happened to have taken a special and I trust somewhat effective part in favoring the State legislation which was in fact the "foundation" of the University. And, in paying homage to the Founder of the University, I should not have forgotten the young Senator who during those early struggles stood courageously by the side of his elder colleague, displaying at all times that marvellous skill and energy without which I fear this Anniversary would have had no *raison d'être.*

In fact it is altogether probable that the bounty of the noble philanthropist who gave his fortune and his name to the institution would have been turned into quite another channel but for the suggestions— I think I may say the persuasions—of the young Senator then chairman of the Senate Committee on Education, who, having conceived the idea of a new and advanced seat of learning, directed not only the thoughts of Mr. Cornell to the founding of such an institution, but, by efforts of the most zealous and intelligent character, succeeded in turning an al-

---

[16] He probably means no way of getting to New York. To get to New York, one could take the Ithaca and Owego railroad to Owego, and from there the Erie Railroad; or one could take a steamer from Ithaca to Cayuga Bridge at the north end of Cayuga Lake, and there connect with the New York Central.

Documents

most insuperable tide of opposition to the support of his project. I speak advisedly when I call it *his* project. The press, or rather the leading newspapers of New York, and many public men were in opposition; and thus the youngest Senator at Albany, by an energy, ability and tact which should not now be overlooked, accomplished a great and noble purpose where rival interests were strong enough to have thwarted a less wise or vigorous man. . . .

I am led to write you these lines, as in reading the published account of the celebration . . . I am amazed to find that the speakers on that occasion, with one or two notable exceptions, scarcely mentioned the name of Andrew D. White. . . .

I can understand how some of the younger speakers or some who were not even acquainted with the founder or with its early history should omit to give due credit to the modest man who did all the literary work, who directed all the legislation, who framed the Charter, whose pen traced the present motto as the language of Ezra Cornell, and who drafted the plan of organization which was adopted by the trustees . . . and which has been the guiding charter of the institution ever since. But I marvel that the principal orators of the day should only once allude to President White and that in a casual manner, and give so much praise to others whose services only began when the University was successfully inaugurated. I feel that a great injustice . . . has been committed; and . . . I feel bound . . . to vindicate the position of Andrew D. White in this behalf. . . .

At the time of the passage of the Cornell charter, I held an official position in Albany which brought me in close relations with Governor Reuben E. Fenton and the members of both branches of the Legislature. I may say that, at the outset of the discussion, my personal sympathies and predilections were not on the side of Cornell. My interest was first excited by listening to a speech of the young Senator from Onondaga in support of the charter of the new University. . . . No one could have heard his arguments or listened to his earnest eloquence without becoming impressed with the power of the orator and the merit of his cause. Two of the older and more prominent Senators, the late Chief-Justice Folger and General James M. Cook, . . . were won over from the opposition. . . . Mr. Cornell, then a Senator, was a reticent and reserved man and not fitted to attract people to his support or to advocate on the floor of the Senate his noble cause. No one who knows me will interpret what I say as derogatory to the honor and merit of Ezra Cornell. . . . I only say what was familiar to all who were cognizant of the contemporary history, that he leaned upon the arm of the younger and more accomplished worker and depended upon him to put into form and urge to success the grand project. . . . There was no rivalry or jealousy between them. And had Ezra Cornell been present at the celebration of his glorious achievement, he would have been the first to give credit to President White and proclaim him the *fidus Achates* in all this work.

As a matter of history, the discussion of educational questions was brought forward in the New York Senate in 1864, on the proposition of Mr. Cornell to divide the . . . Land Scrip Fund which had before been given to the "People's College" at Havana, equally between the People's College and the "State Agricultural College." At this time Mr. Cornell had no idea of founding an institution of learning by the generous gift which has immortalized his name. Senator White opposed Mr. Cornell in this plan, and labored during all the session of 1864 to prevent the disintegration and distribution of the . . . Fund between the two colleges mentioned and the twenty-three other colleges . . . seeking a *pro rata* share of the Fund. It was during these discussions that Mr. Cornell revealed to president White his desire to donate half a million dollars to the cause of education; and Mr. White then suggested the idea of founding a university in the broadest sense. . . . Thereupon Mr. Cornell came forward with his proposition to establish such a university.

The Charter was drawn up by Senator White (except the Land clause, which was framed by Senator Folger . . .); . . . The "People's College" had utterly neglected to comply with the conditions imposed by the State and in fact was seeking relief from such conditions; and that institution, led by the Hon. Charles Cook, of Havana, its patron, opposed Mr. White's scheme. . . . This legislative struggle excited the liveliest interest at Albany. At the outset Mr. Cornell and the young Senator seemed almost alone. . . . I venture to assert that it was through the labors of this young Senator . . . that the opposition gradually melted away. . . . He labored with Senators and members of the Legislature, conducting many of them to Mr. Cornell's room in Congress Hall, where this good man could explain to them his grand project; he brought to his support, at this critical moment, nearly all the prominent newspapers of New York; . . . And when this first battle was won, Senator White, who had wealth and political ambition to lead him to more attractive spheres of activity, left all behind and went to dwell upon the uninviting hillside overlooking the village of Ithaca. . . . And for twenty-three years did president White continue to labor at Ithaca, at Albany, at Washington, and in foreign lands, devoting heart and

brain and the health and vigor of his primal years to the building of
Cornell. . . .

I am not unmindful of the individual labors and material aid given
to the University by other men, some of whom have contributed largely
of their private fortunes. But I think I am correct in asserting that, according to his fortune, President White has contributed as much in
money value to the building of Cornell University as any other man,
apart from its founder. . . .

Yours truly,

GEO. S. BATCHELLOR

ADDRESS

The Cornell Tradition: Freedom and Responsibility

ADDRESS

The Cornell Tradition: Freedom and Responsibility

By CARL L. BECKER

[The seventy-fifth anniversary of the signing of the charter of Cornell University was recognized on April 27, 1940, by the holding of a public meeting of the university and the delivery of the following address by Professor Becker.]

SEVENTY-FIVE years ago today Reuben E. Fenton, the Governor of the State of New York, signed a charter for Cornell University. The founding of the university was made possible, in great part, by the generosity of Ezra Cornell, a citizen of Ithaca. The first faculty was assembled, the university was organized, and instruction was begun under the far-sighted leadership of the first president, Andrew D. White; and in a relatively short time, as such things go, the new institution, as a result of the distinguished achievements of its faculty and the high quality of instruction offered to its students, acquired a reputation which placed it among the leading universities of the country.

In the process of acquiring a reputation Cornell acquired something better than a reputation, or rather it acquired something which is the better part of its reputation. It acquired a character. Corporations are not necessarily soulless; and of all corporations universities are the most likely to have, if not souls, at least personalities. Perhaps the reason is that universities are, after all, largely shaped by presidents and professors, and presidents and professors, especially if they are good ones, are fairly certain to be men of distinctive, not to say eccentric, minds and temperaments. A professor, as the German saying has it, is a man who thinks otherwise. Now an able and otherwise-thinking president, surrounded by able and otherwise-thinking professors, each resolutely thinking otherwise in his own manner, each astounded to find that the others, excellent fellows as he knows them in the main to be, so often refuse in matters of the highest import to be informed by knowledge or

193

guided by reason—this is indeed always an arresting spectacle and may sometimes seem to be a futile performance. Yet it is not futile unless great universities are futile. For the essential quality of a great university derives from the corporate activities of such a community of otherwise-thinking men. By virtue of a divergence as well as of a community of interests, by the sharp impress of their minds and temperaments and eccentricities upon each other and upon their pupils, there is created a continuing tradition of ideas and attitudes and habitual responses that has a life of its own. It is this continuing tradition that gives to a university its corporate character or personality, that intangible but living and dynamic influence which is the richest and most durable gift any university can confer upon those who come to it for instruction and guidance.

Cornell has a character, a corporate personality, in this sense, an intellectual tradition by which it can be identified. The word which best symbolizes this tradition is freedom. There is freedom in all universities, of course—a great deal in some, much less in others; but it is less the amount than the distinctive quality and flavor of the freedom that flourishes at Cornell that is worth noting. The quality and flavor of this freedom is easier to appreciate than to define. Academic is not the word that properly denotes it. It includes academic freedom, of course, but it is something more, and at the same time something less, than that—something less formal, something less self-regarding, something more worldly, something, I will venture to say, a bit more impudent. It is, in short, too little schoolmasterish to be defined by a formula or identified with a professional code. And I think the reason is that Cornell was not founded by schoolmasters or designed strictly according to existing educational models. The founders, being both in their different ways rebels against convention, wished to establish not merely another university but a somewhat novel kind of university. Mr. Cornell desired to found an institution in which any person could study any subject. Mr. White wished to found a center of learning where mature scholars and men of the world, emancipated from the clerical tradition and inspired by the scientific idea, could pursue their studies uninhibited by the cluttered routine or the petty preoccupations of the conventional cloistered academic life. In Mr. White's view the character and quality of the university would depend upon the men selected for its faculty: devoted to the general aim of learning and teaching, they could be depended upon to devise their own ways and means of achieving that aim. The emphasis was, therefore, always on men rather than on methods; and during Mr.

White's administration and that of his immediate successors there was assembled at Cornell, from the academic and the non-academic world, a group of extraordinary men—erudite or not as the case might be, but at all events as highly individualized, as colorful, as disconcertingly original and amiably eccentric a group of men as was ever got together for the launching of a new educational venture. It is in the main to the first president and this early group of otherwise-thinking men that Cornell is indebted for its tradition of freedom.

Many of those distinguished scholars and colorful personalities were before my time. Many of those whom I was privileged to know are now gone. A few only are still with us—worthy bearers of the tradition, indefatigable in the pursuit of knowledge, in the service of Cornell, in the promotion of the public good, young men still, barely eighty or a little more. Present or absent, the influence of this original group persists, and is attested by stories of their sayings and exploits that still circulate, a body of ancient but still living folklore. It is a pity that some one has not collected and set down these stories; properly arranged they would constitute a significant mythology, a Cornell epic which, whether literally true or only characteristic, would convey far better than official records in deans' offices the real significance of this institution. Some of these stories I have heard, and for their illustrative value will venture to recall a few of them. Like Herodotus, I give them as they were related to me without vouching for their truth, and like Herodotus, I hope no god or hero will take offense at what I say.

There is the story of the famous professor of history, passionate defender of majority rule, who, foreseeing that he would be outvoted in the faculty on the question of the location of Risley Hall, declared with emotion that he felt so strongly on the subject that he thought he ought to have two votes. The story of another professor of history who, in reply to a colleague who moved as the sense of the faculty that during war time professors should exercise great discretion in discussing public questions, declared that for his part he could not understand how any one could have the Prussian arrogance to suppose that every one could be made to think alike, or the Pomeranian stupidity to suppose that it would be a good thing if they could. The story of the eccentric and lovable professor of English who suggested that it would be a good thing, during the winter months when the wind sweeps across the hill, if the university would tether a shorn lamb on the slope south of the library building; who gave all of his students a grade of eighty-five, on the theory that they deserved at least that for patiently listening to him while he amused himself reading his favorite authors aloud, and for so amiably submitting to the ironical and sarcastic comments—too highly wrought and sophistically phrased in latinized English to be easily understood by them—with which he berated their indifference to good literature. There is the story of the professor who reluctantly agreed to serve as dean of a school on condition that he be relieved of the irksome task at a certain date; who, as the date approached with no successor appointed, repeatedly reminded the president that he would retire on the date fixed; and who, on that date, although no successor had meantime been appointed, cleared out his desk and departed; so that, on the day following, students and heads of departments found the door locked and no dean to affix the necessary signature to the necessary papers. A school without a dean—strange interlude indeed, rarely occurring in more decorous institutions, I should think; but one of those things that could happen in Cornell. And there is the story of the professor of entomology, abruptly leaving a faculty meeting. It seems that the discussion of a serious matter was being sidetracked by the rambling, irrelevant, and would-be facetious remarks of a dean who was somewhat of a wag, when the professor of entomology, not being a wag and being quite fed up, suddenly reached for his hat and as he moved to the door delivered himself thus: "Mr. President, I beg to be excused; I refuse to waste my valuable time any longer listening to this damned nonsense." And even more characteristic of the Cornell tradition is a story told of the first president, Andrew D. White. It is related that the lecture committee had brought to Cornell an eminent authority to give, in a certain lecture series, an impartial presentation of the Free-Silver question. Afterwards Mr. White, who had strong convictions on the subject, approached the chairman of the committee and asked permission to give a lecture in that series in reply to the eminent authority. But the chairman refused, saying in substance: "Mr. President, the committee obtained the best man it could find to discuss this question. It is of the opinion that the discussion was a fair and impartial presentation of the arguments on both sides. The committee would welcome an address by you on any other subject, or on this subject on some other occasion, but not on this subject in this series in reply to the lecture just given." It is related that Mr. White did not give a lecture on that subject in that series; it is also related that Mr. White became a better friend and more ardent admirer of the chairman of the committee than he had been. It seems that Mr. White really liked to have on his faculty men of that degree of independence and resolution.

Freedom and Responsibility

These stories are in the nature of little flash lights illuminating the Cornell temper. A little wild, at times, the Cornell temper; riding, not infrequently, as one may say, high, wide, and handsome. Some quality in it that is native to these states, some pungent tang of the soil, some acrid smell of the frontier and the open spaces—something of the genuine American be-damned-to-you attitude. But I should like to exhibit the Cornell tradition in relation to a more general and at the same time a more concrete situation; and I will venture to do this, even risking a lapse from good taste, by relating briefly my own experience in coming to Cornell and in adjusting myself to its peculiar climate of opinion.

My first contact with the Cornell tradition occurred in December 1916, at the meeting of the American Historical Association at Cincinnati, where Professor Charles Hull invited me to come to his room in the hotel to meet his colleagues of the history group. Intimations had reached me that I was, as the saying is, being considered at Cornell for a position in European history, so that I was rather expecting to be offered a job, at a certain salary, on condition that I should teach a certain number of courses, assume certain administrative duties, and the like. I took it for granted that Cornell would handle these matters in the same businesslike way that other universities did. But I found that Professor Hull had a manner and a method all his own. He did not offer me a job—nothing as crude as that; he invited me, on behalf of his colleagues, to join the faculty of Cornell University. The difference may be subtle, but I found it appreciable. On the chance that I might have formed a too favorable opinion of Cornell, Professor Hull hastened to set me right by itemizing, in great detail, the disadvantages which, from a disinterested point of view, there might be in being associated with the institution, as well as, more doubtfully, certain possible advantages. Among the disadvantages, according to Professor Hull, was the salary; but he mentioned, somewhat apologetically, a certain sum which I could surely count on, and intimated that more might be forthcoming if my decision really depended upon it. By and large, from Professor Hull's elaborate accounting, I gathered that Cornell, as an educational institution, was well over in the red, but that, such as it was, with all its sins of omission heavy upon it, it would be highly honored if I could so far condescend to its needs as to associate myself with it.

There apparently, so far as Professor Hull was concerned, the matter rested. Nothing was said of courses to be taught, minimum hours of instruction, or the like mundane matters. In the end I had to inquire what the home work would be—how may hours and what courses

I would be required to teach. Professor Hull seemed mildly surprised at the question. "Why," he said, "I don't know that anything is *required* exactly. It has been customary for the Professor of Modern History to give to the undergraduates a general survey course in modern history, and sometimes if he deems it advisable, a more advanced course in some part of it in which he is especially interested, and in addition to supervise, to whatever extent may seem to him desirable, the work of such graduate students as may come to him. We had rather hoped that you would be disposed to do something of this sort, but I don't know that I can say that anything specific in the way of courses is really *required*. We have assumed that whatever you found convenient and profitable to do would be sufficiently advantageous to the university and satisfactory to the students." Well, there it was. Such a magnification of the professor, such a depreciation of the university, had never before, in similar circumstances, come my way. After a decent interval I condescended to join the faculty of Cornell University. And why not? To receive a good salary for doing as I pleased—what could be better? The very chance I had been looking for all my life.

And so in the summer of 1917 I came to Cornell, prepared to do as I pleased, wondering what the catch was, supposing that Professor Hull's amiable attitude must be either an eccentric form of ironic understatement or else a super-subtle species of bargaining technique. Anyway I proposed to try it out. I began to do as I pleased, expecting some one would stop me. No one did. I went on and on and still no one paid any attention. Personally I was cordially received, but officially no one made any plans to entertain me, to give me the right steer, to tell me what I would perhaps find it wise to do or to refrain from doing. Professor Hull's attitude did seem after all to represent, in some idealized fashion, the attitude of Cornell University. There was about the place a refreshing sense of liberation from the prescribed and the insistent, an atmosphere of casual urbanity, a sense of leisurely activity going on, with time enough to admire the view, and another day coming. No one seemed to be in a hurry, except Mr. Burr of course, and sometimes perhaps Mr. Ranum. But that was their affair—a response, no doubt, to the compulsion of some inner daemon. At least I saw no indication that deans or heads of departments were exerting pressure or pushing any one around. Certainly no head of the history department was incommoding me, for the simple reason, if for no other, that there didn't seem to be any history department, much less a head. There were seven professors of history, and when we met we called ourselves the "History

Group," but no one of us had any more authority than any other. On these occasions Professor Hull presided, for no reason I could discover except that we met in his office because it was the largest and most convenient. Whatever the History Group was it was not a department. If there was any department of history, then there were six; in which case I was the sole member, and presumably the head, of the department of Modern European History. The only evidence of this was that twice a year I received a communication from the president: one requesting me to prepare the budget, which consisted chiefly in setting down the amount of my own salary, an item which the president presumably already knew more about than I did; the other a request for a list of the courses given and the number of students, male and female, enrolled during the year. I always supposed, therefore, that there were six departments of history, each manned by one professor, except the department of American history, which ran to the extraordinary number of two. I always supposed so, that is, until one day Professor Hull said he wasn't sure there were, officially speaking, any departments of history at all; the only thing he was sure of was that there were seven professors of history. The inner truth of the matter I never discovered. But the seven professors were certainly members of the Faculty of Arts, the Graduate Faculty, and the University Faculty since they were often present at the meetings of these faculties. They were also, I think, members of the Faculty of Political Science, a body that seemed to have no corporeal existence since it never met, but that nevertheless seemed to be something—a rumor perhaps, a disembodied tradition or vestigial remainder never seen, but lurking about somewhere in the more obscure recesses of Goldwin Smith Hall. I never had the courage to ask Professor Hull about the university—about its corporate administrative existence, I mean—for fear he might say that he wasn't sure it had any: it was on the cards that the university might turn out to be nothing more than forty or fifty professors.

At all events, the administration (I assumed on general principles that there was one somewhere) wasn't much in evidence and exerted little pressure. There was a president (distinguished scholar and eminent public figure) who presided at faculty meetings and the meeting of the Board of Trustees, and always delivered the Commencement address. But the president, so far as I could judge, was an umpire rather than a captain, and a Gallup poll would have disclosed the fact that some members of the community regarded him as an agreeable but purely decorative feature, his chief function being, as one of my colleagues said, "to obviate the difficulties created by his office." I never shared this view. I have a notion that the president obviated many difficulties, especially for the faculty, that were in no sense created by his office. There were also deans, but not many or much looked up to for any authority they had or were disposed to exercise. Even so, the general opinion seemed to be that the appointment of professors to the office was a useless waste of talent. "Why is it," asked Professor Nichols, "that as soon as a man has demonstrated that he has an unusual knowledge of books, some one immediately insists on making him a bookkeeper?" In those days the dean of the College, at all events, was scarcely more than a bookkeeper—a secretary elected by the faculty to keep its records and administer the rules enacted by it.

The rules were not many or much displayed or very oppressive—the less so since in so many cases they were conflicting, so that one could choose the one which seemed most suitable. The rules seemed often in the nature of miscellaneous conveniences lying about for a professor to use if he needed something of the sort. An efficient administrator, if there had been one, would no doubt have found much that was ill-defined and haphazard in the rules. Even to a haphazard professor, like myself, it often seemed so, for if I inquired what the authority for this or that rule was, the answer would perhaps be that it wasn't a rule but only a custom; and upon further investigation the custom, as like as not, would turn out to be two other customs, varying according to the time and the professor. Even in the broad distribution of powers the efficient administrator might have found much to discontent his orderly soul. I was told that according to the Cornell statutes the university is subject to the control of the Board of Trustees, but that according to the laws of the state it is subject to the Board of Regents. It may or may not be so. I never pressed the matter. I was advised not to, on the theory that at Cornell it always creates trouble when any one looks up the statutes. The general attitude, round and round about, seemed to be that the university would go on very well indeed so long as no one paid too much attention to the formal authority with which any one was invested. And, in fact, in no other university that I am acquainted with does formal authority count for so little in deciding what shall or shall not be done.

In this easy-going, loose-jointed institution the chances seemed very good indeed for me to do as I pleased. Still there was an obvious limit. The blest principle of doing as one pleased presumably did not reach to the point of permitting me to do nothing. Presumably, the general expectation would be that I would at least be pleased to do something, and the condition of doing something was that I alone had to decide what that something should be. This was for me something of a novelty. Hitherto many of the main points—the courses to be given, the minimum hours of instruction, the administrative duties to be assumed— had mostly been decided for me. I had only to do as I was told. This might be sometimes annoying, but it was never difficult. Mine not to question why, mine not to ask whether what I was doing was worth while or the right thing to do. It was bound to be the right thing to do since some one else, some one in authority, so decided. But now, owing to the great freedom at Cornell, I was in authority and had to decide what was right and worth while for me to do. This was not so easy, and I sometimes tried to shift the responsibility to Professor Burr, by asking him whether what I proposed to do was the right thing to do. But Professor Burr wasn't having any. He would spin me a long history, the upshot of which was that what I proposed to do had sometimes been done and sometimes not, so that whatever I did I was sure to have plenty of precedents on my side. And if I tried to shift the responsibility to Professor Hull I had no better luck. He too would spin me a history, not longer than that of Professor Burr, but only taking longer to relate, and the conclusion which he reached was always the same: the conclusion always was, "and so, my dear boy, you can do as you please."

In these devious ways I discovered that I could do as I pleased all right. But in the process of discovering this I also discovered something else. I discovered what the catch was. The catch was that, since I was free to do as I pleased, I was responsible for what it was that I pleased to do. The catch was that, with all my great freedom, I was in some mysterious way still very much bound. Not bound by orders imposed upon me from above or outside, but bound by some inner sense of responsibility, by some elemental sense of decency or fair play or mere selfish impulse to justify myself; bound to all that comprised Cornell University, to the faculty that had so politely invited me to join it without imposing any obligations, to the amiable deans who never raised their voices or employed the imperative mood, to the distinguished president and the Board of Trustees in the offing who every year guaranteed my salary without knowing precisely what, if anything, I might be doing to earn it—to all these I was bound to justify myself by doing, upon request and in every contingency, the best I was capable of doing. And thus I found myself working, although without interference and under no outside compulsion, with more concentration, with greater satisfaction, and,

The Cornell Tradition:

I dare say, with better effect, than I could otherwise have done. I relate my own experience, well aware that it cannot be in all respects typical, since it is characteristic of Cornell to permit a wide diversity in departmental organization and procedure. Yet this very diversity derives from the Cornell tradition which allows a maximum of freedom and relies so confidently upon the sense of personal responsibility for making a good use of it.

I should like to preserve intact the loose-jointed administrative system and the casual freedoms of the old days. But I am aware that it is difficult to do so in the present-day world in which the complex and impersonal forces of a technological society tend to diminish the importance of the individual and to standardize his conduct and thinking, a society in which life often seems impoverished by the overhead charges required to maintain it. Universities cannot remain wholly unaffected by this dominant trend in society. As they become larger and more complicated a more reticulated organization is called for, rules multiply and become more uniform, and the members of the instructing staff, turned out as a standardized article in mass production by our graduate schools, are more subdued to a common model. Somewhat less than formerly, it seems, is the professor a man who thinks otherwise. More than formerly the professor and the promoter are in costume and deportment if not of imagination all compact; and every year it becomes more difficult, in the market place or on the campus, to distinguish the one from the other at ninety yards by the naked eye. On the whole we all deplore this trend towards standardization, but in the particular instance the reasons for it are often too compelling to be denied. Nevertheless, let us yield to this trend only as a necessity and not as something good in itself. Let us hold, in so far as may be, to the old ways, to the tradition in which Cornell was founded and by which it has lived.

But after all, one may ask, and it is a pertinent question, why is so much freedom desirable? Do we not pay too high a price for it in loss of what is called efficiency? Why should any university pay its professors a good salary, and then guarantee them so much freedom to follow their own devices? Surely not because professors deserve, more than other men, to have their way of life made easy. Not for any such trivial reason. Universities are social institutions, and should perform a social service. There is indeed no reason for the existence of Cornell, or of any university, or for maintaining the freedom of learning and teaching which they insist upon, except in so far as they serve to maintain and promote the humane and rational values which are essential to the preservation of democratic society, and of civilization as we understand it. Democratic society, like any other society, rests upon certain assumptions as to what is supremely worth while. It assumes the worth and dignity and creative capacity of the human personality as an end in itself. It assumes that it is better to be governed by persuasion than by compulsion, and that good will and humane dealing are better than a selfish and a contentious spirit. It assumes that man is a rational creature, and that to know what is true is a primary value upon which in the long run all other values depend. It assumes that knowledge and the power it confers should be employed for promoting the welfare of the many rather than for safeguarding the interests of the few.

These are the rational and the humane values which are inseparable from democracy if democracy is to be of any worth. Yet they are older than democracy and are not dependent upon it. They have a life of their own apart from any form of government or type of civilization. They are the values which, since the time of Buddha and Confucius, Solomon and Zoroaster, Socrates and Plato and Jesus, men have commonly recognized as good even when they have denied them in practice, the values which men have commonly celebrated in the saints and martyrs they have agreed to canonize. They are the values which readily lend themselves to rational justification, but need no justification. No man ever yet found it necessary to justify a humane act by saying that it was really a form of oppression, or a true statement by swearing that it was a sacred lie. But every departure from the rational and the humane, every resort to force and deception, whether in civil government, in war, in the systematic oppression of the many or the liquidation of the few, calls for justification, at best by saying that the lesser evil is necessary for the greater good, at worst by resorting to that hypocrisy which, it has been well said, is the tribute that vice customarily pays to virtue.

In the long history of civilization the rational and humane values have sometimes been denied in theory, and persistently and widely betrayed in fact; but not for many centuries has the denial in theory or the betrayal in fact been more general, more ominous, or more disheartening than in our own day. Half the world is now controlled by self-inspired autocratic leaders who frankly accept the principle that might makes right, that justice is the interest of the stronger; leaders who regard the individual as of no importance except as an instrument to be used, with whatever degree of brutality may be necessary, for the realization of their shifting and irresponsible purposes; leaders who subordinate reason to will, identify law and morality with naked force as an instrument of will, and accord value to the disinterested search for truth only in so far as it may be temporarily useful in attaining immediate political ends. If these are indeed the values we cherish, then we too should abandon democracy, we too should close our universities or degrade them, as in many countries whose most distinguished scholars now live in exile they have been degraded, to the level of servile instruments in the support of state policy. But if we still cherish the democratic way of life, and the rational and humane values which are inseparable from it, then it is of supreme importance that we should preserve the tradition of freedom of learning and teaching without which our universities must cease to be institutions devoted to the disinterested search for truth and the increase of knowledge as ends in themselves desirable.

These considerations make it seem to me appropriate, on this memorial occasion, to recall the salient qualities which have given Cornell University its peculiar character and its high distinction; and, in conclusion, to express the hope that Cornell in the future, whatever its gains, whatever its losses, may hold fast to its ancient tradition of freedom and responsibility—freedom for the scholar to perform his proper function, restrained and guided by the only thing that makes such freedom worth while, the scholar's intellectual integrity, the scholar's devotion to the truth of things as they are and to good will and humane dealing among men.

BIBLIOGRAPHY

BIBLIOGRAPHY

FOR the first two lectures I have relied chiefly upon secondary works; but for the last four I have examined at least all of the important collections of original sources. Many of these are easily available in published books and collections of official documents; but there are, in Ithaca and elsewhere, considerable collections of unpublished letters and other documents relating to Ezra Cornell and the founding of Cornell University. The collections outside of Ithaca, such as the Morse, Vail, Kendall, O'Reilly, and F. O. J. Smith papers, since they are important chiefly for Ezra Cornell's connection with the telegraph business, I have not examined; but I have been able to make some use of them through the notes collected by the late Charles Henry Hull (see below, *Hull Papers*). The collections of unpublished papers in Ithaca I have examined systematically and used, I hope, to good advantage.

UNPUBLISHED SOURCES

Cornell Papers. This refers to a considerable collection of letters (the greater part letters received) and other documents which the descendants of Ezra Cornell have from time to time given either to Cornell University or to the De Witt Historical Society in Ithaca.

Cornell University has at present, unfortunately, no adequate provision either for the housing, the cataloguing, or the administration of its official records and other manuscript collections. The manuscript records of the proceedings of the meetings of the Board of Trustees, and certain other records, are kept in Morrill Hall in charge of the Treasurer's office. The largest, although not the most important collection, is in the basement of Risley Hall, and can be used only with some difficulty. This collection contains the valuable correspondence between Mr. Cornell and W. A. Woodward in connection with the location of the Wisconsin lands from which the university derived the greater part of its endowment; and Professor Paul Gates, braving all difficulties, has made full use of this correspondence in his *The Wisconsin Pine Lands of Cornell University*. Apart from this correspondence the Cornell

Bibliography

Papers in the possession of the university are all in the university library in what is called "the vault." This is a small basement room in which is set a large steel safe. The safe, long since completely filled with rare books and manuscripts, contains only a few (but these few important) of the Cornell Papers. (1) Mr. Cornell's *Cyphering Book* (see above, Documents, No. 5). (2) A small collection of important papers in a durable cardboard box, catalogued as MSS+ Kc 8. (3) The "Prime Letters." In 1873 the Rev. S. I. Prime, then engaged on his *Life of S. F. B. Morse* (New York, 1875) asked Mr. Cornell for some account of his connection with the building of the first telegraph line from Washington to Baltimore. Mr. Cornell wrote in reply an account of 27 pages, dated April 28, 1873, of which Mr. Prime quoted one or two pages only in his life of Morse. He then asked Mr. Cornell for some account of his early life. Mr. Cornell's reply, a letter of 8 pages, is dated June 9, 1873. The first part of this letter gives much the same account of his early life up to 1828 as that given in a letter of 1855 to Miss Rebecca Chase (printed in full in *The Autobiography of Mary Emily Cornell*, 5–32); but the last two pages carry the story on to 1839. These three letters are all that Mr. Cornell ever wrote in the nature of an autobiography. The originals of the Prime letters are in the Library of Congress; photostat copies are in the Cornell University Library safe, catalogued as MSS++ Kc 9.

Much the greater part of the Cornell Papers in the university library are in the room outside of the safe, mostly in the bundles and boxes in which they were received, so that no more helpful reference to any particular document could be made than "Cardboard Box," "Gray-blue Box," and the like. But besides the letters and papers in these boxes, there are in this room certain records kept by Mr. Cornell in large and small blankbooks. Of these, the most important are the three that I have referred to as *Memorandum Book*. These are leather-bound books, 7 × 12 inches in size. The first volume, unnumbered and without any title, begins with an entry dated April 27, 1835, and closes with an entry dated October, 1860. The book is not a journal in the ordinary sense, but a book in which Mr. Cornell kept a record of various things—business contracts, expenses, copies of important letters written by him, etc. It contains, for example, a copy of the letter, mentioned above, to Miss Rebecca Chase. The second volume is unnumbered, but has on the first page the following: "Ezra Cornell's Mem^d Book, Ithaca, N. Y., Jan. 1, 1861." This volume, most of which is blank, contains entries covering the period from 1861 to 1866, with a few of later date. Volume three has on the first page the following: "Ithaca, May 13, 1863. Memorandum Book to be used for the building of the Cornell Library." It was used chiefly, but not entirely, for that purpose. Besides these three books, there are a few small books in the nature of pocket expense account books. Mr. Cornell also kept a journal in small blankbooks, which the late Franklin C. Cornell placed at the disposal of Professor A. W. Smith, who printed some extracts from them in his *Ezra Cornell,* Chapter 7. A few of these are in the university library, and Mrs Franklin C. Cornell, searching for more among her husband's papers, found only one. This is a cardboard-bound book, 4 × 6 inches, containing 100 pages, entitled: "Journal of Ezra Cornell, President of New York & Erie Telegraph Company." The first entry in it is Sept. 22, 1851; the last June 4, 1852.

The Cornell Papers in the De Witt Historical Society are systematically arranged in durable boxes, labeled "Telegraph Letters," "Lithograph and Miscellaneous Letters," and the like. The box marked "Telegraph Letters" contains many letters from Mr. Cornell's associates and subordinates which exhibit the desperate condition of Mr. Cornell's telegraph companies during the crucial years 1851–1855, and make it clear that Mr. Cornell did not, as is sometimes thought, take a leading part in founding the Western Union Telegraph Company, but was forced into it much against his wishes by the threat of bankruptcy.

White Papers. This refers to the Andrew D. White papers kept in the outer room of the vault in the Cornell University Library. Letters received by Mr. White, by far the larger number, are in 214 ordinary letter filing cases, arranged chronologically; and in a large steel filing case, the drawers of which are labeled according to the initial letter of the writers of the letters within, the folders within each drawer being arranged according to the dates of the letters. From these cases it seems that Professor G. L. Burr removed the letters that he regarded as especially important, and placed them in cases labeled "Family Letters," or in folders labeled with the name of the writer, such as "J. R. Lowell Letter," etc. Letters and papers of especial importance, such as the letter to Gerrit Smith (see above, Documents, No. 6) Professor Burr placed in a tin box. There are also 60 filing cases of various sorts that contain letters and papers written by Mr. White, and other documents, labeled "Collected Writings," "Yale Memorabilia," and the like. Among the "Collected Writings" are some of Mr. White's reports to the Trustees, and the first draft of his autobiography, which contains several interesting statements not included in the published work. Most of the

Bibliography

letters written by Mr. White (an enormous number, judging from the letters received) are probably among the papers, if they still exist, of his numerous correspondents throughout the United States and in Europe. In his letter to Professors Burr and Huffcut (see above, Documents, No. 13) Mr. White refers to "my European diary." This diary is not in the Cornell University Library, and I have not been able to find out anything about it.

Hull Papers. The late Professor Charles Henry Hull made extensive investigations into the life of Ezra Cornell and his telegraph enterprises. Besides the Cornell Papers in Ithaca, he examined the Morse Papers in the Library of Congress, the Henry O'Reilly Papers in the New York Historical Society Library, the Vail Papers in the Smithsonian Institution, and the F. O. J. Smith Papers in the Maine Historical Society Library. From his notes he prepared what may be called an Ezra Cornell Chronology. This consists of two loose-leaf blank-books of about 250 pages each, in which brief statements, with references to the authority in each case, are set down in chronological order indicating for each date what Mr. Cornell was then doing, or noting some event then occurring relating to him or his activities. These books, together with Professor Hull's extensive notes, and many letters of which he made copies, all of which through the generosity of Miss Mary Hull are now in my possession, I have referred to as Hull Papers.

People's College Papers. These consist of: (1) Reference Book No. 1. MS reports, copies of letters, clippings, minutes of meetings, etc., relating to the Mechanics Mutual Protection Organization and People's College, 1848–54. The compilation was made by Harrison Howard, who was largely responsible for the organization of the Mechanics Mutual Protection, and for the movement that led to the establishment of the People's College. Catalogued as MSS+ Kc 5. (2) Sketch of the Origin of the Mechanics Mutual Protection Organization and the Establishment of People's College. MSS+ Kc 6. (3) Papers relating to People's College. Nine manuscripts in envelopes. MSS+ Kc 7.

Brewer MSS. The most important item in this collection is a typed manuscript, divided into sections, giving an account of "the beginnings of agricultural education in New York State, including the People's College and Cornell University." Written, at the request of Professor W. T. Hewett when he was preparing his history of Cornell University, by Professor William H. Brewer, who had formerly been a professor in the People's College, and was in a position to know much about the events relating to that college, to the State Agricultural College, and to

Bibliography

the founding of Cornell University. With this sketch are some other papers obtained, as I suppose, by Professor Hewett at the same time from William H. Folwell of the University of Minnesota. These are all catalogued as MSS+ Kc 258.

Russel MS. This is a manuscript "Sketch of the Beginnings of Cornell University. Read before the Convocation of Regents of the University of New York. July 13, 1876," by William Channing Russel, a member of the first faculty of the university. Catalogued as MSS+ Kc 26.

Cornell University: Miscellaneous MSS. A small collection of papers relating to the university. Catalogued as MSS+ Kc 4.

John Yawger Davis MSS. Photostats of two letters written by Mr. Davis, a student in the university in 1868–69, one to his brother Charles, dated October 9, the other to his sister Cornelia, dated December 6, 1868. Catalogued as MSS+ Kc 276. For the first letter see above, Documents, No. 12.

Cornell University Charter. An exact reproduction, copy or photograph, of the engrossed bill signed by Governor Fenton, April 27, 1865. Framed under glass. Catalogued as MSS++ Kc 1.

PUBLISHED SOURCES

Many works that I have used but incidentally are sufficiently indicated in the notes and references. The following list includes only those publications that I have found most useful, and that are more or less indispensable for any study of the founding of Cornell University.

The statutes, both state and federal, governing the university are most conveniently found in *Laws and Documents Relating to Cornell University* (editions 1870, 1883, 1892; pp. 91, 161, 234). The state statutes are in the annually published *Laws of New York.* The minutes of the legislative bodies are in the Senate and Assembly *Journals.* Reports and other documents are published in *New York Senate* (and *Assembly*) *Documents.* There is no record of debates in either chamber; but Mr. White's speech in the Senate on the Cornell University bill was published in the Albany *Journal,* 1865, and separately: *Speech of Hon. Andrew D. White in Senate, March, 1865.* It is No. 3 in a bound collection of pamphlets in the University Library labeled: "White. Addresses and Essays, 1863–81." Something of what went on behind the scenes when the Cornell bill was pending came to light in the debates in the Constitutional Convention: *New York Constitutional Convention, 1867–1868, Proceedings and Debates,* IV, 2821; V,

Bibliography

2820. Many documents relating to the State Agricultural College, and relevant to the founding of Cornell University, are in the annually published *State Agricultural Society Transactions*.

For the management of the land scrip and the lands acquired by it, an excellent concise account is S. D. Halliday, *History of the Agricultural College Land Grant Act*. Ithaca, N. Y., 1905. But the indispensable work on this subject is Paul Gates, *The Wisconsin Pine Lands of Cornell University: A Study in Land Policy and Absentee Ownership*. Cornell University Press, 1943. For this study Professor Gates has used much unpublished material. The published documents relating to it are in: (1) *Laws and Documents Relating to Cornell University* (which includes the relevant extracts from the State Comptroller's Reports); (2) *The People ex rel. Cornell University v. Davenport, Comptroller* (117 N. Y. 549); (3) *Woodward, W. A., v. Ezra Cornell*, 1871, 2 vols. (suit to recover money for services to Mr. Cornell in locating public lands in Wisconsin); (4) *New York Senate Documents*, 1874, Nos. 92, 93, 103 (evidence and majority and minority reports of the investigation made, at Mr. Cornell's request, into the management of the scrip and the lands). The evidence taken in the Woodward case, and in the Senate investigation, gives much information on other aspects of the founding of the university.

The minutes of the Board of Trustees are in *Proceedings of the Board of Trustees of Cornell University, Including the Minutes of the Executive Committee*, April 1865—July 1885. Ithaca, N. Y., 1940. Reports of committees to the board for the years 1865 to 1868 have not, with one exception, been published. The most important one was published at the time: *Report of the Committee on Organization, presented to the Trustees of Cornell University, October 21, 1866* [according to the *Proceedings* of the Board, this should be November 21]. Albany, 1867. It is in the bound volume of pamphlets: "White: Addresses and Essays, 1863-81."

Of great value is the large collection of pamphlets in the university library. The most important of these are in bound volumes labeled: "Cornell University Pamphlets," Vols. I–III; "White. Addresses and Essays, 1863-81"; "Public Papers and Addresses, Andrew D. White." The last mentioned contains a valuable pamphlet which I have not found elsewhere: *The Cornell University*, pp. 12. It has neither date nor the name of the author; but it was undoubtedly compiled by Mr. White, in connection with the debate on the Cornell bill in March, 1865 (see Mr. White's speech in the Senate, mentioned above, p. 6). It is important

Bibliography

because it prints the letters to Mr. White from Horace Greeley and three other trustees of the People's College assuring him of their hope that the Cornell bill would pass; and also the resolutions adopted at the important meetings at Albany on January 12 and 24, 1865 (see above, p. 86). The bound volumes of pamphlets also include the first general announcements and circulars sent out by the university in 1867 and 1868; and the *Account of the Proceedings at the Inauguration, October 7, 1868*. The University Press, Ithaca. 1869.

The newspapers most worth consulting are: The Ithaca *Journal;* the Rochester *Democrat,* and *Daily Union and Advertiser;* the New York *Tribune;* the New York *World;* the New York *Evening Post;* the New York *Express;* and the Albany *Journal*. For conditions at the university during the first year, *The Cornell Era,* Vol. I., (a student publication) is useful. Especially useful is *The Cornell Era, Ezra Cornell Centennial Number* (May, 1907), which contains much interesting, if fragmentary, information in the form of personal recollections of Mr. Cornell and the beginnings of the university. Of similar value is *Proceedings and Addresses at the Twenty-Fifth Anniversary of the Opening of Cornell University*. Ithaca, N. Y. 1893. A classified list of all officers, members of the faculty, and students of the university from 1866 to 1888 is in *The Ten-Year Book of Cornell University*. Ithaca, N. Y. 1888. Unfortunately, the work is marred by numerous errors.

There are two histories of the university. (1) *Cornell University: An Historical Sketch of its first Thirty Years, 1868–1898*. By Ernest W. Huffcut, Professor of Law in Cornell University. (Published as one of the studies in Sidney Sherwood's *History of Higher Education in the State of New York*. Washington, 1900, pp. 318–425). (2) *Cornell University, A History*. By Waterman Thomas Hewett, Professor of German Language and Literature. New York, 1905; 4 vols. What amounts to a history of the beginnings and early years of the university is the account given by Mr. White in his Autobiography, I. Very useful also is the recent work by Walter P. Rogers, *Andrew D. White and the Modern University*. Cornell University Press, 1942.

There is no life of Mr. White except his *Autobiography of Andrew D. White*. New York, 1905; 2 vols. This is of course of the highest value for a knowledge of Mr. White and the founding of the university; but since there are some things that no man knows about himself, there is need of a critical and interpretative study of this extraordinary man, who probably had a greater influence on the history of higher education in the United States in the nineteenth century than any one else. There

213

Bibliography

are two lives of Ezra Cornell. *Biography of Ezra Cornell, founder of the Cornell University. A filial Tribute.* New York, 1884. This is by his son, Alonzo Cornell. It is especially valuable for the account, based on family papers and oral tradition, of Mr. Cornell's ancestry and early life. It suffers, however, from being a "filial tribute" in the most correct and conventional sense. Alonzo refers to his father throughout as "Mr. Cornell," as to a man for whom he had the highest respect but did not personally know, and Mr. Cornell emerges as a stiff image of perfection rather than as a vivid human being. The most serious defect of the book is in conveying the impression, without explicitly stating it as a fact, that Mr. Cornell took the leading part in forming the Western Union Telegraph Company; which is demonstrably not true, and which Alonzo must have known, from the letters and papers in his possession, including his own correspondence with his father, was not true. This mistake is repeated in Professor Albert W. Smith's *Ezra Cornell, A Character Study.* Ithaca, N. Y., 1934. This work is also a bit too laudatory, but is nevertheless of considerable value, being based on hitherto unpublished letters and other documents, some of which are printed at length in the book. There is need of a critical and interpretative life of Ezra Cornell, a man of sufficient stature to gain rather than to lose by having his foibles and limitations as well as his virtues presented, his rare distinction being after all that he had more talent for founding useful institutions than he had for making the fortune with which to found them. The recollections of Mr. Cornell's daughter, Mary Emily, are given in the small book, *Autobiography of Mary Emily Cornell.* Ithaca, N. Y., 1929. Valuable for the recollections, and also because it contains the long autobiographical letter from Mr. Cornell to Miss Rebecca Chase, which is not elsewhere published. Many letters and documents relating to Mr. Cornell's connection with the telegraph business are in the printed arguments of counsel in the case of "Francis O. J. Smith against Ezra Cornell in the Supreme Court before Judge L. Birdseye, July, 1871" (cited as *Smith v. Cornell*); and in the affidavit of Amos Kendall in the case of "Samuel F. B. Morse and Alfred Vail against Francis O. J. Smith in the Superior Court of the City of New York." New York, 1852.

The most useful maps of Ithaca for the period of the founding of the university are: *Map of the Corporation of Ithaca.* 1868; *New Topographical Atlas of Tompkins County.* 1866; *Birdseye View of Ithaca.* 1873. These are all in the De Witt Historical Society.

Bibliography

The following works I have found especially useful in preparing the first two lectures:

E. P. Cheyney, *History of the University of Pennsylvania, 1740–1940.* Philadelphia, 1940.

E. G. Dexter, *History of Education in the United States.* New York, 1904.

Paul Gates, "Western Opposition to the Agricultural College Act," *Indiana Magazine of History,* XXXII. (This is now incorporated in his *The Wisconsin Pine Lands of Cornell University.* Ithaca, 1943.)

S. E. Morison, *Three Centuries of Harvard.* Cambridge, Mass., 1937.

B. E. Powell, *Semi-Centennial History of the University of Illinois,* Vol. I. Urbana, 1918.

J. D. Reid, *The Telegraph in America.* New York, 1879.

E. D. Ross, "The Father of the Land Grant College," *Agricultural History,* XII.

L. F. Snow, *The College Curriculum in the United States.* New York, 1907.

REFERENCES AND NOTES

REFERENCES AND NOTES

LECTURE I (pages 3–22)

1. Preserved Smith, *History of Modern Culture*, 326 ff.
2. Report of the Board of Trade, 1671, in Hening, *Statutes*, II, 517. Quoted in Channing, *History of the United States*, II, 83.
3. William Bradford, *History of Plymouth Plantation* (Boston, 1898), 476–77.
4. E. G. Dexter, *History of Education in the United States*, 584.
5. *Ibid.*, 590–93.
6. "Advertisement," May 31, 1754; printed in the *New York Gazette*; given in full in L. F. Snow, *The College Curriculum in the United States*, 56.
7. *Works of John Adams*, II, 5–6.
8. John Adams to James Warren, July 17, 1774; *Warren-Adams Letters*, I, 29.
9. E. Edwards Beardsley, *Life and Correspondence of Samuel Johnson*, 6. In his Autobiography, Johnson says: "They heard indeed in 1714, when he [Johnson] took his Bachelor's Degree of a new philosophy that of late was all in vogue and of such names as Descartes, Boyle, Locke, and Newton, but they were cautioned against thinking anything of them because the new philosophy, it was said, would soon bring in a new divinity and corrupt the pure religion of the country, and they were not allowed to vary an ace in their thoughts from Dr. Ames' *Medulla Theologiae* and *Cases of Conscience* and Wollebius." In spite of cautions, "accidentally lighting on Lord Bacon's *Instauratio Magna*, or *Advancement of Learning* (perhaps the only copy in the country, and nobody knew its value), he immediately bought it and greedily fell to studying it." And "about this time, 1714, when he was turned of 18, came over from England a well-chosen library of new books collected by Mr. Dummer, agent for the colony. He had then all at once the vast pleasure of reading the works of our best English poets, philosophers, and divines . . . and . . . Boyle and Newton, etc. . . . All this was like a flood of day to his low state of mind." Quoted in Herbert and Carol Schneider, *Samuel Johnson, President of King's College, His Career and Writings*, II, 5–6.
10. L. F. Snow, *The College Curriculum*, 57.
11. *Ibid.*, 58, 93.
12. *Writings of Benjamin Franklin* (Smyth ed.), II, 386.
13. The ideas of William Smith were expressed in a pamphlet, written by him and published in New York in 1754 in connection with the establishment of King's College, entitled "Idea of the College of Mirania." "With regard to learning, the *Miranians* divide the whole body of the people into two grand classes. The first consists of those designed for the learned professions, by which they understand divinity, law, physic and the chief offices of the state. The second class consists of those designed for the mechanic professions, and all the remaining people of the country. Any scheme, that either proposes to teach both of these grand classes after

References and Notes

the same manner, or is wholly calculated for one of them, without regard to the other, must be very defective." To avoid this the *Miranians* provided a College of Arts for the first class, and for the second a Mechanics School, in no way connected with the College except that it was supervised by the same trustees. The pamphlet is quoted at length in L. F. Snow, *The College Curriculum,* 60–61.

14. *Ibid.,* 69.

15. Jefferson, Notes on Virginia: *Writings Of Thomas Jefferson* (P. L. Ford ed.), III, 256; L. F. Snow, *The College Curriculum,* 74.

16. *Three Centuries of Harvard,* 75, 79.

17. "When he wanted to study German he was obliged to seek a text book in one place, a dictionary in a second, and a grammar in a third." *Life, Letters and Journals of George Ticknor,* I, 25.

18. President Stiles' interests and practices are to be learned from his famous *Diary;* quoted at considerable length in Snow, *The College Curriculum,* 80–81.

19. C. E. Cunningham, *Timothy Dwight,* is the most recent and best life of Dwight. For his work at Yale see Chapters VII–IX.

20. W. T. Tucker, *My Generation,* 50; quoted in W. P. Rogers, *Andrew D. White and the Modern University,* 34. A friendly but judicious estimate of the instruction in Yale in the middle nineteenth century is given by Timothy Dwight, who was both a student and a professor in that college: "We translated the passage assigned to us. We answered, according to our ability, the mathematical or other questions that were put to us. . . . It was useful work. It was work that had a tendency to strengthen our minds. It had its bearing on the future. But it was not very stimulating, or calculated greatly to awaken enthusiasm. It limited itself to the means, if I may so say, instead of reaching out to the end." *Memories of Yale Life and Men,* 22.

21. *Ibid.,* 8, 256. Professor Taylor's "brother" Gibbs was, according to Timothy Dwight, one of the real scholars in Yale at that time—one "who gave the work of his life time to studies in which absolute fairness, as well as honesty, is the governing law, and within the sphere of which the student is led by a sense of duty . . . to look calmly and faithfully at all the possibilities of interpretation."

22. Allan Nevins, *Emergence of Modern America,* 264–65. For Silliman's laboratory, C. F. Thwing, *History of Higher Education in America,* 301; C. E. Cunningham, *Timothy Dwight,* 203–4.

23. *Reports on the Course of Instruction in Yale College,* by a Committee of the Corporation and the Academic Faculty. New Haven, 1828. The report was a defense against the charge "that our colleges must be 'new-modeled'; that they are not adapted to the spirit and wants of the age; that they will soon be deserted unless they are better accommodated to the business character of the nation." The defense was divided into two parts, one of which dealt with the nature of a liberal education, the other defending the ancient languages as the best means of attaining such an education. The report was an able defense of the existing system, and being printed and widely circulated had a great influence in fortifying the conservative tendencies in other colleges.

24. Among American scholars who were influenced by their experience abroad were George Ticknor, Edward Everett, and George Bancroft in the earlier period, and towards the middle of the century, Andrew D. White. The Amherst Report was, like the Yale Report a year later, inspired by the current criticism—the charge

that in "an age of universal improvement and in a young, free, and prosperous country like ours, it is absurd to cling so tenaciously to the prescriptive forms of other centuries." But, unlike the Yale Report, the Amherst Report recommended a "parallel" course "for that large class of young men who are not destined to enter either [any?] of the learned professions." The recommendation was not adopted. L. F. Snow, *College Curriculum*, 156. Josiah Quincy, in his inaugural address at Harvard in 1829, entitled "The Spirit of the Age," discussed in general terms the spirit and "the wants of the age, and the duty of literary seminaries to keep pace with that spirit and supply those wants." *Ibid.*, 163 ff. Francis Wayland, President of Brown University, favored a more liberal course of study, and in 1850 introduced some pretty radical changes at Brown, which, however, were not permanent. C. F. Thwing, *History of Higher Education in America*, 317.

25. C. R. Fish, *The Rise of the Common Man*, 212, referring to J. R. Commons, *Documentary History of American Industrial Society*, V, 99.

LECTURE II (pages 23–42)

1. E. D. Ross, "The Father of the Land Grant College," *Agricultural History*, XII, 170. This article, pp. 151 ff., gives a brief and judicious account of the history of the controversy over the origin of the Morrill Act.

2. The claims of J. B. Turner as the originator of the Morrill Act are ably presented, with references to, and quotations from, many documents, in B. E. Powell, *Semi-Centennial History of the University of Illinois*, Vol. I. The discussion in this lecture is based largely on this account and the article by Ross cited above.

3. J. B. Angell to A. D. White, June 1, 1869; *White Papers*, Steel File, A.

4. B. E. Powell, *University of Illinois*, I, 16 ff.

5. *Ibid.*, 53.

6. "If some of the old states would take hold of the matter, I think it not unlikely that a grant of lands might be obtained from Congress; but coming from the new states, which have already received such large grants for schools and other purposes, it would be likely to meet with less favor." Lyman Trumbull to J. B. Turner, Oct. 19, 1857; *ibid.*, 93.

7. "Dear sir: I am delighted to find your fire, by the letter of the 15 inst. had not all burned out. I presume I recognize Prof. Turner, an old pioneer in the cause of Agricultural education. I have only to say that amid the fire and smoke and embers, I have faith that I shall get my bill into law at this session. I thank you for your continued interest, and am, Very sincerely yours, Justin S. Morrill." Morrill to J. B. Turner, Dec. 30, 1861; *ibid.*, 97. The claim that Turner asked Morrill to introduce his bill rests upon the statement of his daughter, Mrs. Mary Carriel, *Life of Turner*, 159; and of J. R. Reasoner, of Urbana, who told Professor Powell that Turner had told him that "he had taken the matter of having the bill introduced in Congress to Mr. Morrill." *Ibid.*, 95. In February, 1863, Turner wrote to John Kennicott recalling the fact that he and Kennicott and a few others had done much to "get the thing started" and then to guide "the thing through so many years to the first successful notice in Congress and its final passage by that body." *Ibid.*, 99.

8. *Ibid.*, 97.

9. Paul Gates, "Western Opposition to the Agricultural College Act," *Indiana*

References and Notes

Magazine of History, XXXVII, 116. This article is an admirable account of the genesis of the Morrill Act and of the influences for and against it in Congress and throughout the country. The discussion in this lecture is based largely upon this article.

10. *Ibid.*, 12, 124.

11. *Public Laws of the United States*, 1862, Ch. 130. *Laws and Documents Relating to Cornell University*, 1.

12. Paul Gates, *Indiana Magazine of History*, XXXVII, 118.

13. *Ibid.*, 110–111.

14. E. D. Ross, *Agricultural History*, XII, 176–178.

15. Paul Gates, *Indiana Magazine of History*, XXXVII, 130.

16. According to President Angell, the income of the University of Michigan from all sources in 1867 was $76,225. "I may add that at the end of the current year, although our income is $90,000, we shall have to face a deficit of nearly $14,000." J. B. Angell to A. D. White, Oct. 30, 1872; *White Papers*, Steel File, A. "For 1871–72 our [Institute of Technology] income from all sources was about $60,000." J. D. Runkl [?] to A. D. White, Oct. 24, 1872; *ibid.*, R.

17. Paul Gates, *Indiana Magazine of History*, XXXVII, 129, 130.

18. In most accounts May 5, 1863, is given as the date on which New York formally accepted the Morrill Act, and from this it is sometimes assumed that New York delayed its acceptance for nearly a year. This is not correct. The Morrill Act was passed on July 2, 1862. The New York legislature did not meet until January 1, 1863, and on March 4, that is to say, at the first opportunity after the Morrill Act was passed, it declared its acceptance of the act. *Laws of New York*, 1863, Ch. 20. This act contained nothing except the brief statement: "The State of New York, by its Legislature, hereby declares its acceptance of the provisions of an act passed by the Congress of the United States, entitled: An act donating public lands to the several states and territories," etc. The act of May 5 authorized the Comptroller to receive the scrip, and defined in some detail the conditions under which it should be sold. *Ibid.*, Ch. 460. Both of these laws are printed in *Laws and Documents Relating to Cornell University* (edition of 1892), 4–5. The second edition of this work, 1883, contains the act of May 5, but not the other.

19. W. C. Russel, a member of the first faculty of Cornell University, says that there were some who advocated the establishment of five new colleges, to be located in the northern, eastern, southern, western, and central parts of the state. *Sketch of the Beginning of Cornell University, Russel MS*, Cornell University Library, MSS+ Kc 26.

LECTURE III (pages 43–65)

1. What is known about the immediate ancestry and early life of Ezra Cornell is to be found in the *Biography of Ezra Cornell* by his son Alonzo. The account is based on family papers, one of which is a long letter from Ezra, dated Albion, Michigan, December 15, 1855, to his grandniece Miss Rebecca Chase in reply to a request for details about his early life. The letter is printed in the *Autobiography of Mary Emily Cornell*, 5–32. A copy is in Ezra Cornell's *Memorandum Book*, under date of October, 1860. For the genealogy of this branch of the Cornell

References and Notes

family in America, see John Cornell, *Genealogy of the Cornell Family,* New York, 1902.

2. See above, Documents, No. 14.

3. The picture is reproduced in A. W. Smith, *Ezra Cornell,* 26.

4. *Cornell Papers,* Cardboard Box. Bundle marked "Beginning work with Otis Eddy."

5. *New York Senate Documents,* 1874, No. 103, p. 253. "He was never surprised or troubled by anything which any other human being believed or did not believe." A. D. White, *Autobiography,* I, 329.

6. *Cornell Papers,* Memorandum Book, II, Feb. 1, 1861. In a letter to his brother, E. B. Cornell, Nov. 5, 1845, he says: "The first instance I went through with the shaft 15 feet wide and 10 feet high and good seam on the bottom to work on. I recollect that I was six months exactly in carrying this shaft through. The next season we cut it five feet deeper." *Ibid.,* MSS+ Kc 8.

Mr. Beebe appears to have found Ezra indispensable. "Now if you will give your whole attention to my affairs till 1 May, 1836, I will pay you at the rate of $500 per annum from 1 August next." J. S. Beebe to Ezra Cornell, July 21, 1834. *Cornell Papers,* De Witt Historical Society, box marked "Early Railroads." The only indication I have found that Ezra's management was unsatisfactory to Mr. Beebe is the following: "There is so much trouble about your *weighing* that I am discouraged, and have almost concluded not to buy any more wheat and sell the mill. If it was only a few instances when they complained, I could get along with it—say 100 instances—but when it is a continual string of complaints for years, and I cannot get the evil remedied, I do not know any other way to get along but to stop altogether. . . . You know that my wish is to do justice to all, and . . . that I have some *pride* of *reputation,* and if you will not protect it at Fall Creek I will not consent to put it longer in your keeping." J. S. Beebe to E. C., May 26, 1838. *Ibid.,* Cardboard Box.

7. *Hull Papers,* referring to Ithaca *Journal,* Aug. 17, 1836; Ithaca *Chronicle,* Sept. 21, Oct. 12, 1836, May 13, 1837.

8. No doubt building a new mill at the time of the panic had much to do with the failure. There appears to have been some question about completing the mill. "I think you had better go on with the mill as fast as you can with economy." J. S. Beebe to E. C., March 28, 1838. *Cornell Papers,* Cardboard Box. "I need all that can be saved in every way to pay debts. I hope and trust that Mr. Cornell and Mr. Tillotson will settle up the whole Fall Creek accounts in a careful and thorough manner, including Mr. Cornell's account, and they must get along with as little money as possible till I return." A list of directions dated March 23, 1838. *Ibid.* The business was disposed of in 1841. "I took down McElroy and showed him all about it. . . . I settled all questions of title. I have placed the property in the best possible shape to be controlled, and but for losses I should keep it. . . . I have no wish to conceal that my . . . only reason for offering the property this way is that I cannot afford to keep it." J. S. Beebe to E. C., Feb. 15, 1841. *Ibid.*

9. "Adopt that as a rule for life; always carry the book in your pocket, and don't depart from the rule which should be added to the load of the Golden Rule." A. W. Smith, *Ezra Cornell,* 57, 58.

10. These are small books about 4 x 6 inches. Some of them are in the nature of daily memorandum books rather than expense account books; and certainly

none of them contains a full account of every cent spent for the time covered. *Cornell Papers.*

11. See above, Documents, No. 14.

12. The letter to his father and other documents referred to are in *Cornell Papers,* Memorandum Book, III. For the letter to his father, see above, Documents, No. 1. There is ample evidence that Ezra had many irons in the fire. In 1835 he looked over two farms three miles south of Ithaca. "I don't know but I shall buy one of these if I can make the money arrangements." E. C. to Elijah Cornell, Nov. 22, 1835. *Ibid.,* Cardboard Box. "I have to borrow $1,500 this spring to meet my engagements, and I consider myself very fortunate to be able to do it in the present state of the money market. . . . My three lots at Fall Creek that cost me $3,400 are now worth $6,000. . . . The $1,500 that I am about to borrow will pay all my debts." E. C. to Elijah Cornell, May 15, 1836. *Ibid.* The debt was partly contracted by the purchase in 1834 of "the large house and lot that lays between Barnaby's house on the corner and the grocery. I gave 513 and I intend to repair it . . . and put a shed and barn on it and put Elijah B in it to see if he has a faculty of serving the public." E. C. to Elijah Cornell, March, 1834. *Ibid.* When Mr. Beebe sold his property the mill was transformed into a woolen mill, in which enterprise Ezra subscribed for four shares of stock. Receipt dated Jan. 21, 1843. *Ibid.,* Gray-blue Box. He evidently continued to run Mr. Beebe's farm, since Mr. Beebe acknowledges having received "of Ezra Cornell Speed and Co. wheat receipts for three hundred bushels of wheat on account of rent for Fall Creek farm for 1841." *Ibid.* Letters of recommendation for his trip east, and documents concerning the "double mole-board plow" are also in the Gray-blue Box.

13. The first trip to Maine was probably late in 1841, or at least early in January, 1842. He was then apparently trying to interest farmers in the plow, although he had not yet acquired the rights to it himself. E. C. to F. O. J. Smith, January, 1842. *Cornell Papers,* Memorandum Book, I. On Jan. 21, 1843, Mr. Beebe wrote to the Hon. N. P. Talmadge at Washington recommending Ezra, "who is on his way to Georgia to introduce a very valuable improved patent plough." *Ibid.* "I travelled through some of the interior counties of Georgia during . . . April and May last." E. C. to person not named, Oct. 12, 1843. *Ibid.,* Cardboard Box.

14. E. L. Stuvins to E. C., July 19, 1842; Aug. 28, Oct. 8, 1843. *Ibid.* For statement of Otis E. Wood, see above, Documents, No. 14.

15. *Hull Papers,* Bartlett MS, 5–6.

16. *Cornell Papers,* Prime Letters. In one of these letters Ezra gives a detailed account of the efforts to devise a better method of insulation. He professes to have been ignored by Morse and Vail, and to have known before they did that their methods would not work. He says also that the famous message "What hath God wrought?" was by no means the first one sent, if indeed it ever was sent. He at least never heard of it until many years later. The contract by which he became Morse's assistant, signed Dec. 27, 1843, is in *Cornell Papers.*

17. E. C. to Mary Ann, Oct. 29, 1843. *Cornell Papers,* Gray-blue Box. The letter to Mr. Beebe was probably written Jan. 26, 1845. There is a fragment of a letter of that date relating to the settlement of accounts, and it is in his reply to this letter that Mr. Beebe congratulates him on his prospect of being a wealthy man. J. S. Beebe to E. C., Feb. 25, 1845. *Ibid.*

Mary Ann had more than a little to worry about during the next ten years.

Ezra was so infrequently in Ithaca that it is said that one of the children, coming down to breakfast one morning and finding him there, asked: "Father, where do you live when you are at home." *Autobiography of Mary Emily Cornell*, 3. Mary Ann complained very little, but on one occasion she wrote: "I sincerely hope that you will finally succeed in getting together enough of this world's goods so that you can finally make up your mind to settle down. . . . My dear, little do you know how many lonely hours I have passed in your twelve years absence from home, the cares and anxieties of home all resting on me. . . . You may not wonder that my hair has grown gray in those twelve years." Mary Ann to E. C., March 19, 1854. *Cornell Papers*, De Witt Historical Society, Family Letters.

18. A clear, brief account of the early history of the principal telegraph companies in the United States is in J. D. Reid, *The Telegraph in America*. Reid was himself prominently connected with the telegraph business in the early years, and must have had access to many official records, although he gives no references and no bibliography. The agreement between Smith and Kendall is dated June 27, 1847. *Smith v. Cornell*, 10.

19. *Hull Papers;* Chronology, February, 1845. *Smith v. Cornell*, 128.

20. *Hull Papers;* Chronology, February, 1846, referring to the Morse Papers, XXI.

21. Sept. 28, 1847. *Smith v. Cornell*, 119.

22. The contract is in *Smith v. Cornell*, 12.

23. A. W. Smith, *Ezra Cornell*, 62. Other letters to Alonzo are here printed, 52 ff. The originals are in *Cornell Papers*. Copies of some of them are in *Hull Papers*. Cornell told Speed that he was willing to hazard all of his money, and advise all of his friends to do the same, in the New York and Erie. "It is my honest conviction that if I live to be the age of either of our fathers . . . I shall see this line of telegraph that we are now engaged in erecting, become the channel through which England, proud and haughty England, will transmit her orders to her possessions in the East. . . . Remember my motto is, *go ahead*." E. C. to J. J. Speed, Sept. 12, 1847. *Smith v. Cornell*, 134

24. E. C. to Amos Kendall, Sept. 16, 1851. See above, Documents, No. 2.

25. J. D. Reid, *The Telegraph in America*, 293. "The N. Y. and E. line has been sold today without reserve, and I have bid it off at $7,000, which will be enough to pay the debts of the Company. I had tried all sorts of schemes to get up an organization among the stockholders, creditors, etc., etc., to no purpose. As a last resort, I got the Ithaca stockholders together last evening, which resulted in one of our old fashioned stormy times—at about 11 P.M. we adjourned to the Clinton House this morning, and kept up the strife till 2 P.M. in the most boistrous style, until the very moment that the sale commenced, . . . and the line was started at $1,000, which I bid up to $1,200, and I thought several times it would be knocked down to me at the $1,200—but the stockholders, who were pretty numerous, united in saying to me, that if I would bid enough to pay the debts they would all be satisfied, and would not run it up beyond that sum. Even Sage and Woodruff, who had fought all my plans the fiercest, caved in, and said they were satisfied at the result." E. C. to J. J. Speed, Jan. 15, 1852. *Smith v. Cornell*, 92. An account is also in Mr. Cornell, *Journal*, Jan. 15, 1852.

26. J. H. Wade to E. C., Nov. 27, 1853 (see above, Documents, No. 3.)

27. A. W. Smith, *Ezra Cornell*, 79.

28. J. D. Reid, *The Telegraph in America*, 455 ff. Among the able men associ-

ated with Sibley and Selden were Isaac Ellwood, Isaac Butts, and Anton Stager. Letters from Mr. Cornell's operators and associates during 1853–55 (De Witt Hist. Soc., box marked "Telegraph Letters") present a melancholy picture of the poverty and inefficiency of the Cornell lines during these years. "I am obliged to get very near everything I get for the office on credit" (J. W. Carpenter, July 23, 1853). "No telling how long they hang on the hook at St. Louis before they were sent by mail. That is what we have to do when the line is down—send them by mail" (A. Haas, March 20, 1854). "Methinks I would have a sorry thing of it to get only $10 per month and receipts which in seven months have amounted to but [little] more than $50 with expences deducted. I agreed to no such thing" (E. W. Brownell, Oct. 17, 1854). "Mr. Dionell . . . wants his rent certain by Saturday next without fail. The balance due is $10" (C. C. Dickey, Aug. 31, 1854). "I will make you this proposition. I will take the office and keep it for the receipts. You paying the expences of the office and keeping up the line. This you will have to do anyhow. Also $18 a year rent. The wire in this part of the country is being destroyed very rapidly" (C. D. Morgan, Sept. 1, 1854). "Your line has been down between Chi. and here twelve days and good prospect for its remaining so" (C. Sellars, Jan. 1, 1854). "It is hard for a young man to work for $25 per month and then have to wait several months for it" (J. F. Saunders, Jan. 10, 1854). J. Kennan, in reply to a request for an inventory of the property of the company, reported that the property in his office consisted of a table, three Windsor chairs, and one high stool—together worth $2.50; and an old fashioned sending instrument, the value of which he could not estimate. He said that nothing had been added to this for five years (Sept. 1, 1854). "I have sold that inkstand for $1.00 as I found our old one, and inclose the price as the simplest way to balance the account" (C. H. Haskins, June 9, 1854).

Letters from President Faxton, George Curtis, and other officials of the New York, Albany and Buffalo Company indicate that Mr. Cornell was working with them against the House lines. Besides obtaining aid from the company in acquiring control of the Michigan Southern, an agreement was made between the Erie and Michigan and the New York, Albany and Buffalo to unite in paying the expenses of running the New York and Erie (reorganized as the New York and Western Union). *Cornell Papers,* Box marked Telegraph.

Mr. Cornell's efforts at consolidation were all directed against the House lines. On November 30, 1852 he, Speed, and Wade signed an agreement with Henry O'Reilly and Fog Smith to "unite in good faith in bringing about a consolidation of telegraph lines now existing" west of Buffalo on certain terms. *Ibid.* A circular, dated Cincinnati, June 27, 1854, and headed "Grand Combination of Interests," states that "various representatives from telegraph companies built under the Morse patent" were present at the National Telegraph office, Cincinnati, and discussed measures for "promoting increased harmony and cooperation among various Morse companies." Mr. Cornell was elected chairman and J. D. Reid secretary; and the meeting adopted a resolution to the effect that the companies represented would "work together for our mutual prosperity." Eighteen companies are listed, among them the New York, Albany and Buffalo. *Ibid.*

29. The essential facts of the consolidation are given in J. D. Reid, *The Telegraph in America,* 280 ff. The desertion of Speed, Wade, Haviland, and Cobb—all prominent officials at one time or another in the Erie and Michigan—was probably

what convinced Mr. Cornell that the game was up. "According to Col. Speed's version of the transaction, . . . to avert bankruptcy, . . . Col. Speed and Mr. Wade, against Mr. Cornell's emphatic protest, voted to combine their stock with the stock of the competing companies." *Initial Ithacans,* 54. "I have just heard that Col. Speed has sold his interest in the E and M line and Co. I suppose it is so— sold to House folks. Well it aint quite as I would like to have it. . . . Still as I understand it you own a majority of the stock and I am glad of it." C. M. Heaton to E. C., May 20, 1854. *Cornell Papers,* De Witt Hist. Soc., Telegraph Letters. "I had heard of the sale of Speed and Wade's interest to House Co; but had supposed it was with your full knowledge and approval. In Speed's action towards you I am dumbfounded." W. P. Pew to E. C., May 30, 1854. *Ibid.* Cornell protested to Ellwood that the House company was "seducing" his employees. Ellwood replied, "It is true that Messrs Haviland and Cobb have made arrangements to enter the employ of our Co," but said that it was not the result of "any improper inducements." *Ibid.*

According to Reid (p. 280), the offer of consolidation was made "early in . . . 1855." On June 15, 1855, Isaac Butts wrote to Cornell: "I suggested a specific plan for purchasing all your interest in your main competing line and for terminating competition in the west. . . . You decline considering that project and give nothing but vague generalities in reply. . . . If you really desire union you . . . should . . . make some definite proposal. Of our ultimately swallowing up all other lines in the west I entertain no doubt whatever. Our interest . . . must prevail and you must be worse off in the end than you are now. Please look over my former letter and write me more to the point." June 15, 1855. *Cornell Papers;* De Witt Hist. Soc., Telegraph Letters. A little later Cornell drew up a statement showing that the proposed offer would result in a gain for the House companies of $21,000 per annum, and a loss for the Erie and Michigan of $1,000. He then shows what the result would be "if my modification is accepted," and says that if it is accepted "the E and M stockholders might submit to the unjust basis of consolidation that they have assented to by a vote at the stockholders' meeting." The statement has no date, but compares earnings up to Aug. 1, 1855. *Cornell Papers,* Telegraph Box.

The controversy was further complicated by the uncertainty as to patent rights. On June 20, 1853, Speed obtained from Morse and Kendall the Morse patent rights for all unbuilt-on territory in the Northwest, with the assent, presumably, of Fog Smith. *Ibid.* He seems to have disposed of those rights to the House companies without Cornell's knowledge, and contrary to the terms of the agreement with Morse and Kendall. The latter, at all events, protested to Cornell, and said that Cornell, as one of the "guarantors," would be held responsible. Kendall to Cornell, May 7, 1854. *Ibid.,* De Witt Hist. Soc., Telegraph Letters. Shortly after this a printed advertisement, signed by Sibley and others, announced that the House lines had acquired by purchase control of "all patents" for the northwestern states, and "of all lines known as Speed and Wade lines." In reply Cornell issued a printed circular, June 22, 1854, stating that the claim "is false in many particulars," since it is based upon "a pretended purchase of the [patent] right from J. J. Speed . . . my former partner . . . without my knowledge or consent . . . with full knowledge on the part of the House Company . . . that I would not, if consulted, have parted with my interest in the patent." *Cornell Papers,* Telegraph Box. The purchase from Speed, justified or not, enabled the House company to devise the following letterheads, which they were using as late as December, 1854: "Union Telegraph Consolidation of the House, Morse, O'Reilly and Wade Lines: under the control of The New York and Mississippi Valley Printing Telegraph Company." *Ibid.* De Witt Hist. Soc., Telegraph Letters. At that time the House Company had 300,000 shares of stock in the Erie and Michigan; and J. R. Ellwood notified Mr. Cornell that the draft of Speed for the dividend on that stock would be accepted provided the Erie and Michigan made a dividend of five per cent, and provided the draft was guaranteed by J. H. Wade. *Ibid.*

Since Cornell had enlisted the aid of the New York, Albany and Buffalo against the House lines, the officials of that company were surprised and annoyed to learn that he had gone over to the enemy. "When will marvels cease? I have this moment learnt that you are hovering about Rochester . . . and becoming the mouth piece of the same parties that had the rope around your neck not 30 days since, and but for the assistance you got from the 'Morse Co.' would have hung you higher than Haman wanted the Jew." F. S. Faxton (President of the New York, Albany and Buffalo Company) to E. C., May 26, 1855. *Ibid.* Edward Chapman, Secretary of the Board, expressed the same surprise in a letter of the same date. Both men expressed the belief that the New York, Albany and Buffalo would not, as Cornell had evidently suggested, go into the union.

30. A. W. Smith, *Ezra Cornell,* 85.

31. See above, Documents, No. 5.

32. E. C. to Alonzo, Feb. 1, 1846. A. W. Smith, *Ezra Cornell,* 54.

33. Report of the Comptroller on the Agricultural College. New York *Senate Documents,* 1865, No. 39. A brief account of the history of the college is in W. T. Hewett, *Cornell University,* I, 55. There is much interesting material in the *Folwell* and *Brewer MSS* in the Cornell University Library, MSS+ Kc 258. For Ezra Cornell's interest in the college there is material in *Cornell Papers,* De Witt Hist. Soc., Early Railroads and Lithographs. Ezra Cornell's son, Benjamin, entered the college in December, 1860. He wrote to his grandfather that the college was intended to "give a student a good thorough education in English language and chemistry and also in other branches too numerous to mention, with a practical knowledge of agriculture." Dec. 15, 1860. *Ibid.* In October 1861 he went back to Ovid, but returned with the report that the trustees had "decided not to open the College for the winter," but thought of opening it as "a military school." *Cornell Papers,* Memorandum Book, II, Oct. 26, 1861.

34. "Some wished the amount equally divided among all the existing colleges of the state, others that it should be divided into five parts to form five institutions, one at the center, one in the Northern, one in the Southern, one in the Eastern, and one in the Western part of the state." W. C. Russel, *Sketch of the Beginning of Cornell University* (MS). Cornell University Library, catalogued as MSS+ Kc 26.

35. *Laws of New York,* 1863, Ch. 511. In *Laws and Documents Relating to Cornell University,* p. 7. For the history of the People's College: W. T. Hewett, *Cornell University,* I, 39; *Cornell University Pamphlets,* III, No. 2; *Folwell* and *Brewer MSS* in Cornell University Library, MSS+ Kc 258.

36. *Laws and Documents Relating to Cornell University,* 7. A further condition, which later gave some basis for the proposal to divide the grant with the Agri-

cultural College, was that "whenever the proceeds of the investment . . . shall be in excess of the needs of the said college, the Regents of the University, who shall have power to determine the amount of such excess, shall notify the Comptroller, and he shall thereafter withhold the same from said college."

37. Proceedings of the Regents, July 7, 1865. New York, *Senate Documents*, 1865, No. 45; *Laws and Documents Relating to Cornell University*, 32.

38. See below, References and Notes, V, 11.

39. A. D. White, *Autobiography*, I, 102.

LECTURE IV (pages 66–89)

1. Except as otherwise indicated, the account here given of Mr. White is based on his *Autobiography*, and quotations are from that work. Vol. I, Chs. 1, 2, 15–17.

2. *White Papers*, Yale Memorabilia.

3. In his first draft of the autobiography Mr. White says that President Woolsey "consulted a tutor in the college, a classmate of mine, to know whether I was from a religious point of view the right man for the professorship." The tutor, an intimate friend personally, was "rigid" in religion. "Brought up in the Episcopal church, I took no interest in the revivals and prayer meetings which he thought all important. . . . His answer to President Woolsey was unfavorable." *Ibid.*, Collected Writings, I, 4.

4. *The Cornell University: Proceedings at the Inauguration*, 33.

5. For the letter to Smith, see above, Documents, No. 6.

6. In the first draft of his autobiography, Mr. White gives a slightly different account from that in the published work. "On the night previous to our first session the Republican members were called together in private conference. . . . At that meeting I saw for the first time Ezra Cornell. I had never heard of him before save on one occasion when a predecessor of mine in the State Senate, George Geddes, spoke of him to me as a man of noble purpose who had thought of founding a library at Ithaca. . . . My attention was first drawn to him when there was taken up in my committee a bill introduced by him to incorporate a public library . . . in Ithaca." *White Papers*, Collected Writings, I, 14.

7. Senator Folger to Ezra Cornell, Jan. 11, 1864. *Cornell Papers*, Cardboard Box. *Senate Journal*, 1864, 41.

8. Mr. Kelly's resolution is in *State Agricultural Society Transactions*, 1863, p. 39; and in the *Senate Journal*, 1864, p. 194. In the first draft of his autobiography Mr. White says that he "prevented any report on his [Mr. Cornell's] bill." *White Papers*, Collected Writings, I, 17.

9. See above, Documents, No. 8.

10. Professor Brewer thought that Mr. Cornell was influenced chiefly by Mr. White, but that Amos Brown, president of the People's College, may have had some influence too. "I met Mr. Brown . . . in 1868. . . . He then told me at considerable length of his own work for Cornell University after the downfall of the People's College: how that he urged upon Mr. Cornell to found a university rather than an Agricultural College, that the idea of the latter was too narrow for eminent educational success." *Brewer MSS*, Sec. IV. This, however, was in

1868, when Mr. Brown was trying to get some "compensation" from Mr. Cornell for his services in getting the Cornell bill through the legislature. See below, References and Notes, VI, 12.

11. Horace Greeley to Amos Brown, Jan. 9, 1865, *Cornell Papers,* Gray-blue Box. The date on the letter is actually 1864, which must have been a mistake—the kind of mistake one is apt to make in dating letters during the first week in January.

12. The resolution is in *White Papers,* Cardboard Letter File. Printed in a pamphlet, undated, prepared undoubtedly by Mr. White, entitled *The Cornell University,* 11. The pamphlet is in a bound volume of pamphlets in the Cornell University Library, entitled, Andrew D. White, *Public Papers and Addresses.* This pamphlet gives the most precise account of the two meetings at Albany, on Jan. 12 and 24. Other accounts are in: New York, *Assembly Documents,* 1865, Vol. X, No. 203, p. 9; *Agricultural Society Transactions,* 1864, p. 671.

13. A. D. White to E. Cornell, July 10, 1865. *Cornell Papers,* Gray-blue Box.

14. Pamphlet cited above (Note 12), p. 12.

15. For the letters to Mr. White, *ibid.* For Mr. Cornell's statement, see above, Documents, No. 11. According to Professor Brewer, Amos Brown "told Mr. Cornell that all effective opposition of both the People's College and the Agricultural College . . . could be killed by naming on the Board to be created for the new institution a few of the most influential trustees from each; that if their names were put in the act of incorporation . . . they would then work for it. He told me that he had furnished Mr. Cornell with a list of men on the two boards, and discussed with him their merits, and advised that Horace Greeley from the People's College and William Kelly from the Agricultural College be named as two of the corporators of the new institution." *Brewer MSS,* Sec. V.

16. See above, Documents, No. 11.

17. First draft of Mr. White's autobiography. *White Papers,* Collected Writings, I, 25.

LECTURE V (pages 90–110)

1. *Senate Journal,* 1865, p. 155.

2. See above, Documents, No. 9.

3. I, 300.

4. Oct. 29, 1895. *White Papers,* Tin Box.

5. Rochester *Democrat,* March 27, 1865. Rochester *Union and Advertiser,* March 30, 1865. Mr. White was probably misled by the fact that later, Oct. 26, 1869, the *Daily Union and Advertiser* published the most scurrilous article that ever appeared against Mr. Cornell. This article, entitled "The Cornell University Land Job," is printed in *Laws and Documents Relating to Cornell University,* 74.

6. "Last summer the Rochester *Democrat* quarrelled with the Western Union Telegraph Company. Its columns, for a time, were reeking with spleen and bitterness. It would seem that the old wound still rankles for we notice lately that it has made a wicked, personal attack upon Mr. Cornell and the institution he seeks to found." Ithaca *Journal,* April 5, 1865.

7. This was the burden of Senator Murphy's speech in the committee of the whole in reply to Mr. White's speech. Ithaca *Journal,* March 22, 1865.

8. See above, Documents, No. 10.

9. First draft of Mr. White's autobiography. *White Papers,* Collected Writings, I, 31.

10. Mr. White mentions, as especially active in supporting his bill, "Senators Cook of Saratoga and Ames of Oswego, . . . Mr. Andrews, Mr. Havens, and, finally, Judge Folger in the Senate, with Mr. Lord and Mr. Weaver in the Assembly." *Autobiography,* I, 302.

11. Mr. Bell, speaking in the Constitutional Convention of 1867–68, said that Mr. Cook entertained strange and conflicting views. "Having assured the committee [of the legislature in 1863 to which the bill to grant the Morrill land grant to the People's College was referred] that the necessary lands, building, etc., . . . would be furnished at Havana without expense to the State, when the committee called his attention to the bill they had drawn . . . he replied, with strong emphasis, that he would do no such thing. Unfortunately during the pending of the bill in the Senate he fell sick, unable to leave his room. While the bill was still under consideration he sent a relative of his, who assured the committee that Mr. Cook would comply with the conditions of our bill. It was therefore reported and became a law." But afterwards "he made use of the expression in my hearing . . . that he would see the committee and the Legislature in—Heaven before he would do it." *Constitutional Convention, 1867–68, Debates,* IV, 2821. Mr. Alvord, speaking in the Convention, said that before and after he became ill Mr. Cook's position was that until the institution was started, and "received the property [land grant] from the State," he would not *give title* to the property as required by the bill. *Ibid.,* 2822. This amounted to a deadlock: the state would not give the land grant until the college met the conditions; Mr. Cook would not enable the college to meet the conditions until the state gave the land grant. Mr. D. S. Dickinson, one of the trustees of the People's College, told Mr. White that "the People's College, so far as Mr. Cook is concerned, is a standing and impenetrable mystery to me. If its history was written in Sanscrit I could read it as well." Letter to A. D. White, Feb. 28, 1865. *The Cornell University,* 9; a pamphlet prepared by Mr. White, in a bound volume of pamphlets, entitled White, *Addresses and Essays.*

12. Professor W. H. Brewer said later: "According to my recollection of what Mr. Cornell told me as well as what Mr. Brown told me, I certainly have the impression that Mr. Brown did very efficient service in getting over this trouble." The trouble referred to was the opposition of Genesee College, which was supported by the Methodist Church, and Brown, although a Presbyterian, had great influence with the Methodists throughout the state. *Brewer MSS* in Cornell University Library, catalogued as MSS+ Kc 258. On April 26, 1865, Amos Brown wrote to Mr. Cornell: "You will, as I predict, have an open sea; I hope a prosperous voyage. My prayer is that heaven will give you and all connected with you in the great work . . . wisdom equal to your own." *Cornell Papers,* Gray-blue Box. Brown may have been looking forward to the presidency of the new institution. See below, References and Notes, VI, 12.

13. The other trustees were Erastus Brooks, D. S. Dickinson, and Edwin B. Morgan. In 1865 Mr. White obtained from all four letters expressing their views. These letters he published in a pamphlet, *The Cornell University,* 7–10; White, *Addresses and Essays.*

References and Notes

14. The speech was published in the Albany *Journal*, and separately as a pamphlet. The pamphlet is in a bound volume of pamphlets: White, *Addresses and Essays*.

15. See above, Documents, No. 10.

16. *Senate Journal*, 1865, p. 438.

17. *Ibid.*, 678, gives the date of the funeral as April 5.

18. *Autobiography*, I, 332–34.

19. *Ibid.*, 302. The New York *World*, March 16, 18, April 5, 1865.

20. *Autobiography*, I, 303.

21. See above, Documents, No. 11. During the official investigation of the Cornell management of the land scrip, Mr. Cornell referred to this document. Asked on the witness stand whether the university had not been devoted to the "perpetuation of an aristocratic institution," he replied: "The only answer that I could suggest would be to furnish the commissioners with a statement I made when that branch of the subject was under discussion before the Legislature. . . . That was a statement of facts in regard to my aristocratic antecedents." New York, *Senate Documents*, 1874, No. 103, p. 38.

22. *Constitutional Convention, 1867–68, Debates*, V, 3796.

23. *Ibid.*, 2820.

24. August 16, 1865.

25. See above, Documents, No. 13.

26. *The Cornell Era*, XXXIX, 372–73.

27. *Assembly Journal*, 1865, p. 1252. For subsequent action on the bill, see pp. 1280, 1288, 1336, 1393, 1586.

28. *Proceedings of the Trustees*, 1865–1866, p. 1.

29. A. D. White to E. Cornell, July 10, 1865. *Cornell Papers*, Gray-blue Box.

30. A. D. White to E. Cornell, July 12, 1865. *Ibid.*

31. *Laws and Documents Relating to Cornell University*, 32.

LECTURE VI (pages 111–136)

1. *Gazetteer and Business Directory of Tompkins County*, 1868, gives the population of the Town of Ithaca in 1865 as 7,264. This work gives much detailed information about Ithaca and its business enterprises. The best maps for the period 1865–68 are in the De Witt Historical Society. *Map of the Corporation of Ithaca*, 1868. *New Topographical Atlas of Tompkins County*, 1866. *Birdseye View of Ithaca*, 1873. The name of Owego Street was changed to State Street in 1867. *Initial Ithacans* (Ithaca, 1904), 109. The Owego Turnpike ran from Aurora Street up South Hill and along what is now the Coddington Road. Owego (or State) Street ended at Aurora; beyond that was the Catskill Turnpike running past Binghamton to the east. The present Stewart Avenue between State Sreet and the Cascadilla gorge was Factory Street. Above it was Quarry Street, and above that Eddy, so named no doubt because it led from the Catskill Turnpike to Mr. Eddy's cotton mill on the site of the present Cascadilla Hall. Cascadilla Hall (then Cascadilla Place) was constructed about 1865 as a water cure. The list of subscribers, headed by Ezra Cornell with a subscription of $2,400, is in the De Witt Historical Society, Box marked "Lithograph." The Clinton House, in

References and Notes

its present form, was built in 1862. Described by a contemporary as "the most imposing and dignified building in all the beautiful place of Ithaca. . . . Not even the elegant Cornell Library edifice is as impressive to the entering traveller." *The Scenery of Ithaca and the Headwaters of the Cayuga Lake* (Ithaca, 1866), 141.

There is some conflict in the evidence as to where Ezra Cornell lived at different times. His daughter, Mary Emily, says: "When my sister was but a few weeks old [this would be in 1842] the family moved from the 'Nook' to a house on South Hill, where we lived for several years. . . . It was with real regret that we moved once more to a house on Seneca Street. . . . When I was about twelve years old [1859] my father bought Forest Park [where] we went to live." *Autobiography of Mary Emily Cornell*, 1–4. Her recollection was in some respects probably at fault. At all events, Alonzo, who was older and more likely to remember correctly, says that the "Nook," built in 1831, "continued to be their home for more than twenty years . . . until 1852, when they removed into the Village of Ithaca, and there resided until 1857. In the latter year Mr. Cornell . . . purchased the 'Forest Park' property. . . . The dwelling house at Forest Park not fully meeting the demands . . . Mr. Cornell determined to erect a new one as a permanent family residence. Pending the construction of this edifice [the present Llenroc] he occupied the large brick dwelling at the corner of Tioga and Seneca Streets. This was his home from the Spring of 1869 until his death." *Ezra Cornell*, 64–67. Andrew D. White says that "at various periods I passed much time with Mr. Cornell in his farm house." This could only mean at Forest Park, and the various periods must have been between 1865 and 1869. "During the summer before the opening of the university . . . through night after night as I lay in the room next to his at his farm house." *Autobiography*, I, 309, 314. It is significant that Mr. Cornell bought Forest Park in 1857. For six or seven years before that he was too poor to buy anything, and certainly could not have afforded to live in anything as grand as "the mansion" at Seneca and Tioga Streets. There is a picture of this house in *The Cornell Era*, XXXIX, 412.

2. Writing in 1849, Mr. Cornell says: "I arrived home from New York this morning about 4 A.M., having left the metropolis yesterday at 7½ A.M. . . . By either route we are less than 24 hours from New York." A. W. Smith, *Ezra Cornell*, 67. In 1869, according to the author of *Views Around Ithaca*, travellers leaving New York early in the morning arrived at Ithaca early in the evening.

3. New York *Express*, quoted in Ithaca *Journal*, Sept. 13, 1865.

4. *Proceedings of the Trustees*, 2.

5. *Woodward v. Cornell*, I, 2. This suit was brought by Woodward to recover what he claimed Cornell owed him on their agreement. Since much of the testimony was designed to find out precisely what the agreement was, the work is a valuable source of information about the events that led to the employment of Woodward.

6. *Ibid.*, 34–36. Woodward at first suggested that he would like to be a trustee of the new university, and Cornell thought it might be possible; but then on second thought Woodward felt he could "render more essential aid in locating the lands." *Ibid.*, 3, 450, 451.

7. The history of Mr. Cornell's arrangement with the Comptroller, and of his management of the land scrip, is given in brief in S. D. Halliday, *History of the Agricultural College Land Grant*, 20 ff. The most recent and the most authorita-

233

tive account is Paul Gates, *The Wisconsin Pine Lands of Cornell University.* For the essential documents: *Laws and Documents Relating to Cornell University,* Nos. 40, 47, 70, 83, 109; New York, *Constitutional Convention, 1867–68, Documents,* III, No. 47; New York, *Senate Documents,* 1874, No. 103.

8. The testimony taken in the suit is in *Woodward v. Cornell,* 2 vols. (1874). The decision is not given in this work, and I have not been able to find what it was, except that Woodward won the suit. In the official investigation of Mr. Cornell's management of the scrip, Woodward testified that in his suit he claimed that Cornell had paid him something more than $97,000, and that he still owed him $114,000. New York, *Senate Documents,* 1874, No. 103, p. 68. At this time Cornell University took over Mr. Cornell's rights and obligations in respect to the scrip and the lands, and as part of the obligations paid the cost of the Woodward suit, which was $25,000, and paid to Woodward himself $160,831.42. Halliday, *History of the Agricultural College Land Grant,* 61. Of this amount, not more than $114,000 was on account of the suit, since that is all that Woodward claimed, but it is possible, and indeed likely, that Woodward got less than he claimed.

9. Paul Gates, *The Wisconsin Pine Lands of Cornell University,* Ch. V.

10. *Proceedings of the Trustees,* 7. The report was published as a pamphlet, *Report of the Committee on Organization, presented to the Trustees of the Cornell University.* Albany, 1867. It is No. 1 of a collection of pamphlets bound together in a volume entitled, *Cornell University Pamphlets,* I. The first General Announcement is included in a pamphlet entitled, *The Cornell University; Second General Announcement.* Albany, 1868. *Ibid.,* No. 2.

11. *Cornell Papers,* Cardboard Box.

12. Mr. Brown and his friends felt at all events that Mr. Cornell and Cornell University owed him something. Their claims rested on two assumptions. The first was that Brown had exerted a decisive influence in getting the Morrill Act passed. In support of this they obtained a statement, dated February 24, 1863, from nine representatives in Congress from New York, to the effect that "no man did more to impart information and furnish arguments showing the propriety of the law." *People's College MSS* in the Cornell University Library, MSS+ Kc 6. B. F. Wade, writing to G. B. Morgan, said he did not believe the act would have passed but for the work of Amos Brown. *Ibid.* The second assumption was that Brown had been of great help in getting the Cornell University bill through the legislature in 1865, especially in using his influence with the Methodists in connection with the Genesee College demand. On these grounds a "communication" from Mr. Brown was presented to the board of trustees of Cornell University on March 14, 1866. On November 21 the executive committee, to which the communication had been referred, asked to be discharged from further consideration of "the claims of Dr. Brown for compensation," on the ground that "while recognizing the . . . value of those services . . . they do not perceive that there exists any legal or valid claim therefor upon the Treasury of this Institution nor any power on the part of the Trustees to bestow any of the funds committed to their care in gratuity." Erastus Brooks and Horace Greeley, both former trustees of the People's College, of which Mr. Brown had been president, then favored a motion to the effect that the trustees "will endeavor to employ the Rev. Amos Brown in the service of the University in some department where his abilities can be made use of." The motion was lost by a vote of 12 to 4. *Proceedings of the Trustees,* 6, 9, 11–12.

References and Notes

Failing to get anything from the trustees, Mr. Brown then appealed to Mr. Cornell. According to Mr. Cornell, "Mr. Brown wanted to be connected with the new institution in a prominent position." *Brewer MSS,* Cornell University Library, MSS+ Kc 258. Brown denied this, but said he wanted adequate "compensation" for his services. He said that Mr. White had told him that these services were "such that without them the Cornell charter would never have become a law." Brown to E. Cornell, July 10, 1868. *Cornell Papers,* Gray-blue Box. In his reply Mr. Cornell said that the university aimed at employing only the ablest men, which seems to indicate that Brown had asked for something more than compensation. Brown to E. Cornell, July 16, 1868. *Ibid.* At all events, "is there any bar to *your* rating my services at Albany . . . at any value you choose to rate them? . . . Wherein can be the objection legal or moral to paying me such compensation from the interest of the $70,000 in the treasury of the state, the avails of the land sales when the grant passed into your control?" Brown to E. Cornell, July 24, 1868. *Ibid.* Mr. Cornell told Professor Brewer that "Mr. Brown had been paid for his services in accordance with a definite understanding, and that neither he [Cornell] nor the university was under any obligation to connect him with the institution. They felt that Mr. Brown was not just the man they wanted." *Brewer MSS.*

13. "But the *Presidency.* How about Gov. Andrews? He has declined Antioch College. Why may we not secure him if he is desirable? I had already written Allen to get confidential information regarding Gov. Boutwell, but I am inclined to think Gov. Andrews would be better, although I am not sure that Dr. Peabody would not be better than either." A. D. White to E. Cornell, Oct. 5, 1865. *Cornell Papers,* Gray-blue Box. "I have heard of a new candidate, . . . a Massachusetts Judge of high standing. I confess that I would prefer some such man to a clergyman." A. D. White to E. Cornell, July 4, 1866. *Ibid.* Mr. White says he was dissuaded from advocating Dr. Anderson when "Mr. William Kelly President of the State Agricultural Society informed Mr. Cornell and myself that, if we insisted on choosing Dr. Anderson, his duty would be to retire from the Cornell Trusteeship and devote himself to the interest of Rochester as against Cornell." A. D. White to G. L. Burr, Sept. 8, 1893. *White Papers,* Tin Box.

14. *Ibid.* "I was elected Professor of the History of Art and Director of the Street School of Art at Yale College, and all my tastes led me to this position, if I was to resume my career in connection with any institution of learning." *White Papers,* Collected Writings, I, 43.

15. Quoted in W. P. Rogers, *Andrew D. White and the Modern University,* 147.

16. A. D. White to E. Cornell, Oct. 5, 1865, and July 27, 1867. *Cornell Papers,* Gray-blue Box. His ideas are set forth in a Report of the Committee on Appointments to the Trustees, Sept. 26, 1867. *White Papers,* Reports.

17. *Proceedings of the Trustees,* 11, 13.

18. B. Wilder to A. D. White, Oct. 11, Nov. 14, 1867; Feb. 15, March 15, 1868. *White Papers,* Steel File, W.

19. G. C. Caldwell to A. D. White, Sept. 6, 1868, *White Papers,* Steel File, C; R. Hill to E. Cornell, July 6, 1868; Marie Mitchell to E. Cornell, June 11, 1868. *Cornell Papers,* Gray-blue Box.

20. H. Corson to A. D. White, Feb. 16, March 19, Aug. 29, 1868. *White Papers,* Steel File, C. Moses C. Tyler to A. D. White, Sept. 24, 1868. *Ibid.,* T.

21. Act of April 24, 1867. *Laws of New York, 1867,* Ch. 763. Also in *Laws and*

References and Notes

Documents Relating to Cornell University, 94. The postponement of the opening was apparently Mr. White's idea. They needed the time, and besides it would save money. A. B. Cornell wrote to say he agreed. "It was what I suggested at the Albany meeting last winter, but I was pounced upon by the Lieut. Governor in a savage manner, and no one took my side of the question. . . . In five or ten years it will be of very little consequence whether we commence in 1867 or 1868." He added that his father was of course anxious to see the institution opened during his lifetime, but that he would agree to what seemed best for the university, "and in that he will be governed very much by you." A. B. Cornell to A. D. White, Dec. 5, 1866. *White Papers,* Steel File, C.

22. A. D. White to E. Cornell, Jan. 29, 1868. *Ibid.,* W. In accepting the position, Lowell wrote: "I hear your plans spoken of with high commendation on all sides, and I cannot help thinking that even if you partially succeed, you will give an impetus to the true university system which will be felt for good all over the country." J. R. Lowell to A. D. White, Feb. 26, 1868. *White Papers,* Envelope marked "J. R. Lowell Letters."

23. *Proceedings of the Trustees,* 16, 17. Mr. White was strongly in favor of academic freedom, and he knew that one argument in favor of permanent tenure for professors is that it would safeguard such freedom; but he also knew that if permanent tenure is guaranteed deadwood is bound to collect. He was therefore much concerned to devise some method of getting rid of professors who proved incompetent. In the Report of the Committee on Appointments in 1867 he therefore suggested a plan, as a basis of discussion. The plan called for a "scrutiny" of the work of all professors and instructors each year, either by the Board of Trustees or a special board of visitors. Ballots were to be prepared marked "approved," "fair," and "unsatisfactory." A plurality of "unsatisfactory" ballots cast for any instructor meant automatic dismissal; of "fair" for three years in succession meant the same. The "scrutiny" was to be concerned with "faithfulness and capacity alone and is not based on the religious attitude of professors towards a particular belief, nor to the moral character of any professor—that being a matter of direct action." The "scrutiny" was to include the president of the university. *White Papers,* Reports. Quoted in W. P. Rogers, *Andrew D. White and the Modern University,* 161–62. The plan was not adopted, and Professor Rogers hints that Mr. White would not have made the suggestion if he had had at that time "as much experience with faculty and trustees" as he had later. It is certainly true that later he had less occasion for scrutinizing the work of professors than he had for resisting the impulses of certain trustees to dismiss professors for other causes than inefficiency.

24. F. L. Omsted to A. D. White, June 13, 1867. *White Papers,* Steel File, O.

25. E. Cornell to A. D. White, July 9, 1866. *Ibid.,* C. May 2, 18, June 2, 1868. *Cornell Papers,* MSS+ Kc 8.

26. A. D. White to E. Cornell, Sept. 17, 1867. *Cornell Papers,* Gray-blue Box.

27. There are different stories of how the site came to be selected, but probably the most reliable account is that given by Judge Boardman to Professor Hewett. "The late Judge Boardman stated that in company with Mr. Cornell and eleven other gentlemen, he went over the land on East Hill which might be regarded as adapted to the proposed university. The opinion of these gentlemen was, with the exception of Mr. Cornell, unanimously in favor of locating the university buildings on the plateau west of the present site." W. T. Hewett, *Cornell University,* I, 94.

References and Notes

"The first large building is completed with the exception of the heating apparatus and some light work which will be finished early in Spring. The second building had been carried up to the first floor when Winter compelled a closing of the work." Report to the Trustees, Feb. 13, 1868. *White Papers,* Reports. "Building No. 2 [White Hall] is as far advanced as can be without the white stone. The basement . . . is up ready to receive the water tables—and the chimneys and partition walls are up to the third floor or next floor above water tables." E. Cornell to A. D. White, May 18, 1868. *Cornell Papers,* MSS+ Kc 8. In a letter from Mr. Cornell to Mr. White, June 2, 1868, there is a rough sketch of the Shops and Laboratory. *Ibid.*

28. A. D. White to A. B. Cornell, Feb. 25, 1868. *White Papers,* Steel File, C. By the time this letter was written the matter had been settled. It came to Mr. White's attention in July, 1867. On July 9 he wrote to Mr. Cornell that he could not be in Albany that day or the next. "I think you had better sit down with some good lawyer in the convention who is friendly and have Gould with you and some other of our friends and agree on the amendment to be proposed to the committee. . . . I wish that you and Curtis could have a full talk with Folger and ask for his idea regarding an amendment." *Cornell Papers,* Gray-blue Box. The amendment referred to was apparently in the nature of a counterattack. "This morning I took the convention article complete to the committee. . . . We abolish the Regents, etc. Don't say anything of it. . . . Judge Clinton has been absent from the late meetings and may not agree." G. W. Curtis to A. D. White, August 21, 1867. *White Papers,* Steel File, C. In his letter to A. B. Cornell above referred to, Mr. White says: "We scared all the academy men and friends of the Regents by giving them to understand that if they ripped up our part of the educational article we should reopen the question regarding the Regents, etc. The result is that we have again beaten them out of sight."

The article reported by the Educational Committee stated that "The revenues of the College Land Scrip Fund shall each year be appropriated and applied to the support of Cornell University." *Constitutional Convention, 1867–68, Documents,* IV, No. 116, pp. 1–2. In the committee of the whole Mr. Lawrence moved to strike out the words "to the support of Cornell University" and insert "in the mode and for the purposes defined by the Act of Congress . . . of July 2, 1862." *Constitutional Convention, 1867–68, Debates,* IV, 2817. For the debate on this amendment, *ibid.,* 2817–2837. The argument for the amendment was: (1) that otherwise the legislature would have no power to require the university to use the College Scrip Fund for the purposes defined in the Morrill Act; (2) that if the university acquired an endowment beyond its needs it would be only just and wise to devote the Land Scrip Fund to the aid of other colleges. Judge Folger's substitute for the Lawrence amendment is in *Debates,* IV, 2826. This revival of the old controversy was the occasion for the most scurrilous of all the attacks on Mr. Cornell—an editorial in the Rochester *Daily Union and Advertiser,* Oct. 26, 1869, entitled, "The Cornell University Land Job." The founding of Cornell University and Mr. Cornell's control of the land scrip was declared to be "one of the most stupendous jobs ever 'put up' against the rights of the agricultural and mechanical population of the state." The author of the editorial declared that Mr. Cornell would make, on a sale of half of the lands, $24,500,000, and asked, "who would not be willing to found a university under such circumstances." The editorial is printed in *Laws and Documents Relating to Cornell University,* 92. Mr. Cornell's reply, which easily disposed of these fantastic charges by simply stating the essential facts about the land scrip, is in the same collection, 94.

29. A. D. White to E. Cornell, April 8, 1868. *White Papers,* Steel File, W.

30. The state of affairs as late as Aug. 11, 1868, is indicated by a letter from Mr. White to Mr. Cornell. "I regard it as of vast *importance* that a sufficient number of carpenters be put on the laboratory and workshops and the bridge [across Cascadilla Gorge] at the first moment possible. Our great danger is that *large numbers of young men* be disappointed at first, and such a feeling once started will spread among the young men of the state. . . . A man of long experience in building told me yesterday that he thought we could get what workmen we needed by going to the small towns for them—towns like Geneva." A. D. White to E. Cornell, Aug. 11, 1868. *Cornell Papers,* Gray-blue Box. In W. C. Russel's manuscript *Sketch of the Beginning of Cornell University* there is, on one of the blank pages, a note in another hand: "The bridge over Cascadilla Creek was completed only a day or two before the opening of the University. There was no bridge over the second ravine until the next year. [This ravine was where the old University Club house stood, just north of the present law building.] Professors and students descended on one side and clambered up the other with no great difficulty until the snows fell. After that if the unwary foot slipped at the top the descent became more rapid than dignified."

As to the number of professors already appointed at the opening of the university, October 7, 1868, the evidence is conflicting. Professor W. C. Russel, in his manuscript *Sketch of the Beginnings of Cornell University,* says that there were 17 resident and 6 non-resident professors, making 23 in all. *The Ten Year Book of Cornell University* (Ithaca, 1888) records the appointment in 1867–1868 of 19 resident professors and 1 non-resident professor, making 20 in all. *The Cornell Era, Ezra Cornell Centennial Number,* p. 383, prints a group photograph of the "Founder and Original Faculty of Cornell," which includes 28 persons. If we exclude Ezra Cornell the founder, J. M. Hart, Z. H. Potter, and T. F. Crane who were only "Assistants," and J. S. Gould who, according to *The Ten Year Book,* was appointed in 1870, we have 23 professors in all, which is the same as that given by Professor Russel. If we turn to the printed *Proceedings of the Trustees,* which one might think would settle the matter, we find the record of the appointment, up to the end of 1868, of the following resident professors: E. W. Evans, W. C. Russel, Burt G. Wilder, E. W. Blake, G. C. Caldwell, James M. Crafts, Joseph Harris, J. H. Whittlesey, D. W. Fiske, S. H. Mitchell, C. F. Hartt, A. S. Wheeler, A. N. Prentiss, H. B. Sprague, and J. S. Morris—15; and of the following non-resident professors; Louis Agassiz, J. R. Lowell, Fred Holbrook, James Hall, G. W. Curtis, and T. D. Woolsey—6; or 21 professors all told. There is no record in the *Proceedings* of the appointment to professorships, up to the end of 1868, of A. D. White, W. C. Cleveland, James Law, W. D. Wilson, or Goldwin Smith. Yet these men are all included in the list of professors in the *First General Announcement,* issued in 1868, the first four as resident professors, and Goldwin Smith as non-resident professor. Since it is unlikely that either the *Proceedings of the Trustees* or the *First General Announcement* would include the names of any men not actually appointed, we may conclude that at the opening of the university on October 7, 1868, there were 19 resident and 7 non-resident professors—26 in all. If this is correct, then *The Ten Year Book,* which professes to give a complete list of all officers, professors, and students during the first twenty years, together with the date of appointment or matriculation, contains at least seven errors in the record up to January, 1869. I have not checked it beyond that date.

David Starr Jordan, of the class of 1872, speaking in 1888, had this to say of the first faculty. "The faculty was the glory of old Cornell. It was the strength of the men whom, with marvelous insight, President White collected about him in 1868, that made the Cornell we knew. Everything else was raw, crude, discouraging, but with the teachers was inspiration. We cannot look upon the Cornell of 1870 as an inferior school, for it was not, scanty as its material outfit may have been. I have even questioned whether the pioneer work of those times, the work of blazing the educational road, did not make a deeper impression on the student mind than the perfect methods and well-oiled machinery of today. But a visit to the various class rooms shows the old leaven still at work. In no respect, I believe, does Cornell now make so good a showing as in her faculty. . . . Nowhere in this country, I believe, is so able a band of instructors gathered together as in Ithaca." Quoted in W. T. Hewett, *Cornell University*, I, 285.

31. The list of people and newspapers is in the De Witt Historical Society, *Cornell Papers*, box marked "Lithograph." The list of persons includes 115 named "Cornell" and 260 others. Mr. Cornell's article in the *Tribune* was published August 15, 1868. This was not, as Mr. White says in his *Autobiography* (I, 344), "during my absence in Europe," but he may be right in saying that it was published without his knowledge. Mr. White was not really in favor of the scheme for providing students with remunerative manual labor, and he remembered later that much of the student work for the university "had to be done over again," and that it would have been cheaper "to support many of the applicants at the hotel." *Autobiography*, I, 345. This is, so far as I can learn, an exaggeration. The truth seems to be that so long as there was plenty of work to be done in the way of constructing roads, bridges, and buildings, levelling up the campus, and the like, the system of student labor worked well enough, but with the end of such opportunities the plan proved impracticable and was abandoned. The plan was a favorite one with Mr. Cornell. He could see no reason at all for artificial "physical exercise," in which students disported themselves like monkeys. Manual labor was just as good for exercise, besides producing something useful (*Brewer MSS* in Cornell University Library, MSS+ Kc 258). Neither could he think that time and energy spent by students in making a living need interfere with their studies. In his letter to the *Tribune* he said: "I will assure the boys that if they will perform one-fourth as much labor as I did at their ages, or as I do now at sixty years of age, they will find no difficulty in paying their expenses while prosecuting their studies at Ithaca." Quoted in W. P. Rogers, *Andrew D. White and the Modern University*, 184. What Mr. Cornell did not fully realize is that few young men had his physical and mental energy—enough, that is, to do two ordinary days' work in one. The effect of his letter to the *Tribune* was to bring upon him a deluge of some two thousand letters from young men inquiring about the possibilities. New York *Evening Post*, Oct. 2, 1868.

32. W. C. Russel, *Sketch of the Beginning of Cornell University*, in the Cornell University Library, MSS+ Kc 26. Russel says that 332 students were in the first class, and that 80 (transferring probably from other colleges) were "distributed among the three upper classes." Every desirable place was needed, he says, "for

References and Notes

crowded lectures or recitations, and the scientific laboratories were driven into inconvenient apartments in the basement." According to Professor Caldwell, the entrance examinations were held in the basement of the Cornell Library. "The English examinations were held in one corner of the room, the mathematics in another, the geography in another, and, when all the corners were filled in which there was light enough to write by, the lesser examinations were sandwiched in between. In these examinations all helped: a professor of chemistry had charge of the orthography. It might have been wise to have first examined the professor himself in that branch of English. . . . A professor appointed to teach in one of the branches of natural science had, I believe, to look after the examinations in algebra." *Proceedings and Addresses at the Twenty-fifth Anniversary of the Opening of Cornell University* (Ithaca, 1893), 56.

33. See above, Documents, No. 12.

34. "The high wind and my consciousness that I was not heard rather dissipated my speech." G. W. Curtis to A. D. White, Oct. 11, 1868. *White Papers,* Steel File, C.

35. *Account of the Proceedings at the Inauguration,* October 7, 1868. The University Press, Ithaca, 1869. This is number 9 in a collection of pamphlets bound together under the title, White, *Addresses and Essays.*

36. The bells given by Jenny McGraw did not include the great bell, the Magna Maria, which was given by Mrs. White, and arrived June 30, 1869. The inscription on this bell was written by James Russell Lowell:

> I call as fly the irrevocable hours,
> Futile as air or strong as fate to make
> Your lives of sand or granite; awful powers,
> Even as men choose, they either give or take.

The original of this inscription, in Mr. Lowell's hand, is in *White Papers,* Envelope marked "J. R. Lowell Letters."

37. "All that part of our domain which is now devoted to the beautiful lawns about the University Chapel, Barnes Hall, Sage College . . . was then a ragged cornfield surrounded by rail fences." A. D. White, *Autobiography,* I, 344. "Rickety barns and slovenly barnyards offended the sense where the extension of Sibley Hall is now going on." G. C. Caldwell, *Proceedings and Addresses at the Twenty-fifth Anniversary of the Opening of Cornell University,* 57. In the Cornell University Library there is a collection of pictures (A. D. White, *Scrap Book*) which contains one taken in 1868, showing the campus as it was then.

38. *Account of the Proceedings at the Inauguration,* 36.

39. *Autobiography,* I, 344.